Interreligious Philosophical Dialogues

Interreligious Philosophical Dialogues, volume 2 provides a unique approach to the philosophy of religion, embracing a range of religious faiths and spiritualities. This volume brings together four leading scholars and philosophers of religion, who engage in friendly but rigorous cross-cultural philosophical dialogue. Each participant in the dialogue, as a member of a particular faith tradition, is invited to explore and explain their core religious commitments, and how these commitments figure in their lived experience and in their relations to other religions and communities. The religious traditions represented in this volume are:

- Sunni Islam
- Mystical (Kabbalistic) Judaism
- Radical incarnational Christianity
- Shinto.

This set of volumes uncovers the rich and diverse cognitive and experiential dimensions of religious belief and practice, pushing the field of philosophy of religion in bold new directions.

Graham Oppy is Professor of Philosophy at Monash University, Australia.

N. N. Trakakis is Senior Lecturer in Philosophy at the Australian Catholic University, Australia.

Interreligious Philosophical Dialogues
Volume Editors: Graham Oppy and N. N. Trakakis

This set of volumes provides a unique approach to the philosophy of religion – a dialogical conversation embracing a wide range of religious faiths and spiritualities, both western and eastern, in all their multifarious diversity and concrete manifestations. Each volume stages a highly interactive, genuinely comparative and thoroughly cross-cultural dialogue involving leading scholars and philosophers of religion. Each scholar, as a representative of a particular faith tradition, is invited to consider how they think the divine; how they believe they are related to it; and how divinity figures in their lived experience. These dialogues not only traverse the traditional terrain of Judeo-Christianity but also explore an array of religions from across the world, from Islam, Buddhism and Hinduism to traditions which are rarely (if ever) studied in contemporary philosophy of religion, such as Daoism, Shinto, Confucianism and Native American spirituality. In bringing these groups together in meaningful and productive interaction, this set of volumes uncovers the rich and diverse cognitive and experiential dimensions of religious belief and practice.
Available:

Interreligious Philosophical Dialogues: volume 1

Interreligious Philosophical Dialogues: volume 2

Interreligious Philosophical Dialogues: volume 3

Inter-Christian Philosophical Dialogues: volume 4

Interreligious Philosophical Dialogues
Volume 2

Edited by Graham Oppy
and N. N. Trakakis

LONDON AND NEW YORK

First published 2018
by Routledge
2 Park Square, Milton Park, Abingdon, Oxon OX14 4RN

and by Routledge
711 Third Avenue, New York, NY 10017

Routledge is an imprint of the Taylor & Francis Group, an informa business

© 2018 selection and editorial matter, Graham Oppy and N. N. Trakakis; individual chapters, the contributors

The right of Graham Oppy and N. N. Trakakis to be identified as the authors of the editorial material, and of the authors for their individual chapters, has been asserted in accordance with sections 77 and 78 of the Copyright, Designs and Patents Act 1988.

All rights reserved. No part of this book may be reprinted or reproduced or utilised in any form or by any electronic, mechanical, or other means, now known or hereafter invented, including photocopying and recording, or in any information storage or retrieval system, without permission in writing from the publishers.

Trademark notice: Product or corporate names may be trademarks or registered trademarks, and are used only for identification and explanation without intent to infringe.

British Library Cataloguing-in-Publication Data
A catalogue record for this book is available from the British Library

Library of Congress Cataloging-in-Publication Data
A catalog record for this book has been requested

ISBN: 978-1-138-23674-5 (hbk)
ISBN: 978-1-315-11106-3 (ebk)
ISBN: 978-1-138-23718-6 (4 volume set)

Typeset in Sabon
by Apex CoVantage, LLC

Contents

Notes on contributors	vii
Introduction	ix
Position Statements	1
1 Sunni Islam IMRAN AIJAZ	3
2 Mystical (Kabbalistic) Judaism SANFORD L. DROB	25
3 Radical incarnational Christianity LISA ISHERWOOD	49
4 Shinto KOJI SUGA	68
First Responses	83
5 Imran Aijaz	85
6 Sanford L. Drob	93
7 Lisa Isherwood	101
8 Koji Suga	111

Second Responses 123

9 Imran Aijaz 125
10 Sanford L. Drob 134
11 Lisa Isherwood 145
12 Koji Suga 154

Index 164

Notes on contributors

Imran Aijaz is an Associate Professor of Philosophy at the University of Michigan-Dearborn. His areas of research are Islamic philosophy and the philosophy of religion, and he is particularly interested in problems of religious diversity, exclusivism and pluralism. Some of his recent publications on these topics are "Traditional Islamic Exclusivism: A Critique," *European Journal for Philosophy of Religion*, vol. 6, 2014, and "Some Ruminations about Inculpable Non-belief," *Religious Studies*, vol. 49, 2013. He is currently working on a book entitled *Islam: A Contemporary Philosophical Investigation*.

Sanford L. Drob is on the Core Faculty of the doctoral program in Clinical Psychology at Fielding Graduate University in Santa Barbara, California. He holds doctorates in philosophy and clinical psychology and is the author of *Symbols of the Kabbalah: Philosophical and Psychological Perspectives* and *Kabbalistic Metaphors: Jewish Mystical Themes in Ancient and Modern Thought* (1999), *Kabbalah and Postmodernism: A Dialog* (2009), and *Kabbalistic Visions: C. G. Jung and Jewish Mysticism* (2010). His latest book is *Reading the Red Book: A Thematic Guide to C. G. Jung's Liber Novus*, published in 2012.

Lisa Isherwood is Professor of Feminist Liberation Theologies and Director of the Institute for Theological Partnerships at the University of Winchester, UK. Her work explores the nature of incarnation within a contemporary context and includes such areas as the body, gender, sexuality and eco-theology. She has written, co-authored or edited 23 books, including *The Fat Jesus: Feminist Explorations in Boundaries and Transgressions* (2007), *The Power of Erotic Celibacy: Queering Heteropatriarchy* (2006), *Introducing Feminist Christologies* (2001), *Liberating Christ: Exploring the Christologies of Contemporary Liberation Movements* (1999), and *Through Us, With Us, In Us: Relational Theologies in the 21st Century* (co-edited with Elaine Bellchambers, 2010). Professor Isherwood is a founding editor of the international journal *Feminist Theology*, a co-founder and director of the Britain and Ireland School of Feminist Theology, and during 2007–2009 Vice-President of the European Society of Women in Theological Research.

Koji Suga is Associate Professor in the Faculty of Shinto Studies at Kokugakuin University, Japan. His research specialization is religion and nationalism. He is the author of *Nippon tochika no kaigai jinja* (*Shinto Shrines in Overseas Territories of the Japanese Empire*) (2004) and "A Concept of 'Overseas Shinto Shrines': A Pantheistic Attempt by Ogasawara Shozo and Its Limitations", *Japanese Journal of Religious Studies*, vol. 37, 2010, and co-author of *Senso to shukyo* (*War and Religions*) (2004) and *Kyozongaku* (*Coexistence Studies*) (2012–2014), vols. 1–3. Since 1997 he has served as an assistant priest at Tochigiken Gokoku Jinja, a Shinto shrine dedicated to the spirits of fallen soldiers and military employees from the Tochigi prefecture.

Introduction

Religious believers of a certain conservative bent, whether they be simple followers of the faith, or leaders of a religious community, or scholars and theologians, have a distinct tendency to downplay or dismiss the value of discussion and dialogue with individuals and groups of alternative religious faiths (or no faith at all). Even when dialogue is entered into by such believers, it is rarely with the express purpose of seeking to place their own assumptions, beliefs and principles under scrutiny, to have them seriously challenged and even possibly overthrown. Rather, there is either a proselytizing mission of converting the other to one's own faith tradition, or – and this is perhaps more common nowadays within 'ecumenical' circles – only a desire of seeking a better understanding of the other's beliefs and practices, where this might be underwritten by a broader practical or political goal, such as joining together to promote common goods, the public interest or the welfare of the whole, or alternatively to combat common enemies including acts of terrorism, natural disasters, illness or disease, gender and racial inequality, and so on. There is little doubt that centuries-old barriers of misunderstanding, prejudice and animosity between religious communities can be and are being broken down through genuinely open and frank dialogue and also solidarity 'on the ground' in cooperative grassroots projects. But is this as far as we can go? On the 'theoretical' front, is there nothing more that can be achieved from interreligious dialogue than a better (more accurate and more sympathetic) understanding of the history, teachings and practices of the various religions of the world? Is the only model for such dialogue the famous Augustinian–Anselmian precept of 'faith seeking understanding' (*fides quaerens intellectum*), where the faith itself is for all intents and purposes hermetically sealed from challenge or disruption? Indeed, for some hardliners, such as Wittgensteinian fideists and John Milbank's school of Radical Orthodoxy, even the project of seeking understanding is viewed as futile or problematic, since religious language-games are incommensurable (or, at least, have limited commensurability) and so can only be understood, appreciated and evaluated 'from within'. This, as Milbank has proclaimed, spells 'the end of dialogue'.[1]

x *Introduction*

Philosophers, however, tend to take a very different route, one inspired by the 'gadfly of Athens', Socrates. This provocative approach to philosophical problems, known as the *elenchus* (literally, 'examining', 'testing'), had Socrates subjecting his fellow Athenians to a prolonged process of questioning that inevitably infuriated many of them, in large part because it showed up their complacent ignorance and dogmatism. Following Socrates' lead, philosophers often adopt a dialogical model in their inquiries that places everything up for debate, including one's own highly cherished beliefs, whether they be religious or not. This is not necessarily an advocacy of complete skepticism (though even this cannot be excluded from the beginning and may even function as a starting point in the manner of Descartes' meditations); nor is it a vain attempt to philosophize absent any cultural, historical or epistemic horizons. Rather, it is a methodology aimed at overcoming unwarranted biases and blind spots in one's thinking with the hope of arriving at a position that is closer to the truth. Various pressures in contemporary academia, under the influence of the neoliberal ideals of efficiency and productivity, are placing the dialogical model of inquiry at risk. But a delightful (some would say 'quaint') account of what this model looks like in practice is provided by Alvin Plantinga in a festschrift to his one-time colleague at Wayne State University in the late 1950s and early 60s, Hector-Neri Castañeda. Plantinga reminisces:

> In those days the Wayne philosophy department – Nakhnikian, Castañeda, and Gettier the first year, then the next year Robert Sleigh and I, and then a bit later Richard Cartwright and Keith Lehrer – was less a philosophy department than a loosely organized but extremely intense discussion society. We discussed philosophy constantly, occasionally taking a bit of time to teach our classes. These discussions were a sort of moveable feast; they would typically begin at 9:00 A.M. or so in the ancient house that served as our headquarters and office. At about ten o'clock the discussion would drift over to the coffee shop across the street, where it consumed an endless quantity of napkins in lieu of a blackboard. Here it would remain until about lunch time, when it moved back to someone's office. Of course people drifted in and out of the discussions; after all, there were classes to teach.[2]

This vigorous exchange of ideas, at its best, is not an attempt to defeat one's opponent, to 'score points' as in a debating contest and come out victorious. Although this adversarial approach is notoriously common in philosophical and religious discussions, our goal in these volumes has been to create space for discursive exchanges marked by a charitable and cooperative search for understanding and truth.[3] This implies a conception of interreligious dialogue as a form of *conversation*, a talking-with rather than a talking-to, being prepared to listen to the other, to study deeply their texts and traditions, perhaps even imaginatively empathizing with them, walking as far as possible in their shoes in the manner envisioned by phenomenological and hermeneutic approaches to religion. These are approaches which emphasize the importance of description, understanding and interpretation, at least as a first step in coming to terms with or making sense of what is presented by the other. This need not entail a philosophical quietism that, as Wittgenstein advocated, "leaves everything as it is." Explanation, evaluation and judgement, as indicated earlier, are fundamental to the academic and especially the philosophical study of religion. But judgement cannot be immediate or uninformed, otherwise difference and otherness are dissolved or reduced to our terms of reference rather than respected and appreciated in their irreducible particularity. This indeed was Milbank's fear: that dialogue merely masks the hegemonic aspirations of western liberal secularism. Ironically, however, Milbank's substitution of philosophical dialogue with theological contestation reinforces these arbitrary and violent hegemonic and homogenizing tendencies, this time in the name of a premodern Christian worldview that refuses to consider other religious faiths (and secularism) in any other way except through a Christian lens.

The encounters and exchanges in these volumes across multiple religious and philosophical boundaries will hopefully motivate readers to rethink not only the nature of religion and interreligious dialogue but also of philosophy itself and in particular the subdiscipline of the philosophy of religion. After all, the dialogues staged herein are intended as *philosophical* conversations, influenced if not governed by the kind of critical and rational inquiry into the nature of the world and our place in it that is characteristic of the principal texts and figures of the philosophical canon. The American pragmatist philosopher William James, who has had an enduring influence in philosophy of religion, expressed well the distinctive character of philosophical inquiry in the first of a series of lectures he delivered at Oxford in 1908 (subsequently published as *A Pluralistic Universe*):

> [T]here are two pieces, 'zwei stücke', as Kant would have said, in every philosophy – the final outlook, belief, or attitude to which it brings us, and the reasonings by which that attitude is reached and mediated. A philosophy, as James Ferrier used to tell us, must indeed be true, but that is the least of its requirements. One may be true without being a philosopher, true by guesswork or by revelation. What distinguishes a philosopher's truth is that it is *reasoned*. Argument, not supposition, must have put it in his possession. Common men find themselves inheriting their beliefs, they know not how. They jump into them with both feet, and stand there. Philosophers must do more; they must first get reason's license for them; and to the professional philosophic mind the operation of procuring the license is usually a thing of much more pith and moment than any particular beliefs to which the license may give the rights of access.[4]

Truth is not the only or even the chief concern of the philosopher. Equally important is the path traversed on the way to truth, and the way of philosophy – as James states – is reason: "argument, not supposition". This is what sets philosophy apart from other fields and practices, such as theology and religious faiths which do not hesitate to bypass reason and ground their creeds or systems in, say, revelation, sacred scriptures or the pronouncements of a magisterium. While not seeking to exclude confessional commitments, the dialogues in these volumes are chiefly conducted in the philosophical spirit of 'reasoned' discussion, broadly defined so as to consist in (at least at the best of times) a dynamic process of historically informed explication and rigorous rational evaluation of entire religious worldviews and ways of life.

One of the intended effects of these dialogical exchanges is to reorient and renew the philosophy of religion in a fundamental way. The field has traditionally concerned itself almost exclusively with conceptions of God and divinity that have emerged or been abstracted from the Judeo-Christian tradition. This narrow concern with western theistic religions has become narrower still in contemporary philosophy of religion, where very little time is devoted to the embodied experiences and practices of believers. Religion is primarily a form of life centred around participation in corporate worship, liturgical practices and other forms of shared spiritual disciplines. Contemporary philosophy of religion, rather than treating religion in these dynamic terms as a lived experience, tends to 'thin' religious faith down to a cognitive phenomenon, and so attention is diverted to, say, the epistemological status of theistic belief (e.g., Is belief in God rational?) or analyses of the propositional content of specific beliefs (e.g., the goodness of God, God's eternity). While these discussions are significant and legitimate, there is also much to gain from a shift away from narrow preoccupations with generic and highly abstract forms of theism to a philosophical study of *religions* in all their multifarious diversity. This, however, demands a significant broadening of the parameters of the discipline so as to include discussion of a range of 'models of divinity', including comparatively non-standard theistic conceptions of God as well as non-theistic conceptions drawn from eastern, African and Indigenous traditions. Further still, philosophers of religion will need to break away from their habit of restricting themselves to the doctrinal deposit of religious traditions and instead attend also to the various material and symbolic practices of these traditions, including their liturgies and rituals, music and iconography, and myths and poetry. Indeed, models of divinity do not arise *in vacuo* but emerge from philosophical and religious traditions that have a long and complex history which includes both 'cognitive' elements (e.g., scriptures and creeds) and practical and affective aspects (e.g., sacraments and iconography). Both of these dimensions, especially the relatively neglected material and experiential aspects of religious traditions, have to be taken into account as indispensable sources in understanding how a particular religion has arrived at its unique view of the world.

This series of dialogues therefore aims to take the field of philosophy of religion in a bold new direction. To this end, the traditional scope of inquiry is *widened* – by moving the focus away from the theistic religions of the West to non-theistic and non-western religious traditions – and the domain of concern is *particularized* – by taking seriously (both as an object of study and as a source for reflection and insight) the concrete details of specific religious traditions, from their beliefs and scriptures to their rituals, ceremonies and artistic practices. Such a cross-cultural and holistic approach may help to recover the diversity and richness of religion, thus challenging long-standing western theistic biases in the philosophy of religion and perhaps instigating something of a renaissance in the field.

***

In order to broaden the parameters of the philosophical investigation of religion in the foregoing ways, we invited to the discussion table a wide range of philosophers, theologians and religious scholars, each (in some sense) representing a particular religious tradition or a theoretical perspective on religion and divinity. The goal was to be global enough to capture mainstream as well as neglected though significant religious perspectives.

The participants in the dialogue were divided into four groups, with a separate volume dedicated to each:

Group 1

- Bede Benjamin Bidlack (Saint Anselm College, USA): Daoism.
- Jerome Gellman (Ben-Gurion University, Israel): Traditional Judaism.
- Freya Mathews (La Trobe University, Australia): Panpsychism.
- Trichur S. Rukmani (Concordia University, Canada): Non-theistic Hinduism.
- Charles Taliaferro (St. Olaf College, USA): Classical, Christian theism.

Group 2

- Imran Aijaz (University of Michigan-Dearborn, USA): Sunni Islam.
- Sanford L. Drob (Fielding Graduate University, USA): Mystical (Kabbalistic) Judaism.
- Lisa Isherwood (University of Winchester, UK): Radical incarnational Christianity.
- Koji Suga (Kokugakuin University, Japan): Shinto.

Group 3

- Chung-yi Cheng (The Chinese University of Hong Kong): Confucianism.
- Mahinda Deegalle (Bath Spa University, UK): Theravada Buddhism.
- Thurman 'Lee' Hester, Jr. (University of Science and Arts of Oklahoma, USA): Native American spirituality.
- Mark Manolopoulos (Monash University, Australia): Radical-secular Christianity.

Group 4

- John Bishop (University of Auckland, New Zealand): Naturalistic Christianity.
- Heather Eaton (Saint Paul University, Canada): Ecological Christianity.
- Kevin Hart (University of Virginia, USA): Roman Catholicism.
- Michael C. Rea (University of Notre Dame, USA): (Reformed) Protestantism.
- N. N. Trakakis (Australian Catholic University, Australia): Orthodox Christianity.

As will be noticed, the first three clusters are engaged in *multi-faith* dialogues, while the last group undertakes an *intrafaith* dialogue amongst those affiliated, whether loosely or more determinately, with the Christian community. It is worth pointing out here that the initial list of participants was much wider, but – and this is one of the pitfalls of large and ambitious projects such as this – a number of them withdrew during the course of the conversations. The dialogues were therefore originally more representative of the diversity of the world's religious traditions than this list might suggest, and this also explains some important omissions. In particular, we initially had secured representatives from the following religious traditions who eventually withdrew (in all cases inexplicably, without providing any reason, but simply falling off the radar): (group 1) Zoroastrianism; (group 2) African religions, theistic Hinduism; (group 3) Shiite Islam, Sikhism. There were many other groups we would have liked to include in the dialogues – for example, at least one of the schools of Mahayana Buddhism, Sufism and the Australian Aboriginal tradition – but we were obviously limited in how many we could allow to take part, and in some instances it was not possible to secure philosophically adept members of certain religious traditions who were available to speak on their behalf. In any case, these dialogues are merely a first, though positive, step: there is no reason why the experiment cannot be replicated with different mixes of religions.[5]

A word might also be in order about the organizing framework or rationale behind the selection of religions within each of the first three clusters. One of our primary goals was to showcase the diversity and difference that exists within the category of 'religion'. We therefore sought to include an extensive array of faith traditions from across the world, covering not only the world's greatest faiths (in terms of numbers and influence), but also some lesser known, smaller and Indigenous traditions. Clearly, the major world religions have a more pronounced philosophical heritage than some of the smaller or native traditions, but this does not mean that the latter are without philosophical underpinnings; and, moreover, it is not only the cognitive dimensions of religion but the cognitive in connection with the experiential (embodied, affective, practiced, etc.) dimensions that these dialogues are intended to explore. Also, although the groupings within the first three clusters might appear somewhat arbitrary, we were motivated by the desire to provide a unique opportunity for a thoroughly philosophical interfaith dialogue that would not ordinarily take place between diverse groups of religions. The inevitable risk here is that participants, so far removed historically and culturally from one another, may talk past each other rather than engage in meaningful and productive dialogue. It has not of course been possible to completely remove this risk, although it is hoped that it has been minimized by the skill and willingness of participants to enter imaginatively and empathetically into worldviews very different from their own.

A question might also be raised about the framing of these dialogues in terms of specific *religions*, or individual 'believers' as exponents and representatives of specific religions. This penchant for strict and neat categorization might seem misplaced in a postmodern world where identities and boundaries are unstable and permeable. But there was no wish to deny the fluidity of identities in the modern religious marketplace, and indeed criticism of the notion of fixed, self-contained and homogenous religious traditions is a recurring theme in the dialogues of these volumes, which highlight the complicated and circuitous ways by which these traditions have evolved and continue to evolve. And it is not only traditions and institutions that undergo change and occasionally radical reformation but also individuals belonging to and formed by these traditions and institutions. It was not, of course, the aim of these dialogues to convert or deconvert anyone, but changes and transformations in ways of thinking were not ruled out and were even encouraged and expected, and in one case at least the dialogues served as a prompt for a thorough reappraisal that has resulted in the very renunciation of all religious commitment.[6] But even if other participants did not choose to go that far, they have all displayed a commendable ability to look beyond their religious affiliation for inspiration and answers. It is in this vein that some have also sought to express and live out indeterminate or multiple forms of religious belonging, as with Bede Bidlack (in volume 1), who identifies as both a Daoist and a Christian and draws parallels with other recent religious thinkers such as Paul Knitter, author of *Without Buddha I Could Not Be a Christian* (2009).

Turning now to the way in which the dialogues proceeded, the interactions ran over a five-year period (2011–2015) and began with each participant writing a 'Position Statement' (of around 10,000 words) outlining the major contours of the religious tradition they are representing and their involvement in that tradition. Participants were provided with editorial guidelines on how to approach their Position Statements, and this included the following list of questions that we asked each participant to address:

- What are your core (i.e., fundamental or most important) religious beliefs? ('Religious' is here to be understood quite broadly, so as to encompass views about God or the divine, the self or soul, the nature of ultimate reality, the purpose of existence, liberation or redemption, the afterlife, etc.)

- What reasons, if any, do you have for these religious beliefs?
- How do you see the relation between your religious beliefs and reason (or rationality)? In line with this, what is your understanding of rationality? And what role is played by reason (as well as philosophy and science) in informing your religious beliefs and commitments?
- How are your religious beliefs related to your views about the meaning and ultimate purpose of life?
- How are your core religious beliefs related to your ethics, your politics and your everyday life?
- How are your religious beliefs related to your views about other religions, as well as those who do not follow any religion (e.g., secular atheists)?
- How important, if at all, is it to share your religious beliefs with others (to persuade or convince others, or to evangelize)? Do you consider yourself an inclusivist, an exclusivist, or a pluralist?

A similar set of questions was given to the Christian contributors of volume 4, with the addition of Christian-specific questions, such as:

- What is your understanding of such central Christian doctrines as the Trinity, the Incarnation, the Atonement and the resurrection of the dead?
- How would you go about supporting or defending your acceptance of Christianity?
- What are your views regarding the historicity of the New Testament account of Jesus, including his purported miracles and resurrection?
- What is your understanding of the afterlife? Do you accept the traditional Christian teaching of the resurrection of the body? In line with this, how do you view the nature of the human person? For example, do you accept some form of dualism, where the human person consists of a body and a soul?

Once all Position Statements were received, they were circulated to other members of the relevant cluster. Each member of the cluster was then asked to provide a First Response (of around 7,000 words) addressing the other statements within the group. The editors directed respondents to ask for clarifications, wherever necessary; to discuss points of similarity and dissimilarity in (e.g.) conceptions of divinity, the role of reason in religion and views regarding other religious faiths, and to dispute or challenge the ideas and arguments put forward by their interlocutors, thus facilitating a robust and dynamic exchange.

The initial plan was to have all participants at this stage gather in Melbourne, Australia, for a conference where the dialogue would continue in person. Financial constraints, however, did not allow for this, and so the dialogues were undertaken entirely in electronic format.

Introduction xvii

In the next and last stage, participants were invited to write a Second Response (again, of around 7,000 words) in reply to the First Responses, that is, to the critiques made of their Position Statement. All contributions were then collected and edited for publication.

* * *

There are a number of people we would like to thank for helping to bring these volumes to fruition. First and foremost, we are enormously grateful to the dialogue participants themselves, for their patience with a protracted undertaking such as this and for the diligence, respect and charity they exhibited in their contributions.

Secondly, we thank the publishers: Tristan Palmer at Acumen, who initially took on the project and helped mould it into its current shape; the staff at Routledge/Taylor & Francis (including Laura Briskman and Sarah Gore), to whom the project was later transferred; and Katherine Wetzel for overseeing the production process.

Thirdly, we are grateful for the financial support provided by the Australian Research Council through its Discovery Project scheme ('Models of Divinity', DP1093541); for funds provided by the Australian Catholic University as part of a broader project on 'Transcendence within Immanence' (Ref. No. 2013000569); and for two smaller grants provided by the William Angliss Charitable Trust.

Fourthly, we wish to acknowledge those who helped with the preparation of the final manuscripts. Our editorial assistants, Mark Manolopoulos and Tom Cho, took on many of the formatting, copyediting and proofreading duties. Indeed, without Tom's consummate professionalism, the end-product would not have been anywhere near as polished. Karen Gillen again loaned us her expert indexing skills. We are also grateful to Jim Pavlidis for the artwork on the covers.

Apart from these collective debts, Graham Oppy acknowledges ongoing support from friends and family, including, in particular, Camille, Gilbert, Calvin and Alfie. Graham would also like to record his immeasurable indebtedness to Nick Trakakis for his enormous contribution to yet another improbable collaborative venture.

Notes

1 See John Milbank, "The End of Dialogue," in Gavin D'Costa (ed.), *Christian Uniqueness Reconsidered: The Myth of a Pluralist Theology of Religions* (Maryknoll, NY: Orbis Books, 1990), pp. 174–191.
2 Alvin Plantinga, "Hector Castañeda: A Personal Statement," in James E. Tomberlin (ed.), *Agent, Language, and the Structure of the World: Essays Presented to Hector-Neri Castañeda, With His Replies* (Indianapolis, IN: Hackett Publishing Company, 1983), p. 8.

3 We should stress that this was *our* goal, as editors of this series. To what extent this goal has been internalized or even accepted by the participants in their contributions to these volumes is another matter.
4 William James, *A Pluralistic Universe* (Cambridge, MA: Harvard University Press, 1977 [originally published 1909]), pp. 11–12; emphasis in original. James Ferrier (1808–1864) was a Scottish idealist philosopher who taught at the University of St Andrews, and is best known for his *Institutes of Metaphysic* (1854). The passage in Ferrier's *Institutes* to which James is referring is reproduced in the editorial notes to *A Pluralistic Universe* (p. 167).
5 It would also be interesting to allow secular, non-religious perspectives into the mix, and we initially considered doing so by giving Graham Oppy a seat at the dialogue table. But that, as they say, is another project for another time.
6 We will leave it to readers to try to determine who this fortunate, or perhaps unfortunate (depending on one's perspective), fellow is.

Position Statements

1 Sunni Islam

Imran Aijaz

Introduction

In this Position Statement I will begin by stating the core beliefs of the traditional Sunni Muslim community, which I believe to be true. After this, I will devote the substantive part of my Position Statement to matters concerning the *justification* of Islamic belief. In the closing section of my statement, I will briefly address some of the implications that follow from my views regarding the justifiability of Islamic belief.

Statement of religious beliefs

There is, in the Sunni Muslim community, a well-known *hadith* (a report containing a saying attributed to the Prophet Muhammad) that provides a useful reference in thinking about what constitutes Islamic *belief*. The *hadith*, sometimes referred to as the 'Hadith of Gabriel', specifically provides an account of the essential core of Islamic faith and practice. One narration of this *hadith* is attributed to Umar ibn al-Khattab (d. 644), a companion of the Prophet Muhammad and the second Muslim caliph. The relevant portion of this *hadith* begins as follows:

> One day we were sitting in the company of Allah's Apostle (peace be upon him) when there appeared before us a man dressed in pure white clothes, his hair extraordinarily black. There were no signs of travel on him. None amongst us recognized him. At last he sat with the Apostle (peace be upon him). He knelt before him, placed his palms on his thighs and said: Muhammad, inform me about al-Islam. The Messenger of Allah (peace be upon him) said: Al-Islam implies that you testify that there is no god but Allah and that Muhammad is the messenger of Allah, and you establish prayer, pay Zakat [alms tax], observe the fast of Ramadan, and perform pilgrimage to the (House) [the Ka'ba in Mecca] if you are solvent enough (to bear the expense of) the journey. He (the inquirer) said: You have told the truth. He (Umar ibn al-Khattab) said: It amazed us that he would put the question and then he would himself verify the truth.

As stated in this *hadith*, 'Islam' is understood as resting on five different types of *practice*, the famous 'Five Pillars of Islam': (i) testifying that there is no God but Allah and that Muhammad is the Messenger of Allah (the *shahada*), (ii) ritual prayer (*salah*), (iii) paying the alms tax (*zakat*), (iv) fasting (*sawm*) and (v) performing the pilgrimage to Mecca if one is able to do so. The *hadith* continues as follows:

> He (the inquirer) said: Inform me about Iman (faith). He (the Holy Prophet) replied: That you affirm your faith in Allah, in His angels, in His Books, in His Apostles, in the Day of Judgment, and you affirm your faith in the Divine Decree about good and evil. He (the inquirer) said: You have told the truth.

Here, faith (*iman*) is distinguished from 'Islam', which, as stated earlier, focuses on practice. This portion of the *hadith* specifies six articles of faith, which are commonly called the 'Six Pillars of Faith'. Faith consists of having faith in (i) God, (ii) God's angels, (iii) God's revealed books, (iv) God's apostles, (v) the Day of Judgement and (vi) God's determination of affairs that allows for good and evil in the world. After this, the *hadith* mentions a third aspect of the Muslim religion, *Ihsan*:

> He (the inquirer) again said: Inform me about al-Ihsan [the perfection of faith]. He (the Holy Prophet) said: That you worship Allah as if you are seeing Him, for though you don't see Him, He, verily, sees you.

The *hadith* then discusses some of the signs of the Day of Judgement, after which it concludes thus:

> Then he (the inquirer) went on his way but I stayed with him (the Holy Prophet) for a long while. He then said to me: Umar, do you know who this inquirer was? I replied: Allah and His Apostle know best. He (the Holy Prophet) remarked: He was Gabriel (the angel). He came to you in order to instruct you in matters of religion.
> (Sahih Muslim, Chapter 1, Book 1, Hadith #1)

The 'Hadith of Gabriel' thus presents a summary account of what constitutes the religion of 'Islam' – (i) *practice*, (ii) *faith*, and (iii) the *perfection* of faith. Preceding (i) and (iii) is (ii); Islamic practice stems from faith, and the perfection of faith requires that one have faith in the first place. Of the six articles of faith, it is belief in the existence of God and belief in the prophethood of Muhammad that give us the real, core constituents of Islamic belief. This is reflected in the *shahada*, where the believing Muslim bears witness that there is only one God and that Muhammad is His Messenger. In what follows, references to Islamic belief, unless stated otherwise, will be references to two beliefs: (i) the belief that God exists, and (ii) the belief that Muhammad is God's Prophet.

The justification of Islamic belief

In his book *Rationality and Religious Theism*, Joshua Golding provides a useful distinction between a 'rationally compelling' position and one that is simply 'rationally defensible'. He explains this distinction as follows:

> A position is 'rationally compelling' if it can be shown that any rational being ought to adopt that position. A position is 'rationally defensible' if an argument can be marshaled to support that claim or position, and if criticisms and objections to that argument can be rebutted.
> (Golding 2003: 2)

An argument for a position that is rationally defensible may not compel all rational beings to accept its conclusion. One reason for this may be because the argument for such a position rests on certain assumptions that are intuitively plausible to some people but not others. A corollary of Golding's distinction is that, while it is difficult to see how two inconsistent positions can each be rationally *compelling*, it is possible for two inconsistent positions to each be rationally *defensible* (for different people). It is possible, then, that a person who subscribes to a religious position such as Islamic theism can maintain that this position is rationally defensible while allowing that positions that are different from, and perhaps even inconsistent with, it are also rationally defensible.

Are there any good arguments that show that Islamic belief is rationally compelling?

In my view, Islamic belief is not rationally compelling because there are no good arguments that show that all rational beings ought to accept it. More specifically, there are no good arguments which show that all rational beings ought to accept the existence of God or the prophethood of Muhammad. Due to space constraints, I can only briefly sketch out some reasons here that make this claim plausible. I will begin with arguments for the existence of God. Since the religious context that informs the present chapter is specifically an Islamic one, a helpful way to decide on the selection of arguments for the existence of God to examine is to see which ones were prominently discussed in Islamic thought and history. The Qur'an generally refers to the origins of the universe and its apparent design and order as evidence of God's existence (see, for example, 52:35–36; 78:6–16). These two empirical claims form the basis of the two main types of arguments that were discussed in Islamic philosophical thought – cosmological and design arguments. In this section, I will select one variant from each class of argument.

First, let us consider the Leibnizian version of the cosmological argument, according to which there is a sufficient reason (God) why there is something instead of nothing (Craig 2003: 114). Here is a more precise formulation of this argument:

1 Every existing thing has an explanation of its existence, either in the necessity of its own nature or in an external cause.
2 If the universe has an explanation of its existence, that explanation is God.
3 The universe is an existing thing.
4 Therefore, the explanation of the existence of the universe is God.
(Craig 2003: 114)

This argument seems to me to illustrate well the problem that afflicts several arguments for theism. The argument is valid; the premises (1–3), if true, would entail the truth of the conclusion (4). But are all the premises such that they would be plausible for all rational beings? I don't think so. Consider premise 2. Now, theists might (because of their antecedent commitments) think that the only explanation for the universe's existence is God. For, they might argue, if the universe by definition includes all of physical reality, what else could explain its existence other than an incorporeal and powerful being, such as God? So perhaps premise 2 is plausible for theists. But this premise does not appear to be such that non-theists would, if they are to maintain their rational integrity, *have* to agree that it is plausible for them too. Since non-theists are not already committed to belief in the truth of the theistic hypothesis, it seems reasonable for them to be suspicious about the appeal to God as the explanation of the universe's existence. It might be the case that the *explanans* of the universe's existence has to be non-physical, since the *explanandum*, by definition, includes all of physical reality. But the non-theist may object there is no real reason to suppose that a *non-physical* explanation of the universe's existence is *God*. As William Rowe observes, making a point that poses a problem (though perhaps not an irresolvable one) for cosmological arguments in general,

> [I]f the cosmological argument purports to establish the existence of the theistic God when in fact it, at best, establishes the existence of a first efficient cause or a necessary being, then the argument is obviously a failure. . . . Why must a first efficient cause or a necessary being have the properties of the theistic God?
>
> (Rowe 1975: 5)

Because of what might be considered a *non sequitur* by non-theists, premise 2 in the Leibnizian cosmological argument does not appear to be one that would be regarded as plausible by all rational beings. It seems that several non-theists would find it unreasonable to accept (or at least reasonable not to accept). The Leibnizian cosmological argument therefore fails in showing that theism is rationally compelling.

Let me now consider a deductive formulation of the design argument. Although proponents of design arguments typically formulate them in an inductive fashion, there are variants that have been cast in a deductive form. Here is one deductive version formulated by Del Ratzsch and Jeffrey Koperski:

1 Some things in nature (or nature itself, the cosmos) are design-like (exhibit a cognition-resonating, intention-shaped character R).
2 Design-like properties (R) are not producible by (unguided) natural means – i.e., any phenomenon exhibiting such Rs must be a product of intentional design.

Therefore,

3 Some things in nature (or nature itself, the cosmos) are products of intentional design. And, of course, the capacity for intentional design requires agency of some type.

(Ratzsch and Koperski 2015: §2.2)

Does this argument succeed in showing that theism is rationally compelling? The first thing to note here is that, even if this argument were to succeed in showing that its conclusion is rationally compelling, it would not show that *God's* existence is rationally compelling. There is nothing in the conclusion, 3, that identifies the intentional agency as God. If one wanted to use this argument to show that God exists, then an additional step – what Ratzsch and Koperski (2015: §2) call "the natural theology step" – would be required to identify the designer as God. But let me put this aside and consider some further criticisms.

As far as the logical structure of the argument goes, the inference from the premises to the conclusion is valid; if premises 1 and 2 are true, they would guarantee the truth of the conclusion, 3. But, as with the Leibnizian version of the cosmological argument we just saw, this argument does not appear to be such that all the premises would be plausible for all rational beings. In particular, premise 2 seems to be problematic in this regard. One could attempt to argue for the plausibility of 2 on empirical grounds by maintaining that sample cases of things that exhibit Rs and are the product of intentional design give us good reason to suppose that *all* cases of things that exhibit Rs are the product of intentional design. This inductive inference would, however, be questionable on at least two grounds. First, it seems that the majority of cases that exhibit Rs would belong to the category of cases that is being considered, i.e., those R-exhibiting cases belonging to nature. Given the nature of the dialectic in which these cases are being considered, one could not refer to them in drawing up a list of sample cases from which to make an inductive generalization. But, then, we cannot be sure just how representative our sample is if we stick to only those cases we know exhibit Rs *and* are the product of intentional design. Second, this problem is made more acute when we consider that the sample cases with which we can legitimately begin to work will almost certainly be cases that exhibit Rs *and* are the product of intentional human design (i.e., cases involving *human artifacts*). But the cases in which we are interested in extending the generalization to are different in a crucial respect – they are cases involving things that belong to *nature*. This is reason enough to doubt how representative our sample cases are.

Now, in response to such difficulties, those who are sympathetic to the deductive version of the design argument given here might argue that the truth of premise 2 is a conceptual truth and is known *a priori*. The truth of 2 would be known *a priori*, as Ratzsch and Koperski explain,

> in the same conceptual, nearly *a priori* way in which we know that textbooks are not producible by natural processes unaided by mind. And our conviction here is not based on any mere induction from prior experiences of texts. Texts carry with them essential marks of mind, and indeed in understanding a text we see at least partway into the mind(s) involved. Various alien artifacts (if any) – of which we have had no prior experience whatever – could fall into this category as well. Similarly, it has been held that we sometimes immediately recognize that order of the requisite sort just is a sign of mind and intent.
> (Ratzsch and Koperski 2015: §2.2.1)

But would premise 2 in the argument be regarded as something that is known *a priori* by all rational beings? It is not clear that this is the case. It might very well be that many theists, because of their antecedent commitments, find it intuitively obvious that design-like properties are not producible by natural means. Such theists might be accustomed to viewing objects in our world as either (i) devoid of design-like properties and not designed *or* (ii) exhibiting design-like properties and designed (this would include living bodies that theists regard as being the product of intelligent design). Non-theists, however, might introduce a third category in which several objects in our world (iii) exhibit design-like properties but are *not* designed. In his book, *Climbing Mount Improbable*, Richard Dawkins refers to such objects as 'designoid objects'. He explains:

> Designoid objects are living bodies and their products. Designoid objects *look* designed, so much so that some people – probably, alas, most people – think that they *are* designed. These people are wrong. But they are right in their conviction that designoid objects cannot be the result of chance. Designoid objects are not accidental. They have in

fact been shaped by a magnificently non-random process which creates an almost perfect illusion of design.

(Dawkins 1996: 4; emphases in original)

Since many non-theists do not regard living bodies as the product of intelligent design, they would be sympathetic to Dawkin's classification of these bodies as 'designoid' objects; living bodies would exhibit design-like properties although they are (according to many non-theists) producible by natural means. Because of their own particular antecedent commitments, it seems likely that, for many non-theists, premise 2 in the design argument would lack the lustre of an *a priori* truth. While it may justifiably be held *a priori* by many theists, it seems that non-theists can rationally reject this particular premise. Accordingly, this deductive formulation of the design argument fails to show that God's existence is rationally compelling.

In both arguments we have looked at, the Leibnizian cosmological argument and the design argument, there is at least one premise that could reasonably be rejected by non-theists. These arguments therefore fail to show that theism is rationally compelling. A careful analysis of both arguments provides a useful framework to see how similar arguments for theism fail to show that theistic belief is rationally compelling for all rational beings.

What about arguments for the prophethood of Muhammad? Are any of these capable of showing that belief in Muhammad's prophethood is rationally compelling? The focal point of discussions about arguments for and against the prophethood of Muhammad, in past history and in the present, involves the status of the Qur'an. Andrew Rippin gives the following account of an argument that arose in early Islamic history and which continues to be debated and discussed today:

> It would appear that, early on, Muslims had to defend their nascent religion against Christian theological attack in the area of the Fertile Crescent, especially Iraq. The following argument was constructed: miracles prove the status of prophethood and the Qur'an is Muhammad's miracle; therefore, Muhammad was truly a prophet and Islam is a true, revealed religion. All participants in the debate appear to have agreed on the first premise. What Muslims have to prove, and Christians disprove, was the validity [*sic*] of the second, for the conclusion, the truth of Islam, stood or fell on its credibility.
>
> (Rippin 2005: 38)

We can represent the argument Rippin states here in standard form as follows:

1 Miracles prove the status of prophethood.
2 The Qur'an is Muhammad's miracle.

Therefore,

3   Muhammad was a Prophet of God.

As Rippin notes, those who considered this argument in early Islamic history, Muslims and non-Muslims, agreed on the plausibility of 1. Debate focused on 2, with Muslims trying to argue in its favour and non-Muslims (such as Christians) questioning or rejecting it. The classical Islamic argument that emerged to support 2 was based on the alleged 'inimitability' of the Qur'an:

> Over time, the argument became one concerned to prove the 'inimitability' of the Qur'an, an argument which, its proponents were quick to point out, had a basis in the Qur'an itself.... [T]he production of a text 'like' the Qur'an is encouraged but known to be impossible: "Produce a sura like it [i.e., the Qur'an], and call on whom you can, besides God, if you speak truthfully" (Qur'an 10/38); "Well then bring ten chapters the like of it, forged!" (Qur'an 11/13). God has given the Qur'an to Muhammad and because of its divine origin, no text 'like' it can, in fact, be produced. The inimitability of the text proves its divine authorship and thus its status as a miracle, confirming Muhammad's role and the veracity of Islam.
>
> (Rippin 2005: 38)

The classical Islamic argument in support of the Qur'an's status as a miracle has two parts to it. First, there is the hermeneutical component. In several places, the Qur'an challenges those who are skeptical of its claims about being divine in origin to produce something like it. Issa J. Boullata elaborates on this Qur'anic challenge:

> [T]he Qur'an ... [challenged] its opponents and Muhammad's by repeatedly asking them to produce anything like it. When they claimed he invented it, they were challenged by the Qur'an to produce a discourse like it (Q. 52/33–4). And when they claimed he fabricated it, they were challenged to bring forth ten similar fabricated *suras* and seek the help of anybody but God for that purpose (Q. 11/13). On another occasion, the Quranic challenge was even reduced to the production of one *sura* only (Q. 10/38). But in a defiant and authoritative affirmation, the Qur'an said conclusively that if humans and *jinn* [creatures made from smokeless fire] were to combine their efforts, they would not produce a similar Qur'an even if they helped one another (Q. 17/88). And in a later passage, it further asserted that skeptical opponents would definitely never be able to produce even a single *sura* similar to any of its *suras* (Q. 2/23–4).
>
> (Boullata 1988: 140)

Muslim tradition has it that this Qur'anic challenge has never been met successfully, either during Muhammad's lifetime or later on (Boullata 1988: 140–141). But what, exactly, *is* the challenge supposed to be? In reading some of the verses referred to in this quote, one wonders what would be the locus of comparison between these verses and those that skeptics might have produced in response to the Qur'anic challenge (*tahaddi*); what would be the yardstick by which one could measure the degree of similarity between the two classes of verses? By the early part of the ninth century, the alleged phenomenon of the Qur'an rendering humans incapable of imitating it, or any of its parts, came to be known as *i'jaz* (incapacitation) (Boullata 1988: 141). From then on, this term would be used to refer to the inimitability of the Qur'an. According to the early Muslim thinkers who discussed the topic, what constituted the *i'jaz* of the Qur'an was its *stylistic* inimitability. This is the generally accepted interpretation of the term in Islamic thought. Although some of the early Muslim thinkers suggested alternative interpretations, the idea of the Qur'an's *i'jaz* being primarily constituted by its matchless stylistic qualities continued to be upheld by the Islamic majority. And – this is now the second part of the classical Islamic argument in support of the Qur'an's status as a miracle – its stylistic inimitability was said to constitute Muhammad's miracle. Boullata writes:

> [T]he general Muslim consensus . . . continued to hold to the stylistic supremacy of the Qur'an as an inseparable component of the idea of *i'jaz*, constituting with other components of the *mu'jiza* ['that which is ordinarily impossible' – that is, a miracle], the confirmatory miracle of Muhammad's prophethood, specially heightened in view of his illiteracy.
> (Boullata 1988: 142)

The classical Islamic argument in support of the Qur'an's status as a miracle can be presented in standard form as follows:

1 The Qur'an is (stylistically) inimitable.
2 If the Qur'an is (stylistically) inimitable, then it is a miracle (Muhammad's miracle).

Therefore,

3 The Qur'an is a miracle (Muhammad's miracle).

The conclusion of this argument can then be used as a premise in the argument here, which we looked at earlier:

1 Miracles prove the status of prophethood.
2 The Qur'an is Muhammad's miracle.

Therefore,

3   Muhammad was a Prophet of God.

Putting these two arguments together, we get the following argument in favour of Muhammad's prophethood:

P1. The Qur'an is (stylistically) inimitable.
P2. If the Qur'an is (stylistically) inimitable, then it is a miracle (Muhammad's miracle).

Therefore,

C1. The Qur'an is a miracle (Muhammad's miracle). (from P1 & P2)
P3. Miracles prove the status of prophethood.

Therefore,

C2. Muhammad was a Prophet of God. (from C1 & P3)

Many thinkers who argued that Muhammad was not a Prophet of God would centre their argument on the Qur'an, claiming that it was not a miracle at all. And the reason it was not a miracle was because, according to the critics, there was nothing special about its literary qualities. So, does the argument presented earlier succeed in showing that belief in Muhammad's prophethood is rationally compelling? I will now argue that it does not. The argument is certainly valid. But are the premises plausible for all rational beings? No. In particular, it seems to me that P1 is open to being contested by people who are not Muslims. The question that we basically need to ask in judging the plausibility of P1 is: *Is the Qur'an stylistically inimitable?* Throughout history, several people have given varying answers. The typical Muslim answer is, of course, in the affirmative and in agreement with Marmaduke Pickthall's famous description of the Qur'an as "that inimitable symphony, the very sounds of which move men to tears" (Pickthall 1934: 5). Others, however, have disagreed, sometimes sharply. For instance, Edward Gibbon described the Muslim Scripture as an "incoherent rhapsody of fable" (quoted in Warraq 1998), and Thomas Carlyle considered it to be "insupportable stupidity" (quoted in Warraq 1998).

There appear to be two main problems in attempting to argue that all reasonable people should agree with such opinions. To begin with, one could argue that there are no objective criteria by which we can measure something like stylistic inimitability. No such criteria are specified in the Qur'an; that the *i'jaz* of the Qur'an refers to its *literary* qualities is, recall, *an interpretation* of those verses that invite its skeptical readers to produce a discourse similar to it. Assessing the stylistic or literary qualities of a book is to make an aesthetic judgement of some sort. But it is not at all obvious that one requires objective criteria to make an aesthetic judgement. As Oliver Leaman explains,

> What is the difference between a proposition about matters of fact and a proposition about the beauty of something? Many would argue that the former is objective and the latter is subjective. So the argument that Islam is especially rational, since it is based on the overt properties of its central text, needs to be qualified. Determining the aesthetic properties of something is certainly an activity in which reason is involved, but it is not clear how rational it is. The topic is a highly controversial one in aesthetics, of course, with some arguing that aesthetic judgement is almost entirely subjective and others arguing the reverse.
> (Leaman 2004: 142)

Of course, this is not to say that people cannot make objective aesthetic judgements. But the important point to note here is that we are interested in whether the alleged stylistic inimitability of the Qur'an is something that would be agreed upon by all rational beings. Muslims might be entitled to consider the Qur'an as possessing unique stylistic merits, but it is not clear that non-Muslims would be obliged to agree if one thinks that aesthetic judgements are subjective (the point holds *vice versa*, of course). In response to this criticism, one might argue that, on the contrary, aesthetic judgements (which would include those involving the Qur'an) *do* rest on objective criteria. As Leaman observes: "Those who argue that the Qur'an is a miraculously beautiful work tend to support the objective view of aesthetic judgement, with its corollary that one can just *see* the beauty both of the text and of the world for which the text serves as a guide" (2004: 142; emphasis in original).

Suppose that one accepts the general point that aesthetic judgement rests on objective criteria. This still doesn't help us in answering the question whether the Qur'an is stylistically inimitable, because we are now faced with a second problem. One could legitimately ask *what the objective criteria are by which one measures stylistic inimitability*. Referring to the Qur'an is of no help here, because it does not even discuss its alleged stylistic inimitability *simpliciter*. Even if aesthetic judgements, generally speaking, rest on, or can be informed by, objective criteria, this general fact will be of little help in doing away with the problem of subjectivism that we are here trying to avoid. For instance, the Mu'tazilite theologian al-Rummani (d. 996) argues that the concept of *balagha* (aesthetic effectiveness) is a central constituent of the Qur'an's *i'jaz*:

> The elements of *balagha* are ten according to [al-Rummani], namely, (i) concision, (ii) simile, (iii) metaphor, (iv) harmony, (v) periodic rhyme and assonance, (vi) paronomasia, (vii) variation, (viii) implication, (ix)

hyperbole and (x) beautiful rendition. [Al-Rummani] ... [affirms] that the Qur'an is the highest kind of *balagha*, the lower kinds alone being within human powers.

(Boullata 1988: 143)

But why should we think that one of the objective conditions that constitute the stylistic inimitability of a text is aesthetic effectiveness? And, even if this condition is accepted as necessary for a text to be regarded as stylistically inimitable, why suppose that aesthetic effectiveness is constituted by the ten conditions given by al-Rummani? One could object here that al-Rummani's *selection* of allegedly objective criteria is subjective (perhaps another way of putting this criticism across is to say that the alleged objective criteria are not so objective after all).

Unless these difficulties are properly dealt with, it is hard to see how one could reasonably insist that two people (or people in general) should agree on the aesthetic merits (of lack thereof) of the Qur'an. Leaman sums up the problem nicely:

Is the text [of the Qur'an] really so wonderful? Suppose someone was capable of reading it in the original and thought it was not. It could be because he is mean-spirited or prejudiced against it in some way, of course, but surely we must allow for people to read and understand the text, but not appreciate it aesthetically. As is well-known, we cannot compel someone to come to a particular aesthetic judgement, and any glance at the visitors' book in a gallery will reveal a variety of views on any exhibition. The quality of the text, which seemed initially such a strong argument for its inimitability, now seems less powerful, since in so far as the evidence rests on issues of beauty, it appears to be entirely defeasible. We can understand why the love of the Arabs for their language and for what is *fasih* (eloquent) should have made the Arabic of the text so important, but are not judgements of style and beauty rather subjective issues? ... [I]f the style is an aesthetic issue then could we not be unimpressed by it?

(Leaman 2004: 154)

It is hard to see, therefore, how one could reasonably insist that all rational beings should regard as plausible claims about the stylistic inimitability of the Qur'an. What this means, then, is that the argument we have been considering fails to show that belief in the prophethood of Muhammad is rationally compelling.

For the sorts of reasons canvassed here, arguing on the basis of the Qur'an's stylistic merits does not seem to yield a successful argument for (or against) the prophethood of Muhammad. Of course, one could try to provide different kinds of arguments for or against Muhammad's prophethood, those that avoid considerations of stylistic merit altogether. It is difficult to see what alternative, serious candidate arguments there would be, however, since most of the debate about whether Muhammad was a *bona fide* Prophet has concentrated on the stylistic merits of the Qur'an.

Are there any good arguments showing that Islamic belief is rationally defensible?

Although, in my opinion, there are no good arguments showing that Islamic belief is rationally *compelling*, I do believe that there are good arguments to show that such belief is rationally *defensible*. I find the best expression of the general line of argument that I believe is successful in showing that Islamic belief (and religious belief, more generally speaking) is rationally defensible in the work of John Hick (1992). In his discussion of the rationality of religious belief, Hick begins with the supposition that the evidence for and against such belief is (theoretically) ambiguous (1992: 304). This evidence, in his view, would include evidence for and against belief in God's existence and Muhammad's prophethood. Given such ambiguity, having faith, observes Hick, involves making a "basic cognitive choice" that has the characteristics of a wager (1992: 304). Although he does not endorse Pascal's famous Wager Argument, Hick agrees with him in one respect. He explains:

> Pascal was . . . in my view . . . importantly right in seeing that the justification of theistic belief does not consist in an argument moving directly to the conclusion that God exists but rather in an argument for the rationality of so believing despite the fact that this cannot be proved or shown to be in any objective sense more probable than not. The appropriate form of reasoning seeks to establish the reasonableness of religious persons trusting and proceeding to live on the basis of their own religious experience and, through it, of the wider stream of such experience in which they participate.
>
> (1992: 305)

So, in asking the question whether religious belief is rational, we are asking whether religious persons are within their intellectual rights in trusting their religious experience. Hick believes that the right way to answer this question in the affirmative is by focusing on religious experience. He states his thesis precisely, as follows: "[I]t has been rational for some people in the past, it is rational for some people now, and it will presumably be rational for yet other people to believe in the reality of God" (1992: 305). Hick then explains that, in order to make a case for his thesis, he will rely on religious experience:

> [W]hat it is reasonable for a given person at a given time to believe depends in large part upon what we may call, in the cybernetic sense, his or her information or cognitive input. And the input that is most

centrally relevant in this case is religious experience. Here I have in mind particularly the fact that people report their being conscious of existing in God's presence and of living in a personal relationship of mutual awareness with God; and being conscious of their life as part of a vast teleological process whose character as a whole gives meaning to what is presently taking place.

(1992: 305)

In presenting the case for his thesis, Hick makes it clear that he is *not* considering whether a given person's religious experience is genuine as opposed to delusory, since that would require one to first know whether God exists (a possibility that is ruled out on the supposition that the evidence for and against God's existence is ambiguous). Rather, the question is whether a person is rational to trust his or her experience as veridical. A secondary question is whether others can rationally believe in the reality of God based on someone's report about his or her religious experience (Hick 1992: 305–306).

Hick begins his case by observing that we generally regard our perceptual experience of the world as reliable when we participate in ordinary daily activity. Although it is true that our perceptual experience is sometimes delusory, we do in the main regard it as reliable. Indeed, as he points out, we *need* to trust the general bulk of our experience as reliable in order to be suspicious of certain instances of it: "It is only on the basis of this trust that we can have reason to distrust particular moments of it which fail to cohere with the rest" (Hick 1992: 305–306). But such a trust, notes Hick, cannot be supported by proof (in the sense of good arguments). Western philosophy from Descartes to Hume has shown that we cannot prove the existence of an external world. Arguments that appeal to empirical evidence in order to confirm the reliability of our perceptual experience are circular, since they presuppose the reality of the world. Despite this, we continue to believe that there is an external world because "we are so constituted that we cannot help believing and living in terms of the objective reality of the perceived world" (Hick 1992: 305–306).

Following Terence Penelhum, Hick sees that it is possible to offer a parallel account of religious experience that gives rise to religious belief. This parallel account can be expressed in the form of an argument which Penelhum labels 'the Parity Argument' (Hick 1992: 305–306). Very roughly, the parity argument begins by stating that it is no more possible to prove the existence of God than it is to prove the existence of an external world and infers from this that religious (theistic) belief should therefore be regarded just as rationally acceptable as ordinary perceptual belief. Hick states that the parity argument seems to him to be correct, but that more needs to be said before we can take it seriously. Although ordinary perceptual and religious belief might be similar in one respect – neither can be proved to be veridical – there are nevertheless important dissimilarities between the two.

In thinking about the parity argument, an important question comes to mind: Why *do* we regard our fundamental perceptual beliefs to be rational? True, we cannot help but find ourselves believing that, for instance, the sun is shining outside when we have the relevant sort of perceptual experience. But the unavoidability of having such a belief does not seem by itself to provide an explanation as to why it is rational to hold it. Consider: I might find myself in a situation where I cannot help but believe that people who come from a certain culture cannot be relied upon, but this does not help in settling the question whether I am rational in holding this belief. As he continues his discussion, Hick provides an answer as to why we consider it rational to generally trust our perceptual experience. In ordinary life, he says, we operate on what Richard Swinburne calls the 'principle of credulity'. In Hick's own words, this principle states that "it is rational to regard our apparently perceptual experiences as veridical except when we have reason to doubt their veridicality" (Hick 1992: 307). Reasons to doubt the veridicality of our apparent perceptual experiences may be of two kinds. First, one might be aware of positive circumstances that would cause delusion (e.g., a person who has consumed a large quantity of alcohol and who knows the effects of doing so would have reason to doubt her perceptual experience of seeing wobbling walls). Or, second, one's apparent perceptual experience may be too fleeting and discontinuous with the rest of one's experience (e.g., a person who, for a split second, has an apparent experience of seeing a flying saucer would have reason to doubt that it was veridical). So, generally speaking, we regard it as rational to trust our apparent perceptual experiences of the external world unless we have reasons for doubt. Denying this principle, says Hick, "would border upon insanity" (Hick 1992: 308).

Hick continues his discussion by considering the application of the principle of credulity to religious experience, in particular to apparent experiences of God. Initially, he considers those "great souls or mahatmas whose experience lies at the origin of the theistic traditions". Was it rational for a great religious figure such as Jesus, for whom God was an "experienced lived reality", to believe that God is real? Hick answers that it was indeed rational for Jesus, based on his religious experience, to believe in God's reality, and that, in fact, it would have been irrational for him not to do so. Hick's basic argument consists of an application of the principle of credulity to cases of religious experience:

> For unless we trust our own experience we can have no reason to believe anything about the nature, or indeed the existence, of the universe in which we find ourselves. We are so made that we live, and can only live, on the basis of our experience and on the assumption that it is generally cognitive (though perhaps in complexly mediated ways) of a reality transcending our own consciousness. Indeed, what we designate as sanity consists in acting on the basis of our putatively cognitive experience as a whole. We cannot go beyond that; for there is no 'beyond' to go to, since any further datum of which we may become aware will then

form part of our total experience. And if some aspect of it is sufficiently intrusive or persistent, and generally coherent with the rest, to reject it would in effect be to doubt our own sanity and would amount to a kind of cognitive suicide. One who has a powerful and continuous sense of existing in the presence of God *ought*, therefore, to be convinced that God exists. Accordingly, the religious person, experiencing life in terms of the divine presence, is rationally entitled to believe what he or she experiences to be the case – namely that God is real, or exists.

(Hick 1992: 308–309; emphasis in original)

Hick's argument about the general trustworthiness of our apparent perceptual experience appears to me to be correct. Where further questions must be raised, however, is in the application of something like the principle of credulity to cases of *religious* experience. Hick is not unaware of this, observing that "one must add certain essential qualifications" to the argument.

For one thing, it might be argued that the clause specified in the principle of credulity is not met in cases where people claim to have religious experiences of God. This might be because there is strong evidence that there is no God. But such a possibility can be discarded if one considers the evidence for and against God's existence to be ambiguous.

But even on the assumption of such ambiguity, we cannot say that all religious or quasi-religious experiences provide good grounding for religious beliefs: "There are errors and delusions in other spheres, and we must expect there to be such in religion also" (Hick 1992: 309). The possibility of such errors and delusions arises, says Hick, when we look at paradigm cases of religious experience within prescientific cultures. For instance, Jesus not only experienced the presence of God but also experienced certain diseases as being caused by demonic possession (the belief that demons cause disease, as Hick observes, appears to be in conflict with modern medical accounts of how diseases come about). Are we to say, then, that it was rational for him to believe in demonic possession on the basis of his apparent experience of it, if we allow his apparent experience of God to also justify his belief in God's reality? Hick correctly points out that there are, as a matter of fact, two separate questions here:

(a) whether it may have been rational for the participants of prescientific cultures to have held beliefs which we today have reason to think false; and (b), if we answer that question affirmatively, whether it may be rational for us to hold those same beliefs on the ground that it was rational for the participants of another culture to hold them.

(1992: 310)

The answer to (a) is 'yes', notes Hick, since that is what his basic argument has been suggesting: "it *is* rational for people to believe what their experience leads them to believe." The answer to (b), however, will be more difficult. An important condition needs to be met in order to answer (b) in the affirmative: "it can only be rational for us to hold a belief on the basis of someone else's experience if the belief is compatible with our other beliefs, supported as they are by the general body of our own experience" (Hick 1992: 310). By referring to this condition, one could argue that claims about demonic possession fail to cohere with what we believe today, based on our experience as a whole (which would include contemporary scientific views). So, although it might have been rational for people belonging to prescientific cultures to hold beliefs about demonic possession, this will not necessarily be the case for us today. A corollary of applying this condition to cases involving religious belief is that a person will be open to accepting another's report of religious experience only if the religious beliefs to which they point are judged by that person as being possibly true. According to Hick, reason can ascertain that there may be a God and that this is a genuinely important possibility, in which case theistic religious experience deserves to be taken seriously. Now, one might think that there is an inconsistency in taking Jesus' experience of God seriously while not affording the same level of credence to his belief about disease-causing demons. There is no inconsistency, however, because "a person may be correctly experiencing some aspects of reality while falsely experiencing others" (Hick 1992: 311). As Hick nicely puts it, "this is so common a situation that we have to accept it as endemic to our human condition" (1992: 311). Given that this is so, there is no reason to think that the great religious figures, historically and culturally conditioned as they are, will be exempt from this situation.

Hick believes that his discussion of religious experience shows that great religious figures, such as Moses, Jesus and Muhammad, among others, were rationally entitled to believe that God exists. But only a few religious people (if any) claim that they enjoy the sort of powerful religious experiences had by, say, Jesus or Muhammad. "[T]he more common case," as Hick observes, "is probably that of the ordinary believer who does have at least some remote echo or analogue within his or her experience of the much more momentous experience of the great religious figures" (1992: 312). In such a case, although one's religious belief will not be as deeply or solidly grounded as it was for one of the great religious figures, it can be "well grounded enough for it to be reasonable for us to proceed in faith in the footsteps of a great religious leader, anticipating the full confirmation which our faith will ultimately receive if it does indeed correspond with reality" (1992: 313).

What follows next in Hick's discussion is an assessment of an important objection, raised by some philosophers of religion, that cases of religious experience fail to meet the criteria set by the principle of credulity, once this principle is properly explicated. For, according to the critics, an appropriate principle of credulity not only requires that one have an apparent experience of x and have no reason to suppose it is delusory, but also that one's belief that there is no reason to doubt the apparent experience of x must be 'informed'. This informed belief would consist of (i) knowing the sort of circumstances that would give one reason to suspect that one's apparent experience of x is not veridical, and (ii) knowing that these circumstances do not obtain when one has an apparent experience of x. This criterion appears to be an appropriate addition to the principle of credulity. It allows sufficient protection from delusory experienced-based beliefs to make it generally rational for us to hold beliefs on the basis of experience. For instance, one's belief that there is no reason to doubt a tree is present outside the window can be 'informed' because (i) one is aware of various conditions that cause delusions, such as intoxication, sleepiness, etc., and (ii) one is also aware, with a reasonable degree of confidence, that none of these conditions is present. But, the critics have argued, we cannot have 'informed' beliefs about apparent religious experience because we do not know what the possible causes of delusion are. Accordingly, religious experience cannot constitute any sort of rational ground for holding religious belief.

In response, Hick argues that there are criteria in the religious traditions that people have used to distinguish between authentic and delusory religious experiences. One kind of general criterion used in the great world faiths is a moral criterion, for instance. It might be argued that the criteria used by people within a certain religious tradition are only human criteria for what they have decided to *count* as authentic religious experience. We do not know whether such criteria are indicative of genuine religious experience. Indeed, it might be further argued that there are naturalistic theories that account for putative experiences of the divine (e.g., theories according to which theistic experiences are nothing more than projections of the human mind). Hick's reply to this is that, when considered as total explanations, the acceptance or rejection of such naturalistic theories rests on a prior commitment. And, for someone who trusts his or her religious experience, these sorts of naturalistic theories are not very threatening if we regard the universe as religiously ambiguous:

> [F]rom our present standpoint, the universe is religiously ambiguous. Alternative total views confront one another, one interpreting religious data naturalistically and the other religiously. Each may in principle be complete, leaving no data unaccounted for; and the acceptance of either arises from a basic cognitive choice or act of faith. Once the choice has been made, and whilst it is operative, the alternative global view is reduced to a bare logical possibility. This is the status both of the various naturalistic theories of religion from the point of view of one who trusts one's own religious experience, and likewise of theistic theories from the point of view of one who is committed to a naturalistic interpretation.
>
> (Hick 1992: 315–316)

Hick's response to this final objection completes his argument in favour of the rationality of religious (theistic) belief based on religious experience.

In closing, Hick notes that the basic question he has been considering is "whether the possibility, in a religiously ambiguous universe, that religious experience as a whole is illusory renders it irrational for those who participate in a form of such experience to believe in the reality of the divine" (1992: 316). His answer to this question, provided over the course of his discussion, is that it does not. And the argument he provides, as he notes, is analogous to the one given by William James in his famous essay "The Will to Believe". The thesis of James' argument, in Hick's words, "concerns our right to choose how to proceed within an ambiguous situation in which the choice is unavoidable and yet of momentous importance to ourselves" (1992: 316). Hick describes his argument, which he acknowledges is a variant of the one given by James, as

> an argument for our right to trust our own religious experience and to be prompted by it to trust that of the great religious figures. Thus, if in the existing situation of theoretic ambiguity a person experiences life religiously, or participates in a community whose life is based upon this mode of experience, he or she is rationally entitled to trust that experience and to proceed to believe and live on the basis of it.
>
> (1992: 316)

Hick's argument, it seems to me, has merit. I believe it can be further developed to constitute a good argument that shows how religious (Islamic) belief is rationally defensible. Due to limits of space, however, I cannot fully consider how it can be so developed. Still, let me briefly note two criticisms that may be raised against it, and discuss how they may be answered.

One criticism that may be levelled against Hick's argument is that it relies heavily on the supposed similarity between ordinary perceptual beliefs and religious beliefs (even though Hick is aware that there are some differences between these two classes of belief). The justification for the former comes by way of the principle of credulity. And since, according to Hick, perceptual belief is analogous to religious belief, one can try to justify the latter as well by utilizing the principle of credulity. Here, it might be objected that what is actually in operation when we consider the rationality of our ordinary perceptual beliefs is a more *restricted* version of the principle of credulity. This version, one might argue, applies to perceptual experience *only*. The thought might be that beliefs about the existence of an external world, for instance, are paradigm cases of rational belief. Such beliefs are so fundamental and unavoidable that to refrain from affording them the stamp of rationality would in effect lead to radical skepticism about virtually all the beliefs one holds. And the principle of credulity, when applied to such beliefs, provides a good account of why it is rational to hold them. But, the argument might continue, since religious beliefs are by comparison significantly different in this regard, there is no need to try and explain the status of their rationality by something like the principle of credulity. Kai Nielsen explains how one might try to highlight the dissimilarities between basic ordinary (or commonsense) beliefs and religious beliefs:

> Unlike those common sense beliefs that are fundamental, religious beliefs, particularly in our epoch, are not seen as being fundamental and as such universally accepted either intra-culturally or across cultures. But the common sense beliefs in question (beliefs like Moore's truisms) are so accepted. We can hardly avoid recognizing that people require sleep and that water is wet and that we human beings must have it once in a while, but our very noetic structure would not come tumbling down if we ceased believing in God or ceased believing that we are immortal. These beliefs, by now in our culture, as they perhaps are in all cultures, are optional.
>
> (Nielsen 1988: 7)

Here, a defender of Hick's argument might try to respond to this objection by arguing that one's capacity to psychologically avoid holding a belief does not, by itself, provide a reason for thinking that it is *irrational* to hold it (although Nielsen does not draw this conclusion in the quote). A person's religious beliefs may be 'optional' in a way that beliefs about the external world are not, but it may still be permissible to continue holding them even if they cannot be supported by proof. But if there are indeed significant differences between ordinary perceptual beliefs and religious beliefs, one cannot rely (or rely substantially) on claims about parity between these two classes of belief, as Hick does. Further considerations are required to support Hick's argument. Such considerations can be provided, I believe, by some of the arguments given by James in his "The Will to Believe".

A second criticism one could proffer against Hick's argument is that it does not properly appreciate the *ethical* dimension of commitment to religious belief. People's religious beliefs play a considerable role in influencing the way they act. Sometimes, people behave in ways that are morally questionable, if not outright objectionable, being motivated by certain religious beliefs they hold. It does not take much to justify this claim; history bears witness to several crusades and jihads that were carried out, and which were at least partly motivated by the religious beliefs of the participants. Perhaps the most prominent example of this in our contemporary period is the terrorist attack on the World Trade Center carried out by radical jihadists on September 11, 2001, and the subsequent, extended response to it by the American military forces spearheaded by the Bush Administration. In his "Letter to the American people," which was widely circulated after the 9/11 attacks, Osama Bin Laden explained that the main reason why his group was fighting the Americans was as a response to their oppression and injustice. Interestingly, George W. Bush echoed a similar sentiment in claiming that the invasions he launched into Afghanistan and Iraq were motivated by religious experiences in which God told him to fight the terrorists there and end tyranny. Based on examples such as these, critics might argue that Hick's argument for the rationality of religious belief based on religious experience is too permissive; it would license as acceptable cases such as these, in which people acted in morally objectionable ways motivated by religious beliefs that were formed on the basis of religious experiences (e.g., a strong feeling that God is calling one to fight in His cause).

Against this second criticism, one could reply as follows. Given that the moral concern here is legitimate, it seems that the problem with Hick's argument is one of *omission*; if the complaint here is that the argument is too permissive, then this defect can be remedied by *adding* conditions that restrict the ways in which one acts on the basis of beliefs that arise out of one's religious experiences. To be fair, Hick does consider how general moral criteria, those that are internal to a religious system, may constitute conditions that need to be met for a religious experience to be deemed authentic. But because they are internal to the religious system, one could object that such criteria could be problematic from an 'objective' point of view. Consider, for example, the Nazi who considers his actions to enforce an aggressive population policy as morally permissible, or even admirable, because that is how they are regarded from within the belief-system of the Third Reich. To deal with this sort of objection, one could add a further condition or set of conditions to Hick's argument that restrict one's actions, motivated by religious beliefs formed out of religious experiences, to those that conform with correct (i.e., objective) morality (see, for instance, Bishop 2007: 163–166).

Although I have considered Hick's argument only briefly, I think enough has been said to see that the general line of reasoning upon which it is based, *modulo* the fact that it requires supplementary argumentation, is correct. If so, we have good reason for thinking that it is rational for some people to hold religious beliefs under conditions where the evidence for and against such beliefs is ambiguous. This general conclusion *includes* the more specific claim that it is rational for some people to believe that God exists and that Muhammad is the Prophet of God. Accordingly, Islamic belief is a position that is rationally defensible.

Implications and conclusion

In concluding my Position Statement, I will note two implications of my argument for the conclusion that Islamic belief is rationally defensible. First, my argument allows for the possibility that adherents of other religious traditions (e.g., Judaism and Christianity) have positions that are rationally defensible. In this regard, I am a 'pluralist' with respect to the *justification* of religious belief. Second, I do not believe that it is very important to convince others of my own religious beliefs. This is partly based on my view that there are no good arguments that show that Islamic belief is rationally compelling. But there is also the following point. I believe that it probably does not matter a great deal to God that we have true beliefs about His existence, character, revelation, etc. For if it was very important to God that we believe He exists, that Muhammad is His final Prophet, etc., then, probably, God would have made the world in such a way that our present circumstances would better enable us to acquire and hold such beliefs. Discussing the merits of this particular argument falls outside the scope of this Position Statement, so I will simply refer the reader to a more extended discussion of it elsewhere (see McKim 2001: 112–116).

References

Bishop, J. 2007. *Believing by Faith*. Oxford: Oxford University Press.
Boullata, I. 1988. "The Rhetorical Interpretation of the Qur'an: *I'jaz* and Related Topics." In *Approaches to the History of the Interpretations of the Qur'an*, edited by A. Rippin, 139–157. Oxford: Clarendon Press.
Craig, W. L. 2003. "The Cosmological Argument." In *The Rationality of Theism*, edited by P. Copan and P. K. Moser, 112–131. London: Routledge.
Dawkins, R. 1996. *Climbing Mount Improbable*. London: Penguin.
Golding, J. 2003. *Rationality and Religious Theism*. Aldershot: Ashgate Publishing.
Hick, J. 1992. "The Rationality of Religious Belief." In *Contemporary Perspectives on Religious Epistemology*, edited by R. D. Geivett and B. Sweetman, 304–319. New York: Oxford University Press.
Leaman, O. 2004. *Islamic Aesthetics: An Introduction*. Notre Dame, IN: University of Notre Dame Press.
McKim, R. 2001. *Religious Ambiguity and Religious Diversity*. Oxford: Oxford University Press.
Nielsen, K. 1988. "Belief, Unbelief and the Parity Argument." *Sophia* 27, no. 3: 2–12.
Pickthall, M. 1934. *The Holy Qur'an*. New York: A. A. Knopf.
Ratzsch, D. and J. Koperski. 2015. "Teleological Arguments for God's Existence." In *The Stanford Encyclopedia of Philosophy*, Spring 2015 ed., edited by E. N. Zalta. http://plato.stanford.edu/archives/spr2015/entries/teleological-arguments/.
Rippin, A. 2005. *Muslims: Their Religious Beliefs and Practices*, 3rd ed. London: Routledge.
Rowe, W. 1975. *The Cosmological Argument*. Princeton, NJ: Princeton University Press.
Warraq, I. 1998. *The Origins of the Koran*. http://www.sullivan-county.com/x/koran_prob.htm (last accessed July 2012).

2 Mystical (Kabbalistic) Judaism

Sanford L. Drob

Judaism is a religion that is rooted in practice rather than belief, and efforts, such as those of Maimonides, to produce a credo or articles of faith have been met with ambivalence and controversy (Shapiro 2004). According to Jewish tradition, a man or woman is a Jew not by virtue of any set of beliefs or declaration of faith but rather by virtue of his/her having been born of a Jewish mother, or, in cases of conversion, having accepted the obligation of Jewish law, custom and practice. With the exception of one's commitment to a single God and the covenant of law between that God and the people of Israel, Judaism has traditionally tolerated considerable diversity in belief and theory while at the same time providing a narrow prescription for personal and communal conduct. With Judaism's encounter with the Enlightenment and the resultant questioning of the *halakha* (Jewish law), and its later abrogation (Reform Judaism), modernization (Conservative Judaism) and reformulation in terms of Jewish culture (Reconstructionism), there has been a growing interest in the attitudes, beliefs, values and spiritual experiences that constitute the uniqueness of 'being a Jew'.

For many centuries some of those searching for a spiritual and theoretical foundation for their Jewish commitment and practice have turned to the esoteric tradition within Judaism, the Kabbalah. Traditionally, the study of the Kabbalah was restricted by the rabbis to men over the age of 40 who had demonstrated both a strong commitment to the *halakha* and a deep knowledge of the Talmud (the early record of discourses and debates within the rabbinical academies in Babylonia and Jerusalem) and the mode of reasoning and hermeneutics that had developed in the Talmud's wake. This requirement was created in part to ward off the possibility that the seemingly relativistic thinking present in the Kabbalah would undermine the faith and commitment of those less well versed in the tradition.

With the advent of Hasidism in the eighteenth century, the study of Kabbalah, albeit in a somewhat simplified, psychologized form, became the province of even those uneducated Jews who attached themselves to the Hasidic movement. However, during the same period, the attitude towards the Kabbalah taken by educated, *haskalah* (i.e., post-Enlightenment) Jews, was generally one of ignorance or scorn. The great nineteenth-century

Jewish historian Heinrich Graetz (1817–1891) typified this viewpoint when he referred to the Kabbalah as "the babble of a semi-idiot", adding that it wrought great mischief and led to a deterioration of Jewish morals (Graetz 1937: 442–450).

Outside of orthodox Judaism the main interest in the Kabbalah came in Christian circles who saw it as a spiritual foundation for alchemy (Drob 2003a), a justification for the Christian doctrine of the Trinity, or part of a universal theosophy (Dan 1997). It was not until the 1920s and '30s that the Jewish scholar Gershom Scholem (1946, 1969, 1974, 1997) used modern historical and philological methods to begin the process of bringing Kabbalistic texts and ideas into dialogue with contemporary European thought. Scholem and others, including Isaiah Tishby (Tishby and Lachower 1989), Joseph Dan (1998a) and in more recent years Moshe Idel (1988, 2002), Elliot Wolfson (1995, 2003, 2006), Rachel Elior (1987, 1993) and Daniel Matt (1995), created an entire academic discipline devoted to the study of Jewish mysticism, and through them the symbols, metaphors and ideas of the Kabbalah have come to exert a powerful influence on contemporary Jewish thought.

My own meditations and writings have involved comparative studies of Kabbalistic thought and the history of (both eastern and western) religion and philosophy, and the interface between Jewish mysticism and nineteenth- and twentieth-century philosophy and psychology, e.g., Hegel, Derrida, Freud and Jung (Drob 2000a, 2000b, 2009, 2010). I have arrived at the view that the Kabbalah, in particular the theosophical Kabbalah of Isaac Luria (1534–1572), embodies a theosophical system which, when placed into dialogue with contemporary life and thought, promotes an open economy of experience and thought and provides a symbolic lens through which we can formulate a comprehensive understanding of the world and humanity's role within it, one that is spiritually, morally and intellectually satisfying and meaningful, for Jew and non-Jew alike.

My approach to religion and theology is not one in which I seek to produce religious credos or theological positions but is rather one in which I engage theological, philosophical and psychological questions through an encounter with the Jewish mystical tradition. As we will see, the nature of this tradition is such that it promotes multiple perspectives and interpretations, and indeed at times the Kabbalists suggest that the ultimate constituents of reality, the *sefirot*, are 'questions' as opposed to elements (Sperling, Simon, and Levertoff 1931–1934, I: 6; Tishby and Lachower 1989, I: 291–295). One of the guiding principles of Kabbalah and Hasidism is the doctrine of *ha-achduth hashawaah*, the coincidence of opposites, and followers of both frequently held that *Ein-sof* or the *sefirot* were a 'union of all contradictions' (Dan 1966: 94; cf. Elior 1987: 163). Even the very existence of God is subject to a 'bilinear' paradoxical approach, whereby one is prompted to think in one direction and to then (or even simultaneously) think from the opposing direction as well. The thirteenth-century Kabbalist

Azriel of Gerona held that the Infinite (*Ein-sof*) is apprehended through a union of faith and unbelief (Scholem 1987: 441–442). Schneur Zalman of Lyadi (1745–1813), the founder of Chabad-Lubavitch Hasidism, held that there were two opposing paths to understanding 'reality':

> (Looking) *upwards from below*, as it appears to eyes of flesh, the tangible world seems to be *Yesh* [Being] and a thing, while spirituality, which is above, is an aspect of *Ayin* [Nothingness] . . . (But looking) *downwards from above* the world is an aspect of *Ayin*, and everything which is linked downwards and descends lower and lower is more and more *Ayin* and is considered as nought truly as nothing and null.
> (quoted in Elior 1993: 137–138; emphases in original)

In light of such ideas, it can hardly be expected that a definite, fixed theology will emerge from a contemporary engagement with the Jewish mystical tradition. As such, in this chapter, I can only offer a continuation of my encounter with that tradition and in the process offer some general and rather tentative ideas.

In what follows I assume that the reader has little or no knowledge of the Kabbalah, its history and its symbols, and I will provide just enough of this background in order to set the stage for my understanding of what I term the 'New Kabbalah' (Drob 2000–2012), a mode of thinking and way of living that marries traditional Kabbalistic symbols and metaphors with the critical, open-ended worldview of our own age. By way of anticipation, we will see how the Lurianic Kabbalah provides a comprehensive account of God, creation, the world, humanity and the meaning of human existence, while at the same time setting the stage for its own critique, revision and transcendence.

The Kabbalah

Traditional Jewish scholars trace the Kabbalah (which in Hebrew means 'receiving' or more loosely 'that which has been received') to the oral revelation to Moses at Mt Sinai. In their view, the Kabbalah was transmitted from generation to generation and ultimately put into written form by the second-century rabbi Shimon bar Yochai in the *Zohar*, the 'Book of Splendour' (Sperling, Simon, and Levertoff 1931–1934; Tishby and Lachower 1989), which is the *locus classicus* of Kabbalistic symbols and ideas. Modern scholarship, however, understands the Kabbalah to have originated during the eleventh to thirteenth centuries in southern France and Spain as an outgrowth and development of earlier forms of Jewish mysticism. Contemporary scholars are fairly unanimous in their view that the Spanish rabbi Moses De Leon (1250–1305) wrote (or at most redacted) the *Zohar* rather than discovered it in a *genizah* (a burial site for old holy books), as he had claimed (Scholem 1946; Tishby and Lachower 1989). On the modern view, the *Zohar*, while retaining its theoretical and literary eminence, is by no means the earliest Kabbalistic work; some regard the anonymous *sefer ha-Bahir* to be the first work to advance the distinctive Kabbalistic view of the *sefirot*, the value archetypes of creation (Scholem 1969; Kaplan 1989). A period of enormous Kabbalistic productivity in France and Spain from the eleventh to the thirteenth centuries was followed – and in some ways superseded – by a renewal and reformulation of the Kabbalah in Palestine in the sixteenth century. It was there in 1570 that Isaac Luria burst onto the already thriving mystical community in the town of Safed, on the shores of Lake Tiberias.

Kabbalah, prior to Luria, was characterized by the symbolism of the *sefirot*, the archetypal traits (*middot*) of God that are also thought to be the elementary constituents of humanity and the world. Generally regarded to be ten in number, the *sefirot* (a term related to the Hebrew words *sefer* – book, and *separ* – count or number) represent such fundamental values as wisdom, understanding, kindness and compassion, and embody the Platonic notion that the world is essentially comprised of ideals and values as opposed to the material elements that are encountered by our senses. The list of *sefirot* was loosely adapted from the praises to God recorded in Chronicles 29:11, where reference is made to God's greatness, power, beauty, victory, majesty and sovereignty. Luria adopted the theory of the *sefirot* but placed these archetypes in the context of a dynamic theosophical system which accounted for the nature of the deity, the creation of the world and the purpose of humankind. Luria himself wrote very little and died at the age of 37 after only two years of visionary teaching in Safed. His ideas, however, were recorded by his disciples, most notably Chayyim Vital (1543–1620), whose *Sefer Ez Chayyim* (Menzi and Padeh 1999) is the major source of our current knowledge of the Lurianic system.

Luria's theosophical system (Schochet 1981; Scholem 1946, 1974; Drob 2000a) can be described as highly complex and even baroque but in its basic outline is readily comprehensible and serves not only as a foundation for a contemporary Jewish theology but anticipates the thought of later western thinkers, including Hegel, Freud, Jung (Drob 2000b) and Derrida (Drob 2004, 2009), whose ideas would seem to be worlds apart from Jewish mysticism.

Luria once said that it was difficult for him to articulate his thoughts, because his words must be ordered in a sequence and each of his ideas is integrally connected with and can only be understood in relation to each of the others (Fine 2003). With this principle in mind, I will briefly describe the Lurianic symbols and theosophical system. In doing so, I will have occasion to also draw upon Kabbalistic notions that preceded Luria and were assumed by him, as well as by later, particularly Hasidic, thinkers who developed Luria's ideas.

Ein-sof (the Infinite): For Luria, *Ein-sof* is everything and nothing (*Ayin*), the beginning and end of all existence. It is devoid of all specific characteristics, and is ineffable and unknowable to finite minds. The thirteenth-century

Kabbalist Azriel Gerona described *Ein-sof* as the foundation of both faith and unbelief, and manifesting as the "union of all contradictions," a characterization that serves as a template for later descriptions of *Ein-sof* as *ha-achduth hashawaah*, a *coincidentia oppositorum*. *Ein-sof* is both the origin of and completed by the finite world and humanity, and there are places in the Kabbalistic corpus where it is suggested that *Ein-sof* both creates and is created by humanity (Sperling, Simon, and Levertoff 1931–1934, V: 153; Idel 1988: 87). We will return to this radical notion as we proceed through the Lurianic system.

Tzimtzum (Contraction, Concealment): Luria was original in his notion that creation involves a contraction and concealment of the divine plenum. As a result of the *Tzimtzum*, the finite world comes into being in a manner analogous to the way in which celluloid movie film selectively filters out wavelengths emanating from an undifferentiated plenum of white light. For the Kabbalists, the 'undifferentiated plenum', the *Or Ein-sof* (the light of the infinite), must be contracted or concealed in order to give rise to the distinct entities of the finite world. We will later see that the Kabbalists held that the *Tzimtzum* occurs by means of language, and that language, as the vehicle of creation, is both a revelation and a concealment of God.

Adam Kadmon (Primordial Human), *sefirot* (Value Archetypes) and *Otiyot Yesod* (Primordial Letters): The *Tzimtzum* is followed by a second, positive act of creation, in which the light or energy of the infinite (*Or Ein-sof*) is emanated into the metaphysical void that was produced by the divine withdrawal. This energy is conceived in sexual, procreative terms, and the first being to emerge in its wake is *Adam Kadmon*, the Primordial Human, who embodies within himself the divine traits, the *sefirot*. The Primordial Human is a reflection of God and the vehicle through which the archetypal values are revealed and produce the cosmos. The *sefirot*, which are thought of as 'vessels' (*kelim*) for containing the divine light, were thought to be ten (or occasionally eleven) in number, but with the alternate appellations that were in common use by the Kabbalists, they refer to more than ten value archetypes. The *sefirot*, with some variation, are typically recorded as *Keter/Ratzon* (Crown/Desire), *Chochmah* (Wisdom), *Binah* (Understanding), *Da'at* (Knowledge – which in some schemes replaces *Keter*), *Chesed/Gedulah* (Kindness, Greatness), *Gevurah/Din* (Power/Judgement), *Tiferet/Rachamim* (Beauty/Compassion), *Netzach* (Victory), *Hod* (Majesty, Splendour), *Yesod* (Foundation) and *Malchuth/Shekhinah* (Royalty/Feminine Presence). All entities in the world are said to be comprised of combinations of these axiological elements, and the human soul reflects each of them and all of their potential combinations.

An alternative and complementary perspective on creation understands *Ein-sof* contracting into the *Otiyot Yesod*, the twenty-two 'Foundational Letters' of divine speech through which the world was created (Genesis 1:3). Together with the ten *sefirot*, the twenty-two letters of the 'holy tongue' (i.e., the consonants of the Hebrew language) are sometimes said to comprise the 'thirty-two paths of wisdom' through which divine energy is channeled into the finite world. The doctrine of 'Foundational Letters' reflects the ancient midrashic view that the Torah is the 'blueprint' of creation and the later Kabbalistic view that reality is itself a 'text', which like the Torah is subject to a nearly infinite multiplicity of interpretations. An even more radical view was expressed by a follower of Isaac Luria, Israel Sarug, who asserted that the finite world consists of all possible combinations of the letters that comprise the Torah (Scholem 1969: 73), the implication of which is that there is an infinite number of Torahs, an infinite number of worlds and an infinite number of interpretations of each.

Shevirat ha-Kelim (Breaking of the Vessels) and *Kellipot* (Husks): Luria is again original in his view that the *sefirot* and Foundational Letters were *deconstructed* in the course of their emanation. Luria held that the *sefirot* were disjoint and were therefore unable to adequately contain the divine light that was emanated into them. The three 'intellective *sefirot*', Wisdom, Understanding and Knowledge, were displaced, while the lowest seven of the *sefirot*, now conceived as earthenware vessels, shattered and trapped 'sparks' (*Netzotzim*) of divine light as the shards from these vessels tumbled through the metaphysical void. The shards of the broken vessels and the sparks of divine energy together comprise the *Kellipot* or 'husks' which are the actual constituents of our world. The 'heaviest' of the shards, those for which the divine light has been nearly totally obscured, comprise a lower world, the *Sitra Achra* or 'Other Side', a realm of evil and suffering that rises up to inundate a portion of our own world. The Breaking of the Vessels and the entrapment of divine light in the husks are paralleled by a disruption in the coherence of the Foundational Letters, such that a cosmos initially emanated as a meaningful whole falls into a state of linguistic disorder and meaninglessness. In either case, the deconstruction of the original creation results in chaos and evil and places the world in great peril.

Luria held that his ideas were rooted in biblical and historical occurrences which served as symbols for theosophical events and ideas. The Breaking of the Vessels, for example, is symbolized in such biblical events as the expulsion from Eden, the death of the kings of Edom (Genesis 36:31–39), the Flood, and the destruction of the temple in Jerusalem. Indeed, the Kabbalists held that the *shevirah* (as well as each of the other moments in their dialectic) was potentially present at all times and in all things, an idea that we will return to later in this exposition.

Birur (Extraction), *Tikkun* (Emendation), *Partzufim* (Visages): As a result of the Breaking of the Vessels, the worlds are not comprised of the organized combinations of divine values that were originally destined to fill the cosmic void, but rather of the displaced, broken and now meaningless values that are symbolized in the figure of the husks and the disordered letters. It is the individual's divinely appointed task to extract (*Birur*) the sparks of divine light from the husks that are encountered in one's life journey and in the process reassemble, repair and restore the broken values and meanings. This process, which Luria referred to as *Tikkun ha-Olam*, the 'Repair and Restoration of the World', actualizes the *sefirotic* values that existed only *in potentia* prior to the creation of humanity and completes the process which had begun with the *Tzimtzum* or divine contraction. As a result of *Tikkun*, the *sefirot* that were disjoint are brought together, the letters are reassembled into meaningful words and phrases, and the Primordial Human, *Adam Kadmon*, evolves through a series of *Partzufim* (Visages or Configurations) that reflect the maturation of the individual from birth through old age. The Kabbalists, who, as we have seen, spoke of the *Or Ein-sof* or 'divine energy' in sexual/erotic terms, understood *Tikkun* as a restoration of the broken erotic relations between the male and female *Partzufim*, the masculine and feminine aspects of God. This restoration is symbolized by the metaphor of the Celestial Mother and Father, who had turned their backs upon one another as a result of the Breaking of the Vessels, but who now, with the advent of *Tikkun*, resume erotic relations and are again 'face to face'.

For Luria, the human act of *Tikkun* not only completes creation but actually completes *Ein-sof* itself! Indeed, within the Lurianic theosophy, the Infinite God, *Ein-sof*, is not fully actualized in its original form as the totality of being and nothingness that gives rise to a finite world, but rather evolves through and is completed by the entire system, which culminates in the human acts which constitute *Tikkun*. An implication of this view is that while God creates humanity, humanity actualizes and in an important sense creates God.

That humanity serves as a partner with God in the creation, perfection and redemption of the world is a key Lurianic idea that is at the core of Kabbalistic and Hasidic theology. As we have seen, the Kabbalists held that the values symbolized by the *sefirot* exist only *in potentia* within the Godhead and must be actualized through the activities of human beings. Indeed, the purpose of the divine commandments (*mitzvoth*), which according to traditional Jewish accounts number 613, is to spiritualize the world, the self and human relations, thereby contributing to *Tikkun ha-olam*. The contemporary Hasidic/Kabbalistic thinker Adin Steinsaltz has expressed these ideas in a modern idiom through an analogy with race-car driving. According to Steinsaltz, one who wishes to build a superior race car must test it on an extremely difficult track, one on which the car could potentially fail. It is only when it has performed superlatively on such a track that its performance is fully actualized and affirmed. Similarly, it is only in an extremely difficult, dangerous and potentially tragic world that humanity can actualize and 'restore' the *sefirot*. 'Kindness' (*Chesed*) is only actualized in a world where travail and anguish permit kindness to make a difference, and 'Knowledge' (*Da'at*) has its greatest value only when it has been achieved through a hard-won process of discovering nature's secrets. Indeed, Steinsaltz, interpreting Chayyim Vital's claim that the world is mostly evil with only the smallest measure of good, holds that the world we live in is "the worst of all possible worlds in which there is yet hope", and this is, paradoxically, "the best of all possible worlds" (Drob 1990). Only in an opaque, difficult, evil and nearly hopeless world (the very world in which we find ourselves) can humanity exercise its powers of intellect, love, compassion, etc., so as to maximize the values embodied in the *sefirot*. God could not achieve such actualization/maximization him- or herself, nor could humanity have done so in the paradise of Eden. The expulsion from Eden, and more generally the Breaking of the Vessels, was a logically necessary event in the realization of the world's redemption and the actualization of God's very being. That we are on a race track where our vehicle could potentially fail is obvious – yet such a track is essential to the Lurianic view of God, creation and the purpose of human existence. Indeed, this analysis can be regarded as a Kabbalistic theodicy, as it is the Lurianic explanation for why the world is rife with difficulties and suffering.

Here I should point out that, as in Buddhism, compassion plays a pivotal role in the Kabbalah. The *sefirah Rachamim* (Compassion) is central to the '*sefirotic* tree'. *Rachamim*, identified with the 'Holy One, Blessed be He', serves as the vehicle through which the forces of the other *sefirot* are transmitted into the world (via the final *sefirah Malchuth/Shekhinah*). Compassion is also a mediator through which the forces of *Gevurah/Din* (Power/Judgement), which is at the origin of evil, are modified by the forces of *Chesed* (Kindness). *Rachamim* is also identified with *Tifereth* (Beauty), suggesting that the world's aesthetic dimension serves as a compensation for its manifest evil. We will return shortly to the role that values such as compassion and beauty play in the redemption of the world and the 'completion' of God.

The 'logic' of the Lurianic symbols

While the Lurianic theosophy has traditionally been understood as a creative intuition or revelation that is outside the bounds of, or beyond, reason, it can also be understood as a metaphor for an account or theory of the development of human consciousness, creativity and language. The process of human creation, for example, itself moves through a sequence in which a potentially infinite field ('*Ein-sof*') is severely constricted as one focuses upon a problem ('*Tzimtzum*'). One then channels ('emanates') one's energy into an initial creation, idea, value or representation ('*Adam Kadmon*') that typically generates a series of problems and difficulties that lead to its partial deconstruction ('*Shevirat ha-Kelim*'). The problems must be resolved, one's thinking revised ('*Tikkun*') and the germ of the initial notion reconstructed in order to achieve the values, meanings and goals of one's creation.

With regard to language, an individual who is about to speak is analogous to *Ein-sof* prior to creation, as that individual has before him/her a virtually infinite array of possible words, sentences and ideas. It is only by eliminating myriad possibilities, by contracting himself/herself into the letters and words of writing or speech, that a speaker produces a finite meaning or significance (a condition analogous to the act of *Tzimzum* – divine contraction). Indeed, such contraction proceeds through the development of a sentence or thought, and each word and each punctuation in the speaker's language serves as a 'vessel' for the containment and limitation of meaning, in much the same manner as the *sefirot* and 'holy letters' serve as vessels that contain divine thought. However, an individual's thought overflows and ruptures the language he or she utilizes in its expression, just as the divine energy overflowed and ruptured the *sefirotic* vessels and disorganized the Foundational Letters. This 'rupture' results in the ambiguity, failed- and mis-communication that are potentially present in all writing and speech. A condition obtains in which the speaker/writer and her audience are 'back to back', like the Celestial Mother (*Imma*) and Father (*Abba*) after the Breaking of the Vessels. In order for the speaker's 'meaning' to be completed and fulfilled, his/her words/letters must be taken up, interpreted and disambiguated by a reader or listener who in effect performs an act of '*Tikkun*' (repair, restoration, emendation) of what was written or said and thus becomes a 'partner' with the speaker or writer (now 'face to face') in the actualization of the speaker's meaning – just as humanity is a partner with God in the actualization and completion of the world's creation.

The Lurianic metaphors can thus be understood as *logic* as much as *myth*, and the dialectic that Luria articulates through the symbols of *Einsof*, *Tzimtzum*, *sefirot*, etc., can be seen to be at work in virtually all acts of language, consciousness and meaning.

The nature of divinity

The conception of the divine that follows from the Lurianic theosophy is a progressive, even radical one in which God's very nature is integrally related to and interdependent with finite creation and humankind, and where the quest for divinity leads to what might be called an 'open economy' of thought and experience. In her studies of Leibniz, Von Helmont and Locke, Allison Coudert (1995, 1998) has argued that these thinkers took a strong interest in the Lurianic Kabbalah precisely because its concept of *Tikkun ha-Olam* reinforced their faith in humanity's capacity to understand and transform the world. In this section I will revisit several of the Lurianic symbols in order to understand the forms of consciousness and understanding that they imply.

Mysticism in general has been associated with freedom of thought because of its refusal to adhere to a dogmatic, or indeed any particular, understanding of scripture or God (Scholem 1969, Dan 1998b). Indeed, Elior (2007) calls Jewish mysticism "the infinite expression of freedom". The Kabbalists, as is typical of mystics in other traditions, were loath to define God or the Absolute in anything but 'negative theological' terms, and this posture provided them with a degree of freedom to experiment with ideas about the ultimate nature of things, something which would have been more difficult within the framework of normative Judaism. The Kabbalists described *Ein-sof* as that about which nothing can be said or known (Tishby and Lachower 1989, I: 234), and some of them went so far as to hold that the proper mode of apprehending the divine is through "unknowing" or "forgetting" (Matt 1995: 81). Given our understanding of the Lurianic theosophy as an account of creativity and language, we might well say that on the Lurianic view the divine cannot properly be conceptualized as a being or entity but is rather identified with the very process of creative inquiry, open-mindedness and the taking of multiple perspectives that is stimulated by an interest in (and a failure to circumscribe) ultimates and which takes its concrete form in intellectual, spiritual and artistic endeavour.

The Kabbalist's understanding of the Absolute as *Ayin*, 'Nothingness', is a strong impetus to the view that God cannot be characterized or circumscribed by dogmatic theology. The *Zohar* recites that *Ein-sof* is

> the limit of inquiry. For Wisdom was completed from *ayin* (nothing), which is no subject of inquiry, since it is too deeply hidden and recondite to be comprehended.
> (*Zohar* 1: 30a, Sperling, Simon, and Levertoff 1931–1934, I: 114)

At the same time, the Kabbalist's held that this 'no-thing' is also the foundation of 'everything'. In this moment, *Ein-sof* is the mystery that one is faced with when one asks Leibniz's ultimate question, 'How is it that there is anything at all?' *Ein-sof*, at least initially, is the brute fact of existence, before which we stand in wonder and awe and which prompts our inquiry and creativity.

The notion of a 'divine eclipse' symbolized by the *Tzimtzum* further reinforces a theology in which divinity can perhaps be fathomed but never fully circumscribed. Further, as beings created in the Divine Image (*Tzelem Elohim*) we are enjoined to perform our own *Tzimtzum* (contraction) and permit others (and the world as a whole) to develop according to their own essence or *nisus* without imposing our views or desires upon them.

The *Shevirat ha-Kelim* (the Breaking of the Vessels) implies that all things, all conceptions and all systems of thought (including that of Luria himself) are subject to displacement, rupture, emendation and reorganization in response to the influx of divine energy, which we might here reframe as an influx of pre-conceptualized 'reality' or 'truth'. For the Lurianists, all things and all ideas have their own deconstruction and emendation written into their essence.

The notion that divine energy must be 'liberated' from the *Kellipot*, the 'husks' or complexes that entrap it, is further suggestive of an opening up of thought and experience. Indeed, we might say that the *Kellipot* represent a constriction and rigidity of thought and experience, and that it is precisely such rigidity that yields both dogmatic religious belief and the 'evil' of the *Sitra Achra* or 'Other Side'.

The *Otiyot Yesod*, the Primordial Letters, suggest that the Torah and the world are subject to an infinite number of transformations and interpretations. For some of Luria's followers, the 'Supernal Torah', which is a reflection of God and the ultimate blueprint for the world, is equivalent to the totality of recombinations of its letters, each of which is subject to multiple interpretations. While some Kabbalists 'limited' the number of interpretations to 600,000 (Scholem 1969: 76), corresponding to the 600,000 souls who were said to have departed from Egypt during the Exodus, the principle of multiple, if not infinite, interpretations and perspectives was an established Kabbalistic principle. According to Chayyim Vital, the different perspectives that can be taken upon the cosmos are so vast that they generate an unfathomable number of 'worlds' (Menzi and Padeh 1999). Further, the Kabbalists held that the *sefirot* were lenses through which both God and the world can be interpreted and understood. These archetypes were not only conceptualized as divine traits, but also as perspectives that can be taken upon all things (i.e., the world and God can be understood 'under the aspect' of wisdom, kindness, judgement, compassion, etc.).

Taken together, the Lurianic symbols yield an understanding of God, world and humanity that is perhaps as radical in its openness to multiple perspectives and interpretations as that of the most unrelenting advocates of postmodernism, and indeed the concordance between Kabbalah and postmodernism is an area of significant interest amongst contemporary scholars of Jewish mysticism (Idel 2002; Wolfson 2003; cf. Drob 2009). Yet the Kabbalists engaged in 'infinite interpretation' without abandoning their interest and faith in God or sinking into a linguistic or cultural relativism. For the Kabbalists, in accord with their principle of *coincidentia oppositorum*, the 'difference' that results from an open economy of thought and experience ultimately leads to a unity (and *vice versa*). According to the Chabad Hasidid thinker Aaron Halevi Horowitz of Staroselye (1766–1828),

> the essence of His intention is that his *coincidentia* be manifested in concrete reality, that is, that all realities and their levels be revealed in actuality, each detail in itself, and that they nevertheless be unified and joined in their value.
>
> (Elior 1987: 167)

For the Kabbalists, the multiplicity of perspectives and interpretations ultimately emerges from and converges upon a single source. Later in this chapter we will see why, according to the Kabbalistic view, this indeed *must* be the case. Here, we should note that the 'open economy of thought and experience' is our first tentative neo-Kabbalistic definition of divinity.

Divinity and axiology

Like many who expound a negative theology, the Kabbalists could not resist making positive assertions regarding the deity. For the most part these assertions came in the form of descriptions of *Adam Kadmon* and the *sefirot*. Indeed, the Lurianists provided anthropomorphic descriptions of the Primordial Human as if they were describing the physical features of an individual human being (*Luzatto*). Here, however, I would like to focus upon the Kabbalists' descriptions of the *sefirot* as the archetypal values that are *middot* (traits) of humanity, the cosmos and God. On their view, axiology (theory of value) becomes an image or 'map' of God as manifest as *Adam Kadmon*, the Primordial Human, a figure who serves as a sort of middle-point between God and humankind, and which Hegel once spoke of as the "archetype of humanity" (Hegel 1985: 99, 288).

Apropos Hegel, there is a 'logic' to the values of the *sefirot*, as these are implied by the open economy of thought and experience that we have seen to be implicit in the Lurianic theosophy. Many of the values that are embodied in the *sefirot* (and, as such, many values in general) can only be fully actualized in the context of an open economy of thought and experience (i.e. by a consciousness that is free from dogma and prejudice or which is not unduly constricted in its range of experience). Indeed, the intellectual values, those embodied in the *sefirot Chochmah*, *Binah* and *Da'at* and which involve the quest for wisdom, understanding and knowledge, require an open-mindedness and impartiality that we have seen follows from the 'negative' moment of Kabbalistic theology. This is equally the case for the values that proceed from the *sefirah Din*, which again requires a suspension of prejudice and an even-minded 'judgement'. The values of kindness (*Chesed*), compassion (*Rachamim*), saintliness (*Tzaddik*) and community (*Netzach*) require an openness to and respect for the 'other', an openness and respect that follows from the Kabbalist's principle of *Tzimtzum* or self-contraction. The values of contemplation (*Tifereth*), self-transcendence (*yesod/Tzaddik*), reverence, awe and wonder (*Hod*) require an openness to experience that reaches beyond the pragmatics of everyday life. Finally, the values of 'actualization in time' (*Malchuth*) require the respect for difference embodied in Reb Aaron's open-minded principle, which asserts that "all realities and their levels [must] be revealed in actuality" (Elior 1987: 167).

While a catalogue of the *sefirotic* values (like the list of the *sefirot* themselves) is to a degree variable and arbitrary, the *sefirot* and their coordinated values can be roughly tabulated as follows (readers interested in the derivation of this tabulation are referred to Drob 1997):

- *Keter–Ratzon–Tinug* (Crown–Desire–Delight): values of will, desire, Eros and satisfaction
- *Chochmah* (Wisdom): values of wisdom, truth
- *Binah* (Intelligence, Reasoning, Understanding): values of knowledge and creativity
- *Chesed* (Loving-Kindness): values of bestowal and benevolence
- *Gevurah* (Power), *Din* (Judgement): values of power, freedom, justice, ethics, responsibility and equality

- *Tiferet* (Beauty), *Rachamim* (Compassion): values of contemplation, harmony, aesthetics and balance, and values of empathy, sympathy and compassion
- *Netzach* (Endurance): values of commitment and community
- *Hod* (Majesty, Splendour): values of reverence, wonder and awe
- *Yesod* (Foundation), *Tzaddik* (Righteous, Saintly One): values of self-transcendence
- *Malchuth* (Kingdom), *Shekhinah* (Femininity): values of integration, actualization, temporality (having, using, saving time).

The articulation of a Kabbalistic theory of value is, of course, a task that exceeds the parameters of this current treatment. The basic idea, however, is that we can infer the nature of God (the so-called divine *middot*) through an examination of the values that are embodied and instantiated in humanity, a process that the philosopher J.N. Findlay (1961) once described as a map of the "value firmament." For the Kabbalists, the *sefirot* yield such a 'map' and each of the *sefirot* can be understood as encompassing an axiological category that provides a glimpse into the divine nature. By enacting or realizing such values, one not only engages in *Tikkun ha-Olam* but also in what the Jewish mystics called *devekut*, a 'cleaving' to God. Indeed, according to the Kabbalists (and later the Chasidim), the performance of the *Taryag Mitzvoth* (the 613 Torah commandments) instantiates the *sefirotic* values and brings about a closeness or attachment to God. Interestingly, it is a custom amongst religious Jews – mainly those of a mystical bent but of others as well – to cultivate the psychological traits associated with each of the seven lowest *sefirot* (those from *Chesed* to *Malchuth*) during the 49-day period between Passover and the festival of *Shavuout* as a means of readying oneself for the reception of the Torah and thus a relationship with God.

However, as we have seen, the Kabbalists were not so naïve as to hold that values are simply there for the taking or that they can be realized simply through an act of will. Luria held that values are particularly difficult to realize because the sparks of divine light that energize them have been shattered, dispersed, entrapped and obscured in the 'husks' that resulted from the Breaking of the Vessels. As such, values must be liberated from these husks, and it is the process of liberation that is the mark of human endeavour towards *Tikkun ha-Olam*. In 'liberating' values, humanity participates in the completion and perfection of the divine as it is understood through our second neo-Kabbalistic definition, as the source and actualization of the *sefirotic* values.

Coincidentia oppositorum

As we have seen, the Kabbalists held that *Ein-sof*, the Infinite God, is an *ha-achduth hashawaah*, a "coincidence of opposites" (Scholem 1974: 88; Elior 1993: 69) that unites within itself realities, attitudes and ideas that are opposed to or contradict one another (Scholem 1987: 312). The thirteenth-century Spanish Kabbalist Azriel of Gerona held that *Ein-sof* is the union of being and nothingness and the common root of *both* faith and unbelief (Scholem 1987: 441–442). According to the *Zohar*, God creates man, but one who writes a Torah scroll is credited with creating God (Idel 1988: 188). For Isaac Luria, the deity is both infinity (*Ein-sof*) and Nothingness (*Ayin*), creation is both a concealment and a revelation of God, the *sefirot* are only actualized through their displacement and deconstruction (*Shevirat ha-Kelim*), and God Himself is fully actualized only through the deeds of humankind. The Chabad Chasidim, whose thinking is rooted in the Lurianic Kabbalah, asserted that "the revelation of anything is actually through its opposite" (Elior 1993: 64), that the unity of cosmic opposites brings about the completeness (*shelemut*) of God (Elior 1993: 64) and that "all created things in the world are hidden within His essence . . . in *coincidentia oppositorum*" (Elior 1987: 163).

The Kabbalistic notion of *ha-achduth hashawaah*, the coincidence of opposites, is suggestive of a philosophical program in which fundamental dichotomies and oppositions in thought are resolved only when we come to understand that these dichotomies represent interdependent as opposed to conflicting or contradictory ideas. A Jewish mystical understanding of *Ein-sof* applied to the problems of contemporary philosophy and theology implies the interdependence of such disparities as faith and unbelief, idealism and materialism, determinism and free will, essentialism and nominalism, etc. (Drob 2017). While the Kabbalists *asserted* certain of these equivalences, it is the task of a 'New Kabbalah', armed with the tools of philosophical reason and argument, to explore their rational bases.

Word and thing

Space permits only the briefest discussion of the application of this program,[1] and I will focus, in particular, on one philosophical problem which drew the attention of the Kabbalists and is of considerable moment in recent philosophy. The problem I have in mind is the question of whether there is a distinction between language and the world, signifier and signified, words and things. I will show that the Jewish mystics held both that there is and that there is not a sustainable distinction between words and the things they refer to, and I will argue that the two propositions are a *coincidentia oppositorum*. I will begin with a discussion of the Kabbalistic sources that *deny* the distinction between signifier and signified.

A strong connection between language and the world is already present in the Talmud, where we read of the advice of Rabbi Ishmael to a scribe:

> Be careful in your work for it is the work of God; if you omit a single letter, or write a letter too many, you will destroy the whole world.
> (Talmud, Tractate *Eruvin*, 13a)

The notion that the world is created and sustained by divine speech and writing is present as early as the proto-Kabbalistic *Sefer Yetzirah*, which recites:

> Twenty-two foundation letters: He engraved them, He carved them, He permuted them, He weighed them, He transformed them, And with them, He depicted all that was formed and all that would be formed.
>
> (Kaplan 1997: 100)

Similar ideas are expressed in the early anonymous Kabbalistic work, "The Source of Wisdom" as well as in the *Zohar* (Sperling, Simon, and Levertoff 1931–1934, II: 111). Schneur Zalman, the first Chabad-Lubavitcher rebbe, held that

> if the letters (which comprise divine speech) were to depart [even] for an instant, God forbid, and return to their source, all the heavens would become nought and absolute nothingness, and it would be as though they had never existed at all, exactly as before the utterance, "Let there be a firmament."
>
> (Zalman 1981: 287)

Recently, the Kabbalah scholar Moshe Idel has suggested that the philosopher Jacques Derrida may have obtained his famous dictum, "There is nothing outside the text," from the Kabbalistic aphorism, "There is nothing outside the Torah" (Idel 2002: 123), and Elliot Wolfson has argued that the Kabbalists vitiated the distinction between *mashal* and *nimshal*, signifier and signified (Wolfson 2006: xii). With these claims the Kabbalists anticipated the postmodern view that language constructs reality.

What philosophical warrant is there for the view that there is no genuine distinction between words and the objects they presumably signify? The complex answer to this question can only be hinted at here. We might first observe that the vast majority of the words we speak, hear, write and read acquire their meaning through a chain of other words embedded in a linguistic network and 'form of life', rather than through ostensive definition. This is particularly true for philosophical and theological words and concepts. The word 'God', for example, like the word 'king' in chess, obtains its significance from its place within an entire system of discourse. One does not fathom the meaning of the chess 'king' by looking at, handling or pointing to the king on the chessboard but only by comprehending it within the context of the rules, strategies and history of the game of chess, each of which are coded and articulated in language. Similarly, despite (and without doubting the significance of) 'experiences' of the divine, the 'God' of Judaism (or of any other religion) attains its meaning within the context of what Wittgenstein would call the 'form of life', or 'language game', which in the case of Judaism consists of the scripture, traditions and laws of the Jewish people, each of which are again encoded in language (Drob 1988). Perhaps it is this logic that prompted the Italian Kabbalist Menahem Recanti to regard God and the world to be equivalent to the language of the Torah (Idel 2002: 123).

Our knowledge of things that are remote from us in space and time is mediated by language (and to a much lesser extent other forms of *representation*). Without language there could be no meaningful history, culture, science or biography. Indeed, our awareness of virtually anything that we do not know from personal acquaintance is mediated by language, and it is language that provides us with the conceptual matrix through which we even categorize and understand our own experiences and memories. Finally, even the significance of words that presumably refer to things that are directly in our field of perception, like 'gold', 'tree' or 'pencil', is dependent upon the contextualization of these words through a myriad of practical, cultural and even scientific associations that are given in language.

Considerations such as these lead to the conclusion that the signified is (or always leads to) another signifier, and that there is no ultimate distinction between words and things. What we call 'the world' is, as the Kabbalists maintained, inextricably bound to language. Like the 'king' in chess and the Jewish 'God', the meaning of 'world' is not attained through ostensive definition but rather through an extremely complex linguistic and cultural matrix. We might even go as far as the Kabbalists and claim that the 'world' is comprised of language, or as they put it, the "letters of the holy tongue".

The thesis that the world, if not comprised of language, is known only through it has been referred to as 'linguistic idealism' and has been attributed to a range of twentieth-century philosophers. Richard Rorty (1991: 110), for example, has ascribed to Wittgenstein, Derrida and the American pragmatists the thesis that knowledge is a matter of asserting sentences and that "one cannot validate a sentence by confronting an object but only by asserting other sentences." Wilfred Sellars (1963: 160) went so far as to argue "[t]hat all awareness of sorts, resemblances, facts, etc., in short, all awareness of abstract entities . . . indeed, all awareness even of particulars . . . is a linguistic affair."

Yet there is something very unsettling about the claim that language is completely self-contained and that once we begin to speak we are, in effect, sequestered within a "linguistic prison" (Drob 2008), and it is clear that, despite claims like "There is nothing outside the Torah [text]", the Kabbalists held fast to the existence of a God that transcends both language and human experience. Indeed, according to Azriel:

> *Ein-Sof* cannot be an object of thought, let alone of speech, even though there is an indication of it in everything, for there is nothing beyond it. Consequently, there is no letter, no name, no writing, and no word that can comprise it.
>
> (Tishby and Lachower 1989, I: 234)

Common sense, of course, tells us that our knowledge is of things that transcend language. Surely, 'gold' would have no significance if there were no instances of the malleable yellow metal; 'world' and 'God' would be meaningless (even to those who believe in or experience him) if one thought that their significance was a function of their position within a linguistic matrix, unless one believed that with these words we were at least *reaching towards something beyond language*. As Derrida, Mark Taylor and others have suggested, our very use of language is founded upon the distinction between words and things, signifier and signified. The very claim that the signified is another signifier is itself predicated upon our holding the signifier/signified distinction in view. When we speak about objects, referents and signifieds we may be using words to indicate things that are constructed by language and consciousness, yet we could neither speak nor function in the world without assuming the very dichotomy between signifier and signified that we have just deconstructed. We could not even state the thesis that words are constitutive of things unless we assumed the very distinction we believe must be collapsed. We must indeed speak about consciousness, language, things, the world, as if there are entities that stand apart from the language game that provides them with their sense.

We thus see that once we, like the Kabbalists, recognize the ultimate significance of language in constituting the world and its multitude of kinds and particulars, we realize that two opposing perspectives on language and the cosmos must *each be true* if language is to function at all: the signified is a(nother) signifier, and the signified is distinct from all signifiers. Indeed, these propositions exist in *coincidentia oppositorum*. Things are what they are because they have been constructed by words (God created the world through – and its essence is – language), but words (and language in general) only function because things are completely independent of the words that they refer to.

A similar argument can be made with respect to *consciousness* and the *material world*. On the one hand, in today's scientifically minded age, it seems natural to regard the entire world, including the physical apparatus that is our brain, as a causal function of material entities and events. However, when viewed from another perspective, the very material objects we take to be the causes of our conscious experience are themselves a construction of that experience, grounded in the sensations or phenomenology of conscious awareness. Thus, as with the signifier and the signified, consciousness and the material world are interdependent, in *coincidentia oppositorum*. The same reasoning applies to our understanding of 'reality' and 'truth'. On the one hand, these are each constructed on the basis of linguistic convention and, like the king in chess, obtain their significance from their position in culturally-determined linguistic matrices. However, our linguistic conventions are grounded in the assumption (and presumably the actuality) that 'reality' and 'truth' lie beyond language and serve as the foundation of our discourse about them.

The 'echo' of the absolute

The bifurcation between words and things, consciousness and the material world, subject and object, and, ultimately, the sundering of the cosmos into an infinite multitude of entities and ideas is itself, according to the Kabbalists, *a result of language*. The Lurianic Kabbalists maintained that the *Tzimtzum*, the contraction and concealment of the divine essence into the Foundational Letters of the Hebrew alphabet, produces a distinction between words and things that gives rise to the multiplicity of entities and ideas.

For the Kabbalists, it is through the process of linguistic representation that a unified whole (*Ein-sof*) is divided, a finite world comes into existence and specifiable ideas are generated. Because 'representation' is the vehicle that sunders the whole, representation is inherently inadequate as a vehicle for intuiting *Ein-sof*. An imperfect but helpful analogy is the problem inherent in any attempt to map or represent a three-dimensional sphere (e.g., the earthly globe) on a two-dimensional surface (i.e., a map). The effort to do so yields a series of seemingly contradictory projections (e.g., Mercator, dual polar, equal-area projections) each of which is inadequate as a complete representation and (in the absence of a three-dimensional perspective) only correctable through reference to the others. On the assumption that we, like the denizens of Edwin Abbott's 1884 novella, "Flatland" (Abbott 1991), could only perceive the world in two dimensions, our cartographic efforts would create the same diremptive representational problem with the earthly globe that I am suggesting we experience with regard to *Ein-sof*.

However, if representation is the 'problem' that conceals *Ein-sof*, it is also, according to the Kabbalists, the vehicle of its revelation. This is only fully evident, however, if we grasp the interdependence of theological and philosophical ideas that we had hitherto thought to be mutually exclusive; and particularly when we come to understand the interdependence between words and things, subject and object, consciousness and the world. We must not only adopt the multi-valued or dialetheistic logic of a Nagarjuna but must come to understand why '*x*' and 'not *x*' are both true and *why* this must be the case. If representation is the 'Big Bang' that sunders the One into a multitude of finite entities and ideas, the realization of *coincidentia oppositorum* is our means of 'listening to the echo' of the original Unity.

That a coincidence of opposites exists at the very heart of the method (language) we utilize to represent reality as well as the vehicle we use to experience it (consciousness) suggests the pervasiveness of *coincidentia oppositorum* as an inescapable theological/philosophical principle and helps explain the Jewish mystical conception of *Ein-sof* as a 'unity of opposites'. As we have suggested, several important philosophical dichotomies can be analyzed in the same manner as the opposition between language and the world. Relativism *vs.* absolute truth, idealism *vs.* materialism, (the primacy of) interpretations *vs.* facts, even the relationship between mind and brain, are all subject to similar analyses in which, from one point of view, the first term of the dichotomy appears to condition and dominate the second, but from another point of view the second term conditions and dominates the first. The reason for the bifurcation of our fundamental concepts is that these dichotomies are each themselves produced within language, and as long as we remain within language and representation we have sundered (prelinguistic) reality. However, as I have argued, we can 'listen to the echo' of that reality by *thinking* the interdependence of what language presents to us as opposing and conflicting ideas.

It is because language is necessarily diremptive of unity that there is a tendency within many mystical traditions to move away from representation, and, in effect, *close this book* and silence the discursive mind. It is argued that language, while providing us with a pragmatic means for talking about, categorizing and manipulating the world, entangles us in its web and alienates us from 'pure' experience. This view, however, is not prevalent, or at any rate not emphasized, within the Jewish mystical tradition. After all, the Jews are 'the people of the book'. While language is recognized as producing an alienation from the Absolute, it is, as we have seen, this very alienation that is also the means of revelation and redemption. It is through language (and other forms of representation) that we are privy to the infinitely diverse array of things, ideas, cultures and shared experiences that constitute the finite world, and it is largely through language and representation that we can comprehend the values that, on the Kabbalist's view, are the very *raison d'être* of creation.

Earlier we made a comparison between Kabbalistic and postmodern thought and indicated that while the Kabbalists, like postmodernists, acknowledge a multiplicity of perspectives and interpretations, unlike the postmodernists, they held that these perspectives and interpretations ultimately *emerge from* and *converge upon* a single source. For the Kabbalists, behind the multiplicity and fragmentation there is a whole – a unity that exists in *coincidentia oppositorum* with difference, and to use the mapmaking analogy I offered earlier, a 'globe' that we cannot intuit directly but which nonetheless holds together and assures the (partial) validity of each of our 'cartographic' or representational projections. This 'globe' is our third neo-Kabbalistic definition of *Ein-sof* or divinity: the 'unity of all oppositions'.

The Divine Image

On the principle that man is created in the Divine Image (*b'tzelem elohim*), the notion of the coincidence of opposites (like the open economy of thought and experience, and the *sefirotic* values) is reflected in the soul and psyche of individual men and women. The psychologist C. G. Jung described the self as a "coincidence of opposites" (Jung 1968: 186) and at various points held it to be indistinguishable from the unity that is the archetype of God

(Jung 1969: 73, 116, 170). As Jung emphasized, a *coincidentia oppositorum* plays an important role in the process of personal growth and individuation; for, according to Jung, such individuation must involve the reintegration of the 'shadow' and contra-sexual aspects of one's psyche/personality, aspects that run counter to one's 'persona' and which one's ego endeavours to exclude. A similar notion is prominent in the Kabbalah as well, as the *Zohar*, for example, recites that one must pay equal heed to 'evil' as one does to 'good', for both are necessary for the progress and development of the individual and the world (Tishby and Lachower II: 253). By recognizing the coincidence of good and evil, as well as the other oppositions within our own psyche, we avoid the hubris of believing too strongly in our 'selves' and effectively participate in the image of God.

All of this being said, one can also be carried away with the principle of *coincidentia oppositorum*, and this was indeed a danger that Jung fell into when, in the process of heralding the *coincidentia oppositorum* between good and evil, he developed the idea that something genuinely good would emerge from the evils of Nazi Germany (Kirsch 1992: 64). Jung himself arrived at the notion that the *coincidentia oppositorum* must be applied to itself, and there are indeed instances in which we must entertain "absolute opposition" (Jung 1967: 256). As we have seen, our Kabbalistic 'a-theology' must be subject to its own rupture and emendation.

Theological questions

Having described the 'basic metaphor' of the Lurianic Kabbalah, its major symbols, the significance of these symbols for a conception of God as the foundation for an open economy of thought and experience, a 'firmament of values', and the unity echoed in the coincidence of opposites, we are now finally in a position to provide tentative answers to questions regarding fundamental religious beliefs, the role of reason in religion, the relationship between theology, ethics, politics and everyday life, the meaning and ultimate purpose of human existence, the relationship between faith and unbelief, attitudes towards other faiths, and the necessity and manner of religious proselytization.

Several of these questions have been answered implicitly in the course of this chapter, and I will here confine myself to a few brief remarks.

With regard to the role of reason in religion and theology I would note that traditionally the Kabbalah was contrasted with rational philosophy. According to Luria's disciple, Chayyim Vital:

> There is no doubt that these matters cannot be apprehended by means of human intellect, but only through Kabbalah, from one individual to another, directly from Elijah . . . or directly from those souls that reveal themselves in each and every generation to those who are qualified to receive them.
>
> (Fine 2003: 99)

Nevertheless, Kabbalists such as Azriel and Cordovero held that Kabbalah was in accord with philosophical insights. Later Jewish thinkers, including Shlomo Maimon and Moses Mendelssohn, held that the Kabbalists expressed rational and philosophical insights in metaphorical terms. While I appreciate the need to encompass the non-rational in any complete view and experience of the self, world and God, my own predilection is for what J.N. Findlay referred to as a 'rational mysticism', in which mystical and theosophical insights are expressed, as far as possible, in rational terms. My view is that the three pillars upon which I have described the 'New Kabbalah' (Drob 2000–2012) – the open economy of thought and experience, the primacy of value, and the coincidence of opposites – are each reasonable and rational and that in matters of ethics, politics and human action in general, reason must remain the ultimate arbiter.

For the Kabbalists there was no distinction amongst and between the spheres of theology, ethics, politics and everyday life. For them the meaning and ultimate purpose of human existence is to actualize the *sefirotic* values, and they held that the course of any individual's life is such that each moment, each interaction is an opportunity for *Tikkun ha-Olam*. The Hasidim went so far as to hold that all the people and things that an individual encounters in life contain 'sparks' of divinity which that individual is uniquely suited to raise and 'restore'. One leads one's life, according to this metaphor, as a vehicle for the actualization of values, and this was traditionally held to be accomplished through strict adherence to the *Taryag Mitzvoth*, the 613 Torah commandments. If and how the spirit of *Tikkun ha-Olam* can and should be fulfilled outside or beyond participation in the *halakha*, traditional Jewish law, is a critical question that lies outside the scope of this chapter and touches upon the question of a 'universal Torah' (Drob 2010: 158–179). My own perspective on this is that the pursuit of a non-dogmatic, unknowing, 'open economy' of thought and experience is the first and most essential phase in this process.

As we have seen, according to the thirteenth-century Kabbalist Azriel of Gernoa, there is a coincidence of opposites between faith and unbelief in our understanding of the divine. Atheism, by challenging the idols of dogmatic religion and theology and by opening the mind to alternative perspectives and interpretations, is to my way of thinking a necessary stage in the manifestation of divinity as the creative, open economy of thought and experience. There is a sense in which my own understanding of God involves an atheization of theology and a spiritualization of atheism, as I identify divinity with the very values that often prompt an atheistic reaction towards religion. Yet atheism too can become dogmatic and idolatrous and too frequently fails to acknowledge and, moreover, encourage the experience of wonder and awe at 'being' and the sense of sanctity in the world that is at the core of the spiritual life.

Proselytization to an open-minded, multiple-perspective way of thinking and living is to my mind necessary if the world is to advance towards *Tikkun ha-Olam*. Yet such proselytization must occur through respectful discourse and example, and always with a deep respect for the beliefs, traditions and values of other religions and cultures. One must always pay heed to Rabbi Aaron's principle that all things must be revealed in their full actuality, 'each detail in itself', prior to their being unified and joined in their value, and this applies in particular to the diversity of cultures, ethnicities, traditions and religions that characterize the human species. By adhering to this principle and showing our respect for the 'difference' of others and the multiplicities that make up the world, we encourage others to do so as well, and in the process engage in *Tikkun ha-Olam*.

Finally, I would like to comment upon the question of a personal relationship with God. There are certainly elements within my 'New Kabbalah' conception of the deity that are highly abstract and impersonal – the notion of God as a coincidence of opposites between the notions that words are and are not distinct from things is but one example. Yet, there is also a sense in which the God of the Kabbalah is extremely personal, characterized as a firmament of and primordial container of value, and in the figure of *Adam Kadmon*, the Primordial Human, he/she is modeled upon the very traits and values that constitute *personhood*. The access we have to this cosmic person and the values he/she embodies is through the development of ourselves, our relationships with others and our deep concern and engagement with the world as we experience and transform it through the value archetypes of the *sefirot*. We develop a personal relationship with the divine when we relate to ourselves, others and the world, not in a non-pragmatic 'I-it' manner, but personally via 'I and Thou' (Buber 1937). The Indian poet Tulsidas (d. 1623) wrote:

> There is no difference between the Personal and the Impersonal. . . . He who is Impersonal, without form and unborn, becomes Personal for love of his devotees.
>
> (Renou 1962: 220)

Note

1 A full discussion of the 'coincidence of opposites program' in relation to our understanding of mysticism, philosophy and psychology appears in Drob (2017). See also Drob (2003b) in connection with resolving the dilemma of multiple paradigms in psychology.

References

Abbott, E. 1991. *Flatland*. Princeton, NJ: Princeton University Press.
Buber, M. 1937. *I and Thou*, translated by R. G. Smith. New York: Charles Scribner's Sons.
Coudert, A. 1995. *Leibniz and the Kabbalah*. New York: Springer-Verlag.
Coudert, A. 1998. *The Impact of the Kabbalah in the Seventeenth Century: The Life and Thought of Francis Mercury van Helmont (1614–1698)*. Boston, MA: Brill Academic Publishers.
Dan, J. 1966. *The Early Kabbalah*, translated by R. C. Kieber. New York: Paulist Press.

Dan, J. (ed.). 1997. *The Christian Kabbalah: Jewish Mystical Books and Their Christian Interpreters*. Cambridge, MA: Harvard College Library.
Dan, J. 1998a. *Jewish Mysticism*, vols. I–IV. Northvale, NJ: Jason Aronson.
Dan, J. 1998b. "The Name of God, the Name of the Rose, and the Concept of Language in Jewish Mysticism." In *Jewish Mysticism*, vol. II: The Modern Period, edited by J. Dan, 131–162. Northvale, NJ: Jason Aronson.
Drob, S. 1988. "Judaism as a Form of Life." *Tradition: A Journal of Orthodox Jewish Thought* 23, no. 4: 78–89.
Drob, S. 1990. "The Mystic as Philosopher: An Interview With Rabbi Adin Steinsaltz." *Jewish Review* 3, no. 4, March: 14.
Drob, S. 1997. "The Sefirot: Kabbalistic Archetypes of Mind and Creation." *CrossCurrents: The Journal of the Association for Religion and Intellectual Life* 47, no. 1: 5–29.
Drob, S. 2000–2012. "The New Kabbalah." http://www.newkabbalah.com.
Drob, S. 2000a. *Symbols of the Kabbalah: Philosophical and Psychological Perspectives*. Northvale, NJ: Jason Aronson.
Drob, S. 2000b. *Kabbalistic Metaphors: Mystical Themes in Ancient and Modern Thought*. Northvale, NJ: Jason Aronson.
Drob, S. (2003a). "Towards a Kabbalistic Psychology: C. G. Jung and the Jewish Foundations of Alchemy." *Journal of Jungian Theory and Practice* 5, no. 2: 77–100.
Drob, S. (2003b). "Fragmentation in Psychology: A Dialectical Solution." *Journal of Humanistic Psychology* 43, no. 4: 102–123.
Drob, S. 2004. "*Tzimtzum* and 'Difference': Derrida and the Lurianic Kabbalah." http://www.newkabbalah.com/Derrida3.html.
Drob, S. 2008. "James Hillman on Language: Escape From the Linguistic Prison." In *Archetypal Psychologies: Reflections in Honor of James Hillman*, edited by S. Marlan, 153–168. New Orleans, LA: Spring Journal Books.
Drob, S. 2009. *Kabbalah and Postmodernism: A Dialog*. New York: Peter Lang.
Drob, S. 2010. *Kabbalistic Visions: C. G. Jung and Jewish Mysticism*. New Orleans: Spring Journal Book.
Drob, S. 2017. *Archetype of the Absolute: The Unity of Opposites in Mysticism, Philosophy, and Psychology*. Santa Barbara, CA: Fielding University Press.
Elior, R. 1993. *The Paradoxical Ascent to God: The Kabbalistic Theosophy of Habad Hasidism*, translated by J. M. Green. Albany, NY: State University of New York.
Elior, R. C. 1987. "The Contemplative Ascent to God." In *Jewish Spirituality: From the Sixteenth Century Revival to the Present*, edited by A. Green, 157–205. New York: Crossroads.
Elior, R. C. 2007. *Jewish Mysticism: The Infinite Expression of Freedom*, translated by Y. Nave and A. Millman. Oxford: Littman Library of Jewish Civilization.
Findlay, J. N. 1961. *Values and Intentions*. London: George Allen & Unwin.
Fine, L. 2003. *Physician of the Soul, Healer of the Cosmos: Isaac Luria and His Kabbalistic Fellowship*. Stanford, CA: Stanford University Press.
Graetz, H. 1937. *Popular History of the Jews*, 5th ed., vol. 4. Spencertown, New York: Hebrew Publishing Company.
Hegel, G. W. F. 1985. *Lectures on the Philosophy of Religion*, edited by P. C. Hodgson. Berkeley, CA: University of California Press.
Idel, M. 1988. *Kabbalah: New Perspectives*. New Haven, CT: Yale University Press.
Idel, M. 2002. *Absorbing Perfections*. New Haven, CT: Yale University Press.

Jung, C. G. 1967. "The Spirit of Mercurius." In *Alchemical Studies: The Collected Works of C. G. Jung*, vol. 13, translated by R. F. C. Hull, 191–250. Princeton, NJ: Princeton University Press.

Jung, C. G. 1968. *Psychology and Alchemy: The Collected Works of C. G. Jung*, vol. 12, translated by R. F. C. Hull. Princeton, NJ: Princeton University Press.

Jung, C. G. 1969. *Aion: Researches Into the Phenomenology of the Self: The Collected Works of C. G. Jung*, vol. 9, Part II, translated by R. F. C. Hull. Princeton, NJ: Princeton University Press.

Kaplan, A. 1989. *The Bahir: Illumination*. York Beach, Maine: Samuel Weiser.

Kaplan, A. 1997. *Sefer Yetzirah: The Book of Creation*, rev. ed. York Beach, Maine: Samuel Weiser.

Kirsch, J. 1992. "Carl Gustav Jung and the Jews: The Real Story." In *Lingering Shadows: Jungians, Freudians, and Anti-Semitism*, edited by A. Maidenbaum and S. A. Martin, 51–87. Boston, MA: Shambhala.

Matt, D. 1995. "*Ayin*: The Concept of Nothingness in Jewish Mysticism." In *Essential Papers on Kabbalah*, edited by L. Fine, 67–108. New York: New York University Press.

Menzi, D. and Z. Padeh. 1999. *The Tree of Life: Chayim Vital's Introduction to the Kabbalah of Isaac Luria*, trans. Northvale, NJ: Jason Aronson.

Renou, L. (ed.). 1962. *Hinduism*. New York: George Brazier.

Rorty, R. 1991. "Two Meanings of 'Logocentrism': A Reply to Norris." In *Philosophical Papers, Vol. 2: Essays on Heidegger and Others*, edited by R. Rorty, 107–118. Cambridge: Cambridge University Press.

Schochet, I. 1981. "Mystical Concepts in Chassidism." In *Likutei Amaraim-Tanya*, edited by S. Zalman, 810–894. Brooklyn: Kehot.

Scholem, G. 1946. *Major Trends in Jewish Mysticism*, rev. ed. New York: Schocken Books.

Scholem, G. 1969. *On the Kabbalah and Its Symbolism*. New York: Schocken.

Scholem, G. 1974. *Kabbalah*. Jerusalem: Keter.

Scholem. G. 1987. *Origins of the Kabbalah*, translated by R. J. Zwi Werblowski. Princeton, NJ: Princeton University Press.

Sellars, W. 1963. "Empiricism and the Philosophy of Mind." In *Science, Perception, and Reality*, 127–196. London: Routledge and Kegan Paul.

Shapiro, M. 2004. *The Limits of Orthodox Theology: Maimonides' Thirteen Principles Reappraised*. Oxford: The Littman Library of Jewish Civilization.

Sperling, H., M. Simon, and P. Levertoff, trans. 1931–1934. *The Zohar*. London: Soncino Press.

Tishby, I. and F. Lachower. 1989. *The Wisdom of the Zohar: An Anthology of Texts*, vols I–III, translated by D. Goldstein. Oxford: Oxford University Press.

Wolfson, E. 1995. *Circle in the Square: Studies in the Use of Gender in Kabbalistic Symbolism*. Albany: State University of New York Press.

Wolfson, E. 2003. "Assaulting the Border: Kabbalistic Traces in the Margins of Derrida." *Journal of the American Academy of Religion* 70, no. 3: 475–514.

Wolfson, E. 2006. *Alef, Mem, Tau: Kabbalistic Musings on Time, Truth, and Death*. Berkeley, CA: University of California Press.

Zalman, S. 1981. *Likutei-Amarim-Tanya*, bilingual ed. Brooklyn: Kehot Publication Society.

3 Radical incarnational Christianity[†]

Lisa Isherwood

As a feminist liberation, body theologian working within the Christian tradition, the title 'So Here I Stand on Volcanoes and Ruptures' best describes the ground I inhabit in my personal and professional life as I navigate the question of the divine and the implications this may have in my life and beyond. In this chapter I will draw out the implications of each of these parts of my personal and professional identity and demonstrate the impact each has in the private and public arena.

So, first of all, how do I understand *feminist theology*, and how does it impact on what can be called 'traditional theology'? As Rosemary Radford Ruether said before me, feminist theology is the radical and as yet unexplored notion that women are fully human. Ruether was amongst the first to examine where the denial of the female first infiltrated a religion that declared a new social order. She finds the origin of the denial of the feminine in the classical Neoplatonism and apocalyptic Judaism out of which Christianity was born. Here we find the combination of a male warrior God with the exaltation of the intellect over the body. The alienation of the masculine from the feminine is the basic sexual symbol that sums up all the other dualisms, which are mind and body, subjective self and objective world, individual and community, autonomous will (male) and bodily sensuality (female), and the domination of nature by spirit (Ruether 1979: 44).

The Hellenistic influence has shaped concepts such as 'Logos' and 'Christ' in devastatingly androcentric ways (Ruether 1998a: 82). While Christianity has never claimed that God was literally male, the Hellenistic underpinning has led to many assumptions about the nature of God and normative humanity. There has been an unspoken, yet enacted, androcentric bias which has reduced the place of women and men in the world, holding them as it does to very outmoded and reductive notions of humanness. Ruether points out that there was a time when God was far more encouraging in terms of our own freedom; the business of reminding us of our divinity included putting down the mighty, releasing captives and vindicating the oppressed. She says: "If he [God] could be it again he would free slaves, include Gentiles and perhaps even women!" (1998a: 3). Ruether is quite confident that it can happen again, because with the death of Jesus, the Heavenly Ruler has left the heavens and been poured out on the earth. "A new God is being born in our hearts to teach us to level the heavens and exalt the earth and create a new world without masters and slaves, rulers and subjects" (1998a: 11). There can be no claiming of divinity for anyone while injustice and inequality stalk the earth. Ruether is keen to unleash the human potential bound by patriarchy because a tradition that prophetically promised liberation cannot be left in the hands of its manipulators and made into a static set of ideas.

Throughout Christian history there has been what Schüssler Fiorenza calls 'the egalitarian countercultural trend' which has spoken about the equality of women, and Letty Russell is among those who believes that feminist liberation theology does offer women a way to find a usable past, although she acknowledges the difficulty faced in dealing "creatively and faithfully with tradition" (1974: 73). She argues that there is ample biblical evidence which illustrates that a completed and therefore static view of revelation was a late addition to Christianity – a late addition which flies in the face of Jesus' promise of the Spirit which will lead people forward (John 16:13). Russell demonstrates that none of the so-called infallible traditions have actually been cast in stone by the divine, and she illustrates her point by referring to the way in which the divine was imaged in the Hebrew Scriptures. God is often referred to in female terms, and three of the most important ideas in Judaism are spoken of as feminine. These are *Shekhinah* (glory of God), *Chokmah* (pre-cosmic deity) and *Torah* (laws of guidance). The female nature of these ideas was downplayed over the centuries, which illustrates Russell's point that things do change. She says: "the heresy of our time is not that of reexamining the Biblical and ecclesial traditions. It is the refusal of the Church to hear the cry of oppressed people and to speak and act on behalf of liberation for all" (1974: 103).

In the West, Rosemary Ruether was amongst those who declared that Christ was best understood as a liberator, not in the spiritual sense but in real terms in the political and social realm. Aware as she is of the demands for justice in the world, Ruether nevertheless set out a biblically based argument for an understanding of Jesus as liberator. She clearly demonstrated how the Christ of Judeo-Christian tradition was a radical liberative figure. Ruether wished to take seriously the Jewish roots of Christianity and Christian thinking and so was not prepared to merely brush over Hebraic messianic thought with the gloss of Greek metaphysics. Central to Jewish messianic hope was political action, since for the Jews religious life and political life were synonymous. Even when their ideas around the Kingdom became more transcendent, they never lost sight of the importance of politics. The Messianic Kingdom was one with its feet planted deeply in the earth – it was political and social. However, it appears that it was also deeply patriarchal, and this is not entirely surprising given the patriarchal nature of much contemporary Judaism and the increased understanding of the Messiah as a warrior-king. Therefore, a warrior male who would rule from the pinnacle of an elitist hierarchy would supply salvation. Ruether is insistent that this was a story that developed under the pressure of circumstances and was not the entire Jewish heritage from which Christians could draw.

Further, Jesus did not appear to accept such a hierarchical scheme or to evoke Davidic kingly hopes; rather, he praised the lowly and outcasts for responding to his message while the reigning authorities remained encapsulated in their systems of power. Furthermore, he did not envisage the Kingdom as otherworldly, nationalistic and elitist (Ruether 1983: 120). He saw it come on earth when basic needs were met and people could live in harmony. In this new community, we would not simply be servants but brothers and sisters, thus replacing the old idea of the patriarchal family with its inevitable inequalities (Matthew 10:37–38, 12:46–50; Luke 8:19–21). Jesus also declared that God was not speaking in the past but rather speaking now to challenge the Law and its outdated, life-stifling interpretations (John 4:10, 8:4–11; Matthew 9:10–13, 9:18–22; Mark 2:23–28). Ruether argues that once we see Jesus in this light, we find a Redeemer for women. She says:

> Jesus restores a sense of God's prophetic and redemptive activity taking place in the present-future, through people's experiences and the new possibilities disclosed through those possibilities. To encapsulate Jesus himself as God's 'last word' and 'once for all' disclosure of God, located in a remote past and institutionalised in a cast of Christian teachers, is to repudiate the spirit of Jesus and to recapitulate the position against which he himself protests.
>
> (1983: 122)

Against this background, the everyday experiences of women become valuable as disclosers of the divine redemptive process rather than expressions of alienating 'otherness'. Ruether argues that the disciples had not expected such a denouncement of their messianic hopes and patriarchal expectations, and so they began to turn Jesus into a doctrine rather than risk embracing the event of eternal liberation (1983: 110–111). Ruether challenges Christianity to see the events of Jesus' life as eschatological, as realities towards which we are still moving and not as historical events that form the base of an established church. Rita Brock is critical of Ruether, claiming that she places Jesus in the position of a hero, thus disabling his followers. We give away our own power to those we consider heroes, and this is made no better by the fact that we view the hero as benevolent or even the Christ; we are still left bereft of control in our lives. Brock is only too well aware of how dangerous this is and so warns us against casting Jesus in such a role. She is adamant that basing Christology on a historical figure is a mistake since it confuses the concept with the phenomena (see Brock 1988).

While I am in agreement with my fore-sisters, my theological projects are always rooted in a Christology that I call 'radical incarnational theology', which is erotic, sensuous and empowering, one that urges us forward to relationality and flourishing, to life in abundance. Incarnation tells us that our bodies are our homes, that is to say our divine/human desiring dwelling places; therefore our Christological journey is home to the fullness of our incarnation, the co-redemptive, co-creative reality of our fleshly heaven.[1] It is a Christology based on a gospel picture of empowerment, not servitude, and finds inspiration in the life of Jesus and not salvation through the death of Jesus. The Christology that this assumes is not one of denial and narrow boundaries; it is one of embrace and expansion that wilfully wishes to move the edges of the world in which we live! It is a theology/Christology that takes as read that radical politics is not an added extra to an internal relationship with an ethereal Christ but rather radical, countercultural politics is the skin we put on, the Christ we incarnate. It is the world we create through Christological ponderings that is of extreme importance and not the metaphysical workings of essences and hypostatic unions that exercise my mind. Therefore, in my work and personal life I strive for the subjectivity of women to be recognized and valued and of course to be central in the creation of theology, politics, ethics, economics – *life!*

As a *liberation theologian*, issues of the divine are rooted in the concept of freedom from oppression found in the Hebrew Bible and the Christian scriptural notion of life in abundance. As the Bishops at Medellin quickly discovered, scripture alone could not help them with the desperate plight of many of those who they ministered to in Latin America and Africa: the love of God was hard to square with crippling poverty and the pain, suffering and abuse that often comes with it. Many of the bishops who had received western theological education at the time that the grace and nature debates were at their height felt that the usual 'you will get your reward in heaven' answer was not sufficient and indeed was somewhat patronizing to people who clearly understood that their plight was created by human action and not divine dictate. To offer alternatives, they used the biblical concepts of justice, exodus, freedom and liberation but also realized that in order for these theological concepts to be of any earthly good, they needed what might be called 'mediator disciplines', and in the case of poverty in Latin America the chosen discipline was Marxism, and particularly Marxist economics. In this way, from what started as a Marxist understanding of alienation and descriptions of how things came to be humanly made, theologians also found that this in turn had implications for the creation of theology. The method they developed soon became available to many others in the field of theology, and from poverty the liberation method started to be applied to race and ethnicity, and in my own case I applied it to sex and gender. Here too it was possible to see that women and men were being held to a script that was not divinely ordained but rather humanly crafted and, under Christian theology, also oppressively crafted. The question moved from why would God want it this way to who wants it this way and why – for what power and profit? This opened the area of sex and gender within theology in a hitherto unknown way.

It has been argued by feminist theologians that the construction of gender and sexuality and the construction of religion work hand in hand. I will argue that there are heteropatriarchal assumptions underpinning the construction of religion and sexuality/gender which result in narrow and hierarchically driven narratives about both. The split between man and woman has had devastating consequences for women, who have also had to carry the weight of patriarchal disapproval in matters of sexuality, being believed to be the more material of the two genders and therefore more prone to sexual immorality than the more spiritual man. Indeed, the Fathers often warned against intercourse, as the spiritual man would be literally trapped in the material woman, who of course would have enticed him through her lisping speech and devilish flesh. There could then only be dangers involved in anything to do with women, and so salvation and redemption did not tend to include women 'as they are' in the rhetoric or even as a possibility until relatively late (Ruether 1998b).

It is not surprising, then, that Christianity has been historically blind to questions of gender, believing that 'mankind' includes the experiences of women and men and encompasses all that makes us human. This assumption of course works in many ways, and to a certain extent it becomes self-fulfilling in that women do begin to understand themselves through the male lens and in so many respects begin to see themselves as defective, insufficient or as simply experientially deluded. As de Beauvoir realized all those years ago, a woman is not born, she is made, and her making is in order to support the male-dominated status quo – she is made into what is useful. As she also so movingly noted, a woman would apprehend her own body not as an "instrument of her transcendence but as 'an object destined for another'" (Bartky 1990: 38). This destination is usually the physical male but can also be the great Phallus in the sky, the patriarchal father who invades all manner of relationships. Once invading the "intimate recesses of the personality . . . it may maim and cripple the spirit for ever" (Bartky 1990: 58).

Although God plays no part in our secular society, it has to be acknowledged that this making of women has its roots in theology, since the way in which men and women are meant to be supposedly reflects God's design for the universe. For example, the inequality between the sexes has been and still is attributed to the notion of complementarity which can be derived from a patriarchal reading of the Genesis myth. Eve is taken from the side of Adam, thereby signalling that the two halves need to be made whole once more. Woman, being a derivative of man, can never expect to possess the original, holy qualities to the same extent. This is a view that can be lifted not just from the Hebrew scriptures; some scholars argue it is also there in what at first seems a very positive statement for women, the Pauline injunction regarding equality in Christ (Galatians 3:28). On closer inspection, it is argued, what is actually assumed is that woman disappears, the rib slots neatly back into place, and the male image of God is left as it was first placed on this earth. In Christ, the breach that occurred in Genesis is healed and man once again shines in unitary glory (Borresen 1995: 62). Presumably it is not beyond the bounds of speculation to assume that at the eschaton woman will cease to exist, but until that time she will be judged against an androcentric norm. Borresen argues that Christ had to be incarnate as a male if he was to represent perfect humanity, such is the weight of patriarchal ideology (1995: 190). It would have been inconceivable to the Fathers that a woman might be the divine incarnate. Indeed, for them it was often hard to imagine that woman could be holy. This is a trend which started in Ephesians, where we are told that woman's salvational equality is gained by achieving Christ-like maleness (Ephesians 4:13). It was picked up and carried on with vigour, Tertullian imagining that resurrected women would be a mixture of angels and men, while Jerome thought that if a woman wished to serve Christ she had to give up being a woman (*Exposition of the Gospel of Luke* 10: 161) and Ambrose added that a believing woman does indeed progress to complete manhood (*Regula Episcopi*: Preface). This gender-bending for salvation is a rather blunt instrument under which woman's ultimate destiny is to disappear, something which is evident in much Christian doctrine.

Gender is inscribed on the body, and the bodies of women have carried a very heavy burden under patriarchy. The way in which the bodies of women and men have been ascribed gender roles is a question of power and significance in the world. These definitions do not simply show the difference – they make the difference, and as such need much attention by feminist liberation theologies. The way in which the bodies of women and the gender roles given them have been viewed by the churches and traditional theology has meant that women are denied access to the Symbolic Order in any creative and positive way; they are the abject, the ones that have to be rejected in order that the symbolic and political realm can work.

Lacan, as we all know, may well be called the father of the Phallus! For him, the Symbolic Order is what defines us as embodied persons, and, following Freud, he makes it very difficult for women to find a place at all in this Order of the fathers. For him, the acquisition of language is extremely important, and even this is different for boys and girls, since girls do not speak the language of the father which is the dominant currency. Sexual/gender difference, then, is at the centre of the Symbolic Order, and the Phallus reigns supreme as the structuring principle; this, of course, is developed from a very uncritical acceptance of the Freudian notion of the Oedipus complex but also has its roots much further back in our cultural heritage – some would say in Eden itself, when the differentiation of the sexes and the relationship to the Symbolic were first alluded to. These tales we tell ourselves create a world in which women and, of course, our bodies are always lacking; indeed, Lacan speaks of women as absences which need to be filled with phallic signifiers. There is no way to resolve this situation within the world of the Symbolic Order, and Lacan urges women to find their own economy beyond that of the phallus. This can be done through female sexual pleasure (*jouissance*), but it is never likely to be achieved, since it is beyond the phallic and therefore beyond language and meaning itself. There can be no subjectivity, then, and women and their bodies can only find significance through the male body and the male symbolic. This situation permeates the whole of culture, where women are constantly on the outside without a language to call their own. Our bodies, then, have no hope of a voice in the discourses that are played out on them. Irigaray highlights this dilemma by suggesting that there can be no subjectivity until women find a place in culture, since this belonging gives psychic leverage to our personhood (Howson 2005: 103). For Irigaray (1985), this can begin with the body; we can find a language when our genital lips meet and speak. She also feels that we have to find a language of the divine; in fact, the two processes are not that distinct. It is a matter of great urgency that we find a language, because if we do not then we simply repeat the same history through an inability to think otherwise. Irigaray's contribution to religious philosophy is well known to readers, and what is perhaps of most relevance here is her insistence that women have to find a place in culture or have to find a tradition that will empower them. It has been argued by some that sociologists of the body have often forgotten the materiality and social contexts of bodies in their prioritization of Lacan and psychoanalytic discourse, a discourse that gets us in the most intimate parts of ourselves, our psyches.

Both Butler and Braidotti challenge the Lacanian notion that women are outside language. Butler suggests that woman is in process and so not a finally defined other who can be placed outside; she is a body becoming, and this is a language of its own, a language of materiality (Butler 1990: 30). Braidotti speaks of figurations which are politically informed accounts of alternative subjectivity, or living 'as if', which is "a technique of strategic relocation in order to rescue what we need of the past in order to trace paths of transformations of our lives here and now" (1994: 6). She continues: "'as if' is affirmation of fluid boundaries, practice of the intervals" which sees nothing as an end in itself (1994: 6) – not even the Symbolic Order, one suspects! While she does acknowledge that we as women have no mother tongue, we do have linguistic sites from which we both see and fail to see. For this reason, then, we need to be nomads, taking no position or identity as permanent but rather trespassing and transgressing, making coalitions and interconnections beyond boxes. We have no language, but we do have bodies, bodies that have been "the basic stratum on which the multilayered institution of Phallocentric subjectivity is erected. . . . Woman is the primary matter and the foundational stone, whose silent presence installs the master in his monologic mode" (Braidotti 1994: 119). These same bodies can be radically subversive of culture when they find their voice beyond the fixed language and meaning of the masters' discourses.

Braidotti anticipates the objection that total nomadism will never allow for coalitions by suggesting that the only way to find a larger vision is to be somewhere in particular, to engage in a politics of positioning (1994: 73).

However, this does not require us to be static or defined by male definitions because, as she tells us, it is the feminine which is a "typically masculine attitude, which turns male disorders into feminine values" (1994: 124) and not the female body – this is free to roam and to express itself, to find new ways of being by thinking through the body. The nomadism of which Braidotti speaks perhaps enables the feminist theologian to pick up the notion of Christians as resurrection and pilgrim people, especially in the light of our nomadic cross-dressing fore-sisters. Should we take seriously the possibility of shifting and moving within gender and sexual identities, that could free us from the oppressive repetitions required by religion and culture. Perhaps by highlighting the constructed nature of gender categories we begin to draw attention to their foolishness and restricting (non-redeemed) nature and begin to enflesh the Galatian baptismal formula: "In Christ there is neither male nor female" – is this a Christian politics of positioning?

With the adoption of feminist methodology in theology, we have a revolutionary situation in which embodied subjectivity is placed at the heart of knowing, and this declares invalid 'objective absolute rationality', which has been the 'norm' within patriarchal mythology.

Butler is provocative when she declares that multiplicity is not the thing that makes agency impossible, but is rather the very nature of agency, precisely the condition under which agency flourishes. Further, she suggests that it is in the fear of the questions posed by multiplicity that we find the creation of the rhetoric of morals as a defence of politics (Butler 2004: 180). She illustrates her point through considering how the Catholic Church deals with issues of gender and sexual difference. In 1995, the Curia called for the United Nations to eliminate the language of 'gender' from its platforms to do with the status of women, declaring that the word was simply a cover for homosexuality, which they condemn and do not see as having a place in a rights agenda. They insisted on a return to the word 'sex', and their rhetoric attempted to indisputably link sex with the maternal and feminine, reflecting, as they saw it, the divinely ordained 'natural goodness' of things.

To those observing, the agenda was very clear: it was an attempt to reverse many of the gains that women had made in relation to human rights, and it was a narrow defining that could be once again placed at the service of containment and control. Butler puts it as follows: "The Vatican fears the separation of sexuality from sex, for that introduces a notion of sexual practice that is not constrained by putatively natural reproductive ends" (2004: 184). It is, then, no surprise to her that the Vatican considers the inclusion of lesbian rights in United Nations legislation as 'anti-human'. Given the Vatican's understanding of the relation of sex and the human person, it is then correct to make such a statement, since the inclusion of lesbian into the realm of the universal would be to expand the boundaries of what has thus far been defined as 'human' beyond the conventional limits. In order, then, that all humans may be recognised, it seems that "the human . . . must become strange to itself" (2004: 191).

Butler goes on to say that this new human "will have no ultimate form but it will be one that is constantly negotiating sexual difference in a way that has no natural or necessary consequences for the social organisation of sexuality" (2004: 191). Is this what those early Christian fore-sisters were attempting to embody in their interpretation of the declaration in Galatians? Is it in this enactment of the beyond, the becoming strange to oneself, that all the possibilities of incarnate life find root? Butler reminds us that the body is the site on which language falters (2004: 198), and the signifiers of the body remain, for the most part, largely unconscious, which in itself is a language but one ever unfolding and of many tongues. Performativity is a whole body engagement, just as incarnation is, and both resist the deadening claws of narrow and controlling definitions of personhood – both expand the edges of where it is we think we inhabit.

The other massive contribution offered by feminist theologies is in the area of sexuality. The traditional interpretation of Christianity has not looked kindly on sexuality, particularly the sexuality of women, which lives in the Christian psyche as the cause of the Fall of Man! Many of the early feminist scholars illustrated for us how women, sexuality, spirituality and the sacred were not always at odds in our human history – indeed, how women's sexuality was for many centuries intimately and positively connected with the sacred and the divine itself (see, e.g., Tessier 1997).

This recovery of the erotic within theology has been a significant contribution of feminist theologies. For theologians, Audre Lorde – although not a theologian herself – stands out as the provider of the essential canon on the erotic. For Lorde, the erotic is the intense kernel of our being that when released "flows through and colours my life with a kind of energy that heightens and sensitizes and strengthens all my experience" (Lorde 1984: 57). It is a form of outreaching joy that connects us to all things and transforms all experiences into delight. Not quite how the Fathers saw it!

Rita Brock (1988) and Carter Heyward (1989a) are the two feminist theologians who expand this understanding and are most associated with the notion of Christ as erotic power. Brock believes that when speaking of Jesus as powerful, we have to be quite clear that this is erotic power; this is no abstract concept but is power deeply embedded in our very core. This kind of power is wild and cannot be controlled, and living at this level saves us from the sterility that comes from living by the head alone. *Eros* allows us to feel our deepest passions in all areas of life, and we are enjoined to reclaim it from the narrow sexual definition that has been used by patriarchal understanding. Christianity has always encouraged *agape*, which Brock sees as heady and objective and therefore not as something that will change the world. Indeed, it is part of the objectifying discourse which allows us to stand by as though powerless in the face of many of the horrors of our world. Both Brock and Heyward show how, in fearing passion, traditional Christianity has made us a passionless and therefore largely impotent people.

For Heyward, intimacy is the deepest quality of relation, and she sees no reason why it should be left out of our theological story. Heyward believes that to be intimate is to be assured that we are known in such a way that the mutuality of our relation is real, creative and cooperative, and so it has a fundamental part in any theology and religious practice. Heyward's original work was rooted in a close analysis of Mark's gospel and a rereading of the meaning of *exousia* and *dunamis* as used in that gospel. Her conclusions led her to assert that it is the power of *dunamis*, that raw dynamic energy that attracts us to each other and the world, that is the transforming and thus salvific power that Jesus points us towards through his life and engagement with just such a passion. Heyward's grounding of passion and erotic power within the Christological arena opened the way for much creative and revolutionary sexual theology, and with it the rethinking of women's sexuality in general. If the central core of Christian belief, Christology, is indeed rooted in the erotic, which has some expression through the sexual, then Christian theologians will have to think again about their naïve division of these deeply human, deeply divine elements of humanity. Heyward stunned the theological world when a preface to her book noted that she could not write theology unless she was grounded in sensuous pleasures, including making love to one of her women lovers who would bring her forth to herself and the world, and, in so doing, to God. Strong words in so many ways for an Episcopalian priest. This feminist engagement with Christology and ways of interpreting actually gave female sexuality ways in which women could lift their bodies and sexuality out of the mire of male clerical dictate and once again declare the sacredness of their sexual lives. Of course, in turn, this also highlighted how, under patriarchal rules (both clerical and secular), the lived reality of women's sexuality was not always as free or sacred – many a woman has had her body made the object of blasphemous treatment by clerical declaration as well as by physically harsh and disrespectful treatment. By suggesting that the embodied reality of *eros* is central to the life of Christ as it is to our own becoming and relating, Heyward opened the gates for sexual lives to be part of the basis for the unfolding of the divine and the reflection that becomes doctrinal.

In recent years, queer theory has impacted on feminist theology. The postmodern agenda makes it imperative that we look with new eyes at the old questions and, especially in the light of rethinking what it is that women may be, that we do not come to easy and safe answers – sexual theology asks that we be bold in order to fully explore the depths of our human/divine nature. If Heyward is right, then it is in the depth of our relationality, a relationality that is tested, stretched and enabled through skin-on-skin engagement, that we find the depth of the divine. Incarnation is not for the faint-hearted! Of course, there is a difference between not being faint-hearted and actually being blind to some of the old ways creeping in under another and seemingly more inclusive name. Although Sheila Jeffreys (2003) is not a theologian, she is an activist with a keen eye for the pitfalls lurking in sexuality and gender. She is concerned that, in considering gender as a performance, we are still stuck within binary opposites when looking for ways to perform and that, in perhaps being afraid to question such things as butch/femme relationships and transsexual surgery, we are reinforcing all that we say we have stood against for years, that is, the binary opposition of male and female and the unequal power structure that it enables.

While some feel that feminist liberation theological interventions in the area of sexuality may have broken open the narrow boundaries too wide, there are others such as Marcella Althaus Reid (2001) who call feminist liberation theologies to task for not having the honesty to face the full reality of women's lives. She claims that much liberation theology, of which feminist sexual theology was a part, can only deal with 'decent women', that is to say, those who are seen as suffering and sexually pure. The married mother who is the victim of domestic abuse is within the remit, but the poor woman who likes sex, all kinds of transgressive and beyond-the-pale sex, is a test for feminist liberation theology. Althaus Reid points out that the experiences of many women are not included in the activity of feminist sexual theology, and she urges a new look and a move beyond. She offers us Xena the leather lesbian warrior as a salvific figure, as an image of Christ. The drag queens of her home town Buenos Aires are brought into the theological conversation and are no longer held at the edges in a morally disapproving cage; rather, their lived experience and what they signal about sex and gender are at the centre of theological considerations. Back-street prostitutes become images of Christ as they give their bodies for the lives of others, normally their children, and the child prostitute becomes Christ since her suffering calls us to redemptive action, that is, to deep and transforming action within ourselves and the systems that create such suffering. If we are declaring the sacredness of female sexuality, it is counterproductive to place a ring around good sex and bad sex. Feminist theologians have to get far more comfortable with sex, all kinds of sex, and not run and hide behind gender discourse (Isherwood and Reid 2009). Incarnation is much rawer than that!

So raw, in fact, that it is constantly challenging the edges of any discourse in theology. In the area of sexuality, it does seem that there is tension in feminist theology, particularly over whether the discipline can carry forward the harder questions. There is, though, a more disturbing notion, and that is that sexuality is once again a private matter, one that is concerned with integrated, happy people doing whatever gives them pleasure. Feminist theology for these people has helped to make sexuality a broader playing-field and contributed to the political move for more rights and the social movement for more acceptance regarding a range of sexual preferences. It is therefore alarming, since the political goes much deeper than more diverse pleasures being accepted across a greater range of society; in my opinion, it would benefit us to keep the thoughts of Heyward (1989b) in mind: she understood love to be revolutionary rather than simply romantic; we fight for change for the world we say we love and those within whom we love. This is no statement of simple self-acceptance and contentment; it is a fundamental declaration of the personal as political and a commitment to embodied justice-seeking between two people and far beyond into the whole social order. It is the kind of revolution that is spoken of in the Song of Songs, where the lovers challenge all convention, race, class and economics, and place their sex – there is very little mention of love and certainly no marriage envisaged – within the widest possible context: that of the cosmos itself as an act of revolution (Isherwood 2006). Feminist theology has always been concerned with freeing people from the narrow confines of patriarchally constructed discourses, but it has also seen links between many of these discourses; in this way, free expression in the body should also be linked with social change.

As a *body theologian*, that is to say, one who understands the body as central in revelation and the revolutions that the creation of radical theology requires, I understand every 'body' to be a source of countercultural radical incarnation. Of course, they are also objects within a consumer society and a theology that does not always view them as positive.

In my view, an example of very poor theology involving the politics of the body can be found in the 'Slim For Him' and 'Weigh Down' programs, which are billion-dollar industries which extol the religious virtue of being slim and see fat as sin. One may wish to argue that although they have theology at their heart, they are not far removed from secular medical and social arenas that also wish to punish fat women, particularly for daring to be outside the norm. These movements are particularly popular with women, and becoming slim for Jesus appears to be almost part of what good Christian womanhood implies in some circles. These programs would perhaps be less of a concern for me if it was not for the ever-increasing number of deaths from anorexia that are sweeping through our world. We are really at crisis-point, yet the world does not appear to notice. We have young women walking amongst us whose bones are on display, yet they are not stricken with a wasting disorder and they do not live in countries where food is hard to find. In 2017, a web search I carried out revealed that 1.6 million people in the UK were suffering from anorexia, with those in the 14 to 25-year-old range being most affected (Priory Group n.d.). Further, it is the biggest killer of those with psychological conditions in the UK. As a feminist liberation body theologian, I find myself asking what has happened that these young women and girls cannot imagine their lives without a life-threatening condition? What is it that makes it so hard for our young women to live life in abundance on this planet at this time?

As a body theologian, I have some ideas and further theological baggage that I bring in answer to this: it is difficult for women to be fully embodied under patriarchy, as has been demonstrated in works relating to sexuality; however, the rhetoric of over-sensual women can, I believe, extend to eating and the enjoyment of food by women. The whole idea of sensuous enjoyment can set off alarm bells in many Christian circles for both sexes. Of course, there is a paradox here since the Messianic banquet, which is thought to be at the end for all, is heralded through the Eucharist meal shared between believers. Christianity, like many religions, has in this respect understood the powerful way in which food acts as a language of memory: in celebrating with bread and wine in memory of Christ, we are drawing believers into a fully embodied experience. They take into themselves that which they are remembering, and that, in turn, acts as a series of ongoing memories, their own and that of the generations before them, all of whom shared that same meal with that same memory. Catholics have always believed that a profound change takes place at the Eucharist, not only to the elements themselves but also to those who ingest them – they become drawn into a totality of life that is both public and private. Those who share this table are asked to accept a set of radical values that are in opposition to those of the world and the respectable and established order of things. More than the brain is connected here: the whole body is engaged. In the Eucharist, food is not just what we do as part of a celebration: it is the core of what it is we are remembering, engaging, ingesting.

The Bible, tradition and doctrine use food as a sign of many matters of divine importance; it is a sign of love, community and the sacred. The question arises that if women are at odds with food through the cultures we have created, are they also at odds with the love, community and sacredness of life itself? If women are not honoured guests at those tables of love, community and the sacred, where are they to find full humanity? Understanding incarnation as I do, I find the politics of eating and not-eating to be as important as any other matter – it is a theological issue. Eating, like any other human activity, becomes an incarnational matter too, one that enables or restricts our divine becoming and the glorious explosion of our *dunamis* through our embodied, lived realities.

In primitive society, the act of eating symbolised the partaker being eaten by the community and through sharing food becoming a companion (*com panis*, shared bread), an equal in that society. This simple and basic act, then, carries historically a great deal of significance: at the heart is a notion of sharing, not exchange, in which subjects are born through the powerful symbolism of food (Falk 1994: 20). Falk argues that, although one became a member of a group self through being eaten by the community and sharing with them, there always remained "an oral type of self autonomy" (1994: 21): there was subjectivity and group identity in harmony through the primitive understanding of food as a symbol. He goes on to argue that, with the collapse of the primitive systems, eating changed from an open to a closed activity, thus moving away from an eating community to that of a bounded individual eating. Of course, the Christian church can argue that the eating community never went away within its walls, since the Eucharistic meal has always been there. Norbert Elias has argued that, with the shift from eating community to bounded self, there also comes an armouring of the self, a level of control put in place that is not seen in eating communities (cited in Falk 1994: 25). This also signals a shift from values lying in the community to a new and imaginary inwardness of emotional experience where value may be found, as well as the notion that what is outside may harm this inner depth. The shift in understanding of the symbolic nature of food leads to a crucial shift in the place of the individual in relation to others: there is much more emphasis on the bounded self, which in terms of Christian theology can be understood as personal salvation, the relationship between an ethereal God and the self-defined individual. I wonder if this may explain the almost entirely fundamentalist Protestant diet industry? In broader terms, this individual sense also disconnects people from the wider community and leaves them vulnerable – indeed, primed to be genocidal consumers, by which I mean their bounded selves need things and the cost is not counted: there is no 'eating community' to which they are attached, only a bounded self to be served.

The consumer capitalism that is embedded in many of these programs is truly disturbing to me, as we find God turned into an 'ultimate shopper' with great taste so that 'he' is a heavenly fashion consultant. His pockets are deep; he will provide you with the funds to be beautiful so that his name may be praised. What kind of Christ is emerging here? He appears to be one of the beautiful people who cannot countenance anything less than narrow perfection. We see before us the very God and Christ that liberation theology has unmasked as unjust and exploitative; it is as though the last forty years of experiential theology never existed. Although there is an experiential element lurking here, it is the kind that never gets beyond what is good for the individual; it is not an eating community that is being entered into and shared, but rather it is the bounded individual self which is being served. Modern Christian diet rhetoric has moved on from notions of health based upon good and bad food to the idea of prosperity. Such notions of health and beauty are not only the key to eternal salvation but also to a very good life here. The bodies of women, and some men, are being used in just the way Mary Douglas tells us: they are to create a bounded identity for a group, in this case the saved. But, of course, what is also happening is the creation of the body of Christ, and this Christ is being projected onto the world through the practices of the believers. For feminist liberation theology, Christ is always ethical rather than an abstract set of metaphysics. What world emerges if we lived 'as if' this diet-Christ called us to do his will? A very narrow world devoid of the glorious rainbow of incarnational diversity and divine potential that is our birthright: a very phallic thinking and a politically aggressive one attempting to project the pale face of vanilla womanhood on a global screen for the economic advantages that such a projection ensures.

As Nelle Morton told us, the journey is home, and under the cosh of a disempowering Christian diet rhetoric, this is a journey back to our bodies, to a place of once again inhabiting this flesh that holds within it the divine incarnate. We are asked to once again touch and revel in our passions and desires, to touch, taste and see it is good, and I believe this invitation is laid out before us at the Eucharistic table – a table that has become sterile and bounded but in its inception was the radical space of sensuous engagement and commitment. It was here that the exchange model of a patriarchal society was challenged, and the sharing of bread and politics ensured that patriarchy would always be challenged through this radical sharing. It is here that we are invited to refuse the assimilation of norms and to instead find countercultural ways of radical praxis, of living 'as if', that is to say, as if the fullness of divine/human incarnation was enfleshed. It is through these repeated incarnational performances that co-creation and co-redemption become lived realities.

Monica Hellwig has argued that the way in which we view the 'hunger of the world' should always be within the context of the Last Supper, which was, as she sees it, the foundational meal of Christianity. The context was one of oppression, and the act of communal eating a commitment of ultimate fellowship – the kind that would be embodied through these continued acts of eating and radical praxis.

Body, feminist and liberation theology compelled me to engage with the question of the new cosmology and theology as a way to further investigate identity and notions of divinity hitherto contained and controlled within the Christian understanding of the One All-Powerful God. This led to an investigation of the Deep, which is the very ground of who we are, though, as we shall see, the Deep does not offer a fixed identity relying on and embedded in the One. It is a Deep situated in the cosmos itself that gives the lie to *creatio ex nihilo* and opens before us the God who is of intimate/infinite entanglements (Keller 2012). The God who is the All in All of Corinthians is not beyond, not distant, but entangled. Keller visits Paul's writings in 1 Corinthians on the body of Christ and reminds us that, in the Greek, *energeia* is used in 12:4–6 when Paul tells us that there are differences, but it is the same God who is in all. For Keller, this disables any theology of distance and separation: God is not above, nor is the divine simply androcentric, but rather the very bible itself declares God to be eco-centric, All in All. Energy, then, is not something we have but something we are (Keller 2012: 12), and it is the same energy that gives life to all, it is the stuff of entanglement. Keller writes: "feeling the pulsations of our bodies in our planet and the pulsations of the planet in its universe our earthly interactions are rendered simultaneously intimate and virtually infinite" (2012: 13). This is the energy of eternal delight which comes from the free-flow of these energies uninhibited by repression, exploitation and denial. One may add: and uninhibited by a desire to see distinctions between it and God. Just as Heyward before her accused theology of making us less than we are by dampening and denying desire within us, so Keller suggests that the exploitation and denial of entanglement block energy, which leads to depression and lack of meaning. The Mono-God, who has dragged us from our cosmic home in order to find salvation, has done us no favours; as Keller puts it: "God in heaven who we create without a body to do work for us and who in the name of religion represses the rhythms of the human body and pulsations of desire" leaves us adrift (Keller 2012: 15).

Engaging with our enfleshed cosmic story moves us away from a search for perfect origins and back to beginnings; there is no place from which we were cast out by a disapproving Father but rather a place that grew us, that nurtured us and generously gave and gives us life. Edward Said reminds us that beginnings are always relative, contested and historical, whereas origins are absolute and power-laden. Beginnings, then, give the Christian theologian the chance to decolonize this space of origins in creation and the inevitable creator who sits apart and to challenge, as Catherine Keller puts it, "the great supernatural surge of father power, a world appearing zap out of the void and mankind ruling the world in our manly creator's image" (Keller 2003: 6). We are thrown back to cosmic beginnings, to void and chaos, and we are asked to make our theology from that ground – to understand who we are and who we might be from *tohu vabohu*, the depth veiled in darkness. Once we give agency to void and chaos, there can be no creation out of nothing as our power-laden dualistic origin. Creation ceases to be a unilateral act, and the theological vista is cosmic! The divine speech in the pages of Genesis is no longer understood as a command uttered by the Lord and warrior King who rules over creation, but, as Keller (2003: 56) tells us, 'let there be' is a whisper of desire, and what comes forth emanates from all there is rather than appearing from above and beyond. In this shift we also see the possibility for incarnation to be understood as the rule rather than exception of creation because the whisper desires enfleshment. Keller certainly moves us significantly from creation out of nothing to a place where the divine is more humble and entices ever-unfolding acts of becoming grounded in the chaos at the heart of the cosmos. However, she perhaps still leaves that gap between the divine and material order that the cosmic story itself seems to challenge – there is, after all, nothing outside the unfolding of the multiverse.

It is this gap that secular theorists have no difficulty challenging. Val Plumwood (2002), an eco-philosopher, is amongst those who insist that it is this gap that continues to harm both us and the planet. While we understand ourselves as something other than the rest of the created order, we will inevitably see ourselves as 'better' or 'higher', and this false consciousness leads to alienation and destruction. Plumwood is quick to point out to us the logical absurdity of such a position: monological relationships will eventually weaken the provider, the earth on which we rely. We need to move to dialogue between mutually recognizing and supporting agents, or, as Thomas Berry puts it, we need to realize we live in a communion of subjects rather than a collection of objects. Plumwood argues that removing agency from the cosmos, a technique we have so often used in our colonial history in relation to the discovery of 'new lands', makes it – and all that lives in it – an empty space, one that can be used for profit through the maximization of its development potential. She reminds us of the knock-on effect of this way of thinking: nature is no longer viewed as a creator of our environment, and the land and those who depend most directly on it are relegated to the realm of 'Other'. They are backgrounded, which means that we deny our reliance on both the land and those who toil in it – we live as though they have no impact on our lives and as though we lived outside the biosphere.

Plumwood argues for a return to what she calls the "heart of stone" in order to overcome the "sado-dispassionate rationalism of scientific reduction" (2002: 49). This involves a re-enchantment of the realm designated as material, the re-materialization of spirit as speaking matter. She warns that this project should not slide into the world of the romantic, and in order to guard against this it needs to be ever mindful of the spirit/matter dualism and resist it at every turn. Western culture has placed speaking matter in the rarefied world of fairy tale and legend from where it cannot really impact on ethical or philosophical thinking, but it is this world that we need to foreground if we are to return intentionality and agency to matter. By journeying to the heart of stone, we have to walk a different path, one that moves stone (the material world of nature) from the background of consciousness to the foreground, from silent to speaking, and from the ordinary to the extraordinary, to the wonderful and even to the sacred. This move is needed in order to challenge the false consciousness of the western world, so rooted in our Christian heritage that tells us we no longer live in nature but in culture. Environmental philosophy is attempting this through stressing that attention must go 'all the way down', or, as Deborah Bird Rose puts it, 'Nothing is nothing'. This move, Plumwood claims, opens the door to a wide range of interspecies dialogues, dramas and projects that would otherwise be unimaginable but which free us to rewrite the earth as sacred, earth exploration as pilgrimage and earth knowledge as revelation. The political and economic implications of this are, I think, quite clear. What impact would such thinking have on logging companies, chemical companies and the bodies of those who labour to make £2.50 T-shirts?

Interestingly, engaging (as Plumwood suggests) enables us to embed in the cosmos but also come home to millions of women whose relationship with nature is direct and harsh. Our industrialized world has widened the gap between rich and poor, and women bear the brunt of this since they and their children make up the largest number of the poor. Vandana Shiva (2008) has highlighted for us how economic growth has become another form of colonialism that drains the resources from those who need them the most. Many women are actually being removed from the means of growing food through such activities as cash cropping. This simply highlights how productivity for survival is very different from productivity for the capitalist market. In our coming home to the cosmos, we are not propelled into some safe and fluffy existence but rather into ongoing political struggles for economic justice. John F. Haught explains that there are three persistent elements in cosmic evolution: gratuity, extravagance, and surprise. This, he believes, suggests that we should move to a more humble and receptive mode of being, accepting all as gift and changing our way of living accordingly. The extravagant life in abundance that the cosmos offers to all does away with a select heaven for the faithful and economic and resource prosperity for the few – once again, a call to political action.

The cosmos did not emerge from Platonic forms but rather from *tehomic* chaos; there was no blueprint but instead the glorious outpourings of surprise and novelty. Christian theology has been so used to divinely laid out intentions that this comes as something of a surprise. Keller offers a proposition for a *tehomic* ethic, and it is this: that we bear with the chaos, neither liking it nor fostering it but recognizing that *there is* the unformed future

(2003: 29). This unformed future is made up of repetition, but from very early in cosmic development this repetition always adds something new – every repetition is a transgression, our bodies and that of the cosmos are in constant flux: as they regenerate, they change; they are, in essence, transgressive. This is, of course, a challenge to Christian theology, accustomed as it has been to Platonic forms.

Embedding ourselves in the universe as spiritual home is pitching our tent on earthquakes and seismic shifts. Cosmology shows us that all new reality emerges from "explosive volatile exuberance" (David Toolan, quoted in O'Murchu 2002: 85), which offers us big dreams and futures as well as dangers and risks. However, I have argued elsewhere that incarnation itself signals to us such uncertain and ever-changing ground and invites us to continue the discontinuity of cosmic ruptures (Isherwood 1999). To commit to flesh is to commit to change and risk, but it is also to dream big, to embrace the reality of the future. We should not make the mistake of supposing that, although the cosmos may be this volatile, our theology can be more stable – rather, our theology needs to be one of ruptures and new emergences. There are, in short, endless possibilities, and the energy in this is the energy of All in All.

I hope this chapter illustrates that my life and work are committed to expanding the space in which we create theology together and that none of these creations are set in stone – rather, they, like us and the cosmos that birthed us, are forever in transgressive change, set as they are on earthquakes of cosmic/divine becoming. In this way, I hope to be inclusivist but not evangelizing, since each process is distinct. And why do I continue this work with passion? It is a question I cannot fully answer, but it seems to me that life is to be free and full, not reduced by systems and dogmas; and as a woman within Christianity, I have experienced many attempts at reduction physically, emotionally and spiritually – it is the rage at this injustice that keeps me going. Of course, liberation theologies are committed to changing the world – not just praying for it; and as an academic I hope my contribution, based as it is in lived experience of women and men, offers other ways to think and be.

Notes

† This paper uses material from the following publications: Lisa Isherwood, *Introducing Feminist Christologies* (London: Sheffield Academic Press, 2001); Lisa Isherwood, "Feminist Critique of Sexuality and Religion," in Stephen J. Hunt and Andrew K. T. Yip (eds.), *The Ashgate Research Companion to Contemporary Religion and Sexuality* (Farnham, Surrey: Ashgate, 2012), pp. 31–43; Lisa Isherwood, "Will You Slim for Him or Bake Cakes for the Queen of Heaven?", in Marcella Althaus-Reid and Lisa Isherwood (eds.), *Controversies in Body Theology* (London: SCM Press, 2008), pp. 174–206; Lisa Isherwood and David Harris, *Radical Otherness: Sociological and Theological Approaches* (Durham: Acumen, 2013; Abingdon: Routledge, 2014). All material used with permission.
1 Those who have read *Liberating Christ* (1999) will understand that this is far from the individualistic statement that it appears to be; it is rather a cry for heaven on earth, a cry both biblical and doctrinal. It is a call for the radical nature of incarnation to be taken seriously, to be lived, to be put on. I have my critics!

References

Althaus Reid, M. 2001. "Outing Theology: Thinking Christianity out of the Church Closet." *Feminist Theology* 27: 57–67.
Bartky, S. L. 1990. *Femininity and Domination*. London: Routledge.
Borresen, K. 1995. *The Image of God*. Minneapolis, MN: Fortress Press.
Braidotti, R. 1994. *Nomadic Subjects*. New York: Columbia University Press.
Brock, R. 1988. *Journeys by Heart: A Christology of Erotic Power*. New York: Crossroad.
Butler, J. 1990. *Gender Trouble*. London: Routledge.
Butler, J. 2004. *Undoing Gender*. London: Routledge.
Falk, P. 1994. *The Consuming Body*. London: Sage.
Heyward, C. 1989a. *The Redemption of God*. Washington, DC: University of America Press.
Heyward, C. 1989b. *Touching Our Strength: The Erotic as Power and the Love of God*. San Francisco: HarperCollins.
Howson, A. 2005. *Embodying Gender*. London: Sage.
Irigaray, L. 1985. *This Sex Which Is Not One*. Ithaca, NY: Cornell University Press.
Isherwood, L. 1999. *Liberating Christ: Exploring the Christologies of Contemporary Liberation Movements*. Cleveland: Pilgrim Press.
Isherwood, L. 2006. *Erotic Celibacy*. Edinburgh: T & T Clark.
Isherwood, L. and M. Althaus Reid. 2009. *Trans/Formations*. London: SCM.
Jeffreys, S. 2003. *Unpacking Queer Politics*. Cambridge: Polity.
Keller, C. 2003. *Face of the Deep: A Theology of Becoming*. London: Routledge.
Keller, C. 2012. "The Energy We Are: A Meditation in Seven Pulsations." In *Cosmology, Ecology and the Energy of God*, edited by D. Bowman and C. Crockett, 11–25. New York: Fordham University Press.
Lorde, A. 1984. *Sister Outsider*. Freedom, CA: Crossing Press.
O'Murchu, D. 2002. *Evolutionary Faith: Rediscovering God in Our Great Story*. Maryknoll: Orbis Books.
Plumwood, V. 2002. *Environmental Culture: The Ecological Crisis of Reason*. London: Routledge.
Priory Group (n.d.). "Eating Disorder Statistics." Accessed July 24, 2017. http://www.priorygroup.com/eating-disorders/statistics.
Ruether, R. R. 1979. "Mother Earth and the Megamachine: A Theology of Liberation in a Feminine, Somatic and Ecological Perspective." In *Woman Spirit Rising: A Feminist Reader in Religion*, edited by C. P. Christ and J. Plaskow, 43–51. San Francisco, CA: Harper and Row.
Ruether, R. R. 1983. *Sexism and God-Talk*. London: SCM.
Ruether, R. R. 1998a. *Introducing Redemption in Christian Feminism*. Sheffield: Sheffield Academic Press.
Ruether, R. R. 1998b. *Women and Redemption: A Theological History*. Minneapolis, MN: Fortress Press.
Russell, L. 1974. *Human Liberation From a Feminist Perspective: A Theology*. Philadelphia, PA: Westminster Press.
Shiva, V. 2008. *Soil Not Oil: Climate Change, Peak Oil and Food Insecurity*. London: Zed Books.
Tessier, T. 1997. *Dancing After the Whirlwind: Feminist Reflections on Sex, Denial, and Spiritual Transformation*. Boston, MA: Beacon Press.

4 Shinto

Koji Suga

Is Shinto a religion?

Before stating my own beliefs, it would be worthwhile to examine a simple but difficult question: Is Shinto a 'religion'?

Of course, Shinto has its own ritual forms (*matsuri*) observed at shrines to worship unique spiritual beings called *kami* – deities exhibiting supranormal vitality and character. *Kami* are ordinarily referred to in the plural and often described with the prefix 'eight hundred myriads'. Each *kami* is also identified by his/her/its proper name, which usually describes the *kami*'s characteristics and functions. Having their origins in ancient shamanistic cults, *matsuri* normally consist of phases including purification, offerings, prayer and entertainment. Purity, in terms of both one's spiritual condition and physical status, plays a very important role in Shinto.

Although Shinto has no canon of holy scriptures, in their place ancient Japanese mythological episodes in *Kojiki* (compiled 712 CE) and *Nihon shoki* (compiled 720 CE), together with other classics and fragments of folk tales, have been used as materials for interpreting the divinity of the 'eight hundred myriads of *kami*'. From this point of view, Shinto, literally interpreted as 'the way of *kami*', is certainly a religion of sorts. Shinto could be classified as a type of polytheistic religion, consisting of such elements as animism, ancestor worship and veneration for great persons. At the same time, I think the question 'Is Shinto a religion?' is still worth considering in the context of present-day Japanese society. The question can be approached on several levels, but here I want to focus on two aspects, namely, the political and the philosophical.[1]

The well-known Japanese Buddhist philosopher Daisetsu T. Suzuki has stated:

> One remarkable fact deserving notice . . . is that Shintoism, which is regarded as the official embodiment of the national spirit of Japan, did not assert itself as doctrinally independent of either Confucianism or Buddhism. The most probable reason for this is that Shintoism has no philosophy of its own to stand on; it is awakened to its own

consciousness and existence only when it comes into contact with one of the others and thereby learns how to express itself.

(Suzuki 1959: 57)

In contrast to sophisticated world religions and their philosophies, Shinto is occasionally described as lacking revelations, eschatological dogmas or a well-articulated theology. In extreme cases, Shinto has been described as a hodgepodge of folk traditions somehow related to undeveloped superstitious customs in Japan. While some Shinto sects and new religious movements derived from Shintoist traditions have official founders and teachings, 'Shinto' in the narrower sense – hereinafter referred as 'Shrine Shinto' or the beliefs and practices of Shinto shrines – indeed has no founder.

A further contrast with Buddhism is that in matters of ethics and politics Shinto is frequently associated with Japanese militaristic tendencies, or at least secular-based nationalist policies, rather than with the rich spiritual world of Japanese history. Here, a debate from the political perspective on the question of Shinto's religious status can easily lead to the question, 'Is Shinto a religion?' However, in the minds of scholars with some knowledge of modern Japanese history, the question also inevitably raises associations with the so-called State Shinto system of pre-war twentieth-century Imperial Japan. During that period, Shinto shrines were officially classified as nonreligious institutions for state ritual and thus discriminated from other religions, while the government simultaneously claimed that Japan had no state religion. The state also advocated certain Shinto-derived moral values in public education as a means of inculcating Japanese national identity, using ancient Japanese mythology to emphasize the divine origins of the Japanese emperor, the Japanese people and even the very land of Japan. As the American scholar Daniel C. Holtom claimed at the time, the 'Shinto shrines as nonreligious' policy could be understood as the government's attempt to camouflage Japanese racism, employing secular history and tradition to disguise the religious elements derived from mythological episodes. Holtom had lived in Imperial Japan as an educator for almost three decades after his arrival as a Baptist missionary and was responsible for coining the term 'State Shinto' (Holtom 1947). After the defeat of Imperial Japan in World War II, the allied occupation authorities made use of Holtom's coinage and interpretation of State Shinto as they worked to abolish Shinto shrines as a nonreligious system. The occupation authorities' goal was to stamp out State Shinto, which they perceived as lying at the root of Nazi-like Japanese racism.

As a result, Shinto has been regarded since the end of World War II as a religion, legally speaking. But even today the claim that 'Shinto is not a religion' continues to attract advocates in Japanese society. To some degree this situation is connected to particular historical circumstances. Needless to say, the word '*shinto*' has a long history, going back to ancient times. The term appears in the classics in certain cases to discriminate *kami* from other objects of worship. On the other hand, as a generic term for thought and practice related to *kami* worship, the word '*shinto*' was rather new to vernacular speech at the time the concept of 'religion' was imported from the West (Hardacre 1989: 34–35). That occurred around the time Japan entered its modern period in the latter half of the nineteenth century. This fact also means that the set of basic criteria as to what counts as a 'religion' was modeled at the time principally after Christianity. Such criteria include the existence of a founder, a canon of scriptures, and established dogma. In addition, any particular personal awareness of faith by the individual believer was missing, or was at least very obscure, in Shinto.

Today, following the custom of *hatsumode* or 'first worship', tens of millions of Japanese visit Shinto shrines during the first few days of each year. Likewise, many students preparing for school entrance examinations visit shrines to pray for success. And despite the declining birth-rate in Japan, considerable numbers of babies are brought to Shinto shrines shortly after birth to receive a blessing. Yet if someone were to ask those people who visit shrines, "What are your religious beliefs?" most would likely offer the paradoxical reply: "I'm just visiting here to pray. I'm not a believer of any religion."

How can someone pray without any consciousness of belief in a divine object? Is it a type of secular faith? No, I don't think so. What we see here may be an example of the possibility of religious practice without belief. And though it may sound strange to concede this, my own religious beliefs regarding Shinto are strongly reinforced by this phenomenon. When compared with the world religions, it is surprising that such an obscure religious practice without an established consciousness of faith has managed to survive to the present day.

What role does consciousness of faith play in religious practice? Followers of monotheistic religions appear to possess a strong religious identity with their own faith, but identity formation of this type may be found in other religions as well, including Shinto. On the other hand, it is frequently noted that there has been no particular increase in the proportion of Christian believers (regardless of their sectarian affiliation) in Japan's population for more than a century since its legalization. This situation is quite different from the cases of other East Asian countries such as Korea and Taiwan.

It was in light of these circumstances that a Japanese Christian scholar once told me: "I conclude that the fact that modern Shinto has thrived despite being a religion with such vague, uncertain faith and beliefs is nothing but the result of the state's former support for it. Shinto has managed to survive in the postwar period only as a result of the wealth of past state patronage." Although straightforward remarks of this kind are somewhat unusual, it seems that any discussion that adopts the term 'State Shinto' in regard to the political aspect of the question 'Is Shinto a religion?' tends to imply just such a connection between Shintoism and former Japanese imperial policy. But, again, how essential is this connection for the popularity of Shinto shrines today?

My religious development

I am never convinced by opinions that seem to ascribe the current popularity of Shinto shrines to a remnant of the secular political faith of the past. On the other hand, in a totally different manner, the question 'Is Shinto a religion?' is one that I also direct at myself. As a student of religious studies, my research focuses on the relationship between politics, nationalism and religion, particularly the case of Shinto in modern Japan but beyond the very convenient – yet vague – term 'State Shinto'. What I am examining is the historical background to the social situation I described earlier. At the same time, I am also a part-time priest at a Shinto shrine. I decided to become a Shinto priest and received clerical training after I began my academic research on Shinto.

I was born and raised, in fact, in a Roman Catholic family – not the most desirable background for a Shinto priest. A certain proportion of the Shinto priesthood consists of hereditary families, but most of the approximately 20,000 priests, who likely recognize themselves not as experts in Shinto theology but as professional Shinto ritualists, have come from 'Buddhist families'. By this expression I mean ordinary Japanese families which observe regular rituals to pray for the repose of ancestors according to the liturgical style of various Buddhist sects. Many of the members of such Japanese 'Buddhist families' do not view themselves as having 'faith in Buddhism'. And although many Shinto priests come from such 'Buddhist families', it may seem paradoxical that few feel they have converted from one religion to another, unless they have completely changed their observance of ancestral rituals to the Shinto style (not a given).

The shrine where I currently serve as a part-time priest is the Gokoku Shrine in the Tochigi Prefecture. Established in 1872, this shrine was renamed in 1939 to reflect its role in enshrining the spirits of war dead who were specifically from the Tochigi Prefecture (Suga 2010a). While the spirit of each individual is memorialized by his or her name, they are collectively enshrined as the tutelary *kami* for people living in the prefecture and, by extension, the whole nation. I am not one of the bereaved with a direct relationship to the souls enshrined there. In fact, I had no connection at all to the Tochigi Prefecture before becoming a priest at the shrine, located in a city north of Tokyo.

The essential elements of worship at Gokoku shrines on the prefectural level are, in general, the same as the faith directed toward the Yasukuni Shrine on the national level. Established in 1869 and sometimes referred to as a 'Japanese war shrine' in the media, the Yasukuni Shrine lies at the crux of the debate regarding Shinto's 'religious' status. As a result, it has been frequently viewed not as a religious shrine but as a secular institution for memorializing the dead of a modern nation-state. As a graduate student I studied certain historical aspects of the Yasukuni faith before being accepted to serve at the Tochigi Gokoku Shrine. From that time, the experiences I received through service at this shrine have given me another perspective of Shinto faith as a whole. I have come to the conviction that faith in the deified spirits of the war dead enshrined in Yasukuni and regional Gokoku shrines is, in fact, a crucial part of *kami* beliefs in contemporary Japan. At the same time, I recognize the fact that the faith directed toward these shrines may also stimulate Japanese political chauvinism, as many critics have pointed out.

I would like to discuss here the philosophical aspects of the question 'Is Shinto a religion?' while deferring to my academic interests in Shinto to help elucidate this matter further. In the final section of this chapter, I will restate my conception of the war dead *kami* as I return to the political aspects of the question.

During my time as an undergraduate student at university, I became very interested in existentialist philosophy as found in the works of Søren Kierkegaard, Friedrich Nietzsche and Martin Heidegger. I was initially deeply impressed by Kierkegaard's view of 'the single individual'. In spite of my Christian beliefs at the time, the focus of my interest gradually shifted from Kierkegaard to Nietzsche's thought. In particular, Nietzsche's philosophical repudiation of an absolute God and his ideas regarding life-affirmation, the death of God, perspectivism and the will to power exerted a strong impact on my thinking. I was particularly impressed (in part due to typical adolescence angst, youthful heroism and an affectation of nihilism) by his understanding of the relation between *ressentiment* and religion.

But I also learned how the 'discovery' of Buddhist philosophy among the classics of colonized India had shocked the western intelligentsia in the late nineteenth century. Reading moreover Nietzsche's last work, *The Anti-Christ*, I deliberated on his denunciation of Christianity (despite his undoubted affection for Jesus the man), his valuation of Buddhism and his interpretation of Greek polytheism.

At that time, I also wanted to know more about how my country Japan had created a western-style nation-state in East Asia. I traced the historical process of the state authority's interest in the indigenous value of Shinto for enhancing Japanese national unity in the latter half of the nineteenth century. Simply speaking, in my eyes, the construction of the so-called 'State Shinto' system was a process of disenchantment or *Entzauberung* of 'the way of *kami*' for the purpose of forging a type of faith in the nation with imperial authority at its centre.

History provides multiple examples where the religious dimension of national identity asserts itself when the independence or unity of a nation is threatened. In my estimation, one of those cases was exemplified by Japanese Shinto in the late nineteenth century, namely, when Japan's independence and seclusion policy were threatened by the encounter with the industrialized West. Later, I discovered that an authority on nationalism studies, Ernest Gellner, had already briefly spoken to this philosophical-political position I had arrived at:

> But even religions which might be thought to have had little inherent potential for such 'protestant' interpretation, could nonetheless be turned in that direction during the age when the drives to industrialism and to nationalism were making their impact. Formally speaking, one would not expect Shintoism to have any marked resemblance to, say, English nonconformity. Nevertheless, during the Japanese modernization drive, it was the sober, orderly, as it were Quaker elements in it (which evidently can be found or imposed anywhere if one tries hard enough) which were stressed to the detriment of any ecstatic elements and any undue private familiarity with the sacred. Had ancient Greece survived into the modern age, Dionysiac cults might have assumed a more sober garb as Hellas lurched forward along the path of development.
> (Gellner 1983: 41)

At the end of my intellectual quest, I came to seek my way not in Buddhism but in Shinto. The main basis for this decision was that Shinto seemed to me to maintain a primitive, unsophisticated and unaffected native simplicity within my own culture. Shinto also offered an interpretation of the universe without any clear horizon of ultimate truth, while the possibilities to access it could be found in each occasion. Although it might sound somewhat odd, since then I have felt that the evolution of my faith has been an experience of 'moulting' rather than 'conversion' *per se*.

Shinto as agnostic pantheism?

By that time, I found myself as an agnostic pantheist of a Shinto sort. While I would not want to disparage other people's faith in God, I no longer feel the need for any belief in an absolute being. Rather, the only necessary and sufficient object of faith is truth figured in vague and unsteady fashion, and this provides adequate space for optimism. In my view, an optimistic faith that can keep evil away by means of purification rituals offers a secure way to happiness. The relativistic incompleteness of the theological dimension of Shinto, which has no concept of supernatural creation from outside the universe, is therefore something I have found pleasing.

According to Japanese mythology, the Shinto pantheon is inhabited at its core by Amaterasu-o-mikami, the sun goddess and imperial ancestor. While central in significance, she is not omnipotent. At times in Shinto history, certain theological tracts have proposed other *kami* as representing the ultimate origin of the universe, but none of them has achieved orthodoxy. At any rate, the Shinto pantheon lacks any supreme being as the creator of the entire universe.

A notable Shinto theologian – and thankfully my first instructor in Shinto studies – Ueda Kenji (1927–2003) pointed out that, among the several mythological creation episodes, we find that every event in the course of universal creation occurs on the condition that something already exists before it (Ueda 1991: 31–40). Ueda notes that even in the very first verse of Japanese mythology, the whole world is generated from what is not narrated. Since its point of departure is agnostic, Ueda's theory seems to avoid any metaphysical arguments in its philosophy of Shinto. Ueda discusses beliefs in unknowable noumena beyond the physical universe while simultaneously denying any fundamentally monist tendency in Shinto. He contends that the divinity of a *kami* can only be observed in particular finite beings.

This agnostic view that we can never know the ultimate origin and cause of the universe is one I find satisfactory. In any case, it is the philosophical dimensions of Shinto that I would like to discuss further with scholars of other religious traditions. Indeed, is Shinto a religion even worth consideration from a philosophical perspective? To tell the truth, I feel unsatisfied with the present state of virtually all research on Shinto, whether it be research in support of Shinto or in criticism of it, and irrespective as to whether the studies originate from within or outside of Japan; the limitations in such research remain so long as it is concerned with nothing more than historical or social phenomena within the material universe. In this respect, I find most current Shinto research wanting, even that which attempts to examine the shamanistic aspects of Shinto from a rationalist framework. This signals, overall, a significant shortcoming in rational inquiry into Shinto belief. In my estimation, this situation is likely evidence of a severe hangover from the political situation of Shinto within Imperial Japan, namely, its status as so-called State Shinto. This applies both to the character of Shinto as it was subjected to 'disenchantment' for the purpose of building a modern form of nationalism as well as to the subsequent re-mythicizing of the nation under Japanese fascism. In fact, these three elements – the two dimensions of State Shinto and the issue of rationality – form the subjects of my research. But I confess that my research on the last issue has not progressed sufficiently for me to address it here.

Another comment regarding Shinto mythology: following the first several generations of single heavenly deities, the first mated couple of deities appears. The heavenly deities, then, mandate the couple to "make, order, consolidate, and accomplish". In line with this mandate the divine couple marry, and after an initial mistake, give birth to the Japanese islands as well as to celestial and terrestrial deities. Amaterasu is produced as their noblest daughter. Who is the real initiator behind this divine mandate? Ueda again discusses this point, or more precisely his discussion revolves around the heavenly reply to the divine couple's inquiry after their initial mistake in attempting to follow the mandate (Ueda 1991: 146). He concludes that the reply must be an exact reflection of the collective will of the heavenly deities.

To further examine the polytheistic nature of Shinto, we can observe the mythic episode of the 'Heavenly rock cave' of Amaterasu, which is quite popular in Japan. As the sun *kami* and ruler over Heaven, Amaterasu is challenged by her younger brother Susanoo (a tempestuous *kami* representing masculinity). The two *kami* engage in a contest in the form of a trial by pledge. In that process, they give birth to five male *kami* and three female *kami*; Amaterasu declares that the five male *kami* produced from the 'seed' of her necklace are her own divine children. The Japanese imperial genealogy later claimed to have its origin in one of these sons. Having proved his innocence in the trial, Susanoo next goes on a rampage, causing his sister to hide away in the heavenly rock cave and throwing the world into darkness and chaos. In response, the *kami* Takamimusuhi calls a divine conference of the other heavenly *kami* to discuss how to lure Amaterasu from the cave. Finally, it is decided that a program of festival worship and votive entertainment will be undertaken. Lured by the excitement outside, Amaterasu emerges from her cave, and light returns to the world once again. The cave is then sealed to prevent her from returning inside.

In general, this episode is interpreted as describing the origin of *matsuri* (festive worship) as the way of appealing to *kami*, but here I want to place additional emphasis on the 'divine conference'. The conference is convened by the deity Takamimusuhi, who belongs to the first generation of creation and whose name includes the ancient term '*musuhi*', meaning 'spiritual producer' or 'generating soul', thus indicating his eminent status within that early generation. But Takamimusuhi does not appear to be the sole deity responsible for making the decision to hold a *matsuri*. Here once more the decision is portrayed as being the result of the collective will of a community of *kami*. '*Kami*', it might be noted, is an appellation for those beings which possess extraordinary and surpassing ability and which are awesome and worthy of reverence, though they are beings that might be evil as well as good (Motoori 1968: 53).

Motoori Norinaga (1730–1801) was an outstanding Shinto scholar in the *Kokugaku* ('National Learning') school in early modern Japan. His definition of *kami*, referenced in part earlier, suggests that all spiritual beings lying behind any awe-inspiring phenomena in the world must be considered *kami*, regardless of their moral status as good or evil. The way in which I understand this description is that any spiritual objects that can be worshiped, revered or appeased using the ritual forms of *matsuri* in shrines are to be viewed as *kami*. At the same time, interaction with *kami* through *matsuri* worship or prayer provides a transcendental path toward the vague yet ultimate reality. Also, I can accept *kami* as individually imperfect though mutually supplementing each other's shortcomings to comprise a harmonious whole.

Everything in the world possesses features that exceed the ability of others to perceive. This is suggested by the famous ancient Greek aphorism attributed to Heraclitus, *panta rhei* or "everything flows", and by the Buddhist idea of impermanence, that all phenomena in the universe are characterized by ever-present change. No individual can be aware of and control his or her own personality perfectly. In my interpretation of Shinto belief, this fluidity in the phenomenal world can also be conceived as a complex relationship among innumerable coexisting *kami* as they work toward a harmonious future resolution. The imperfection of any individual *kami* demonstrates a transcendental path for the 'lives' of animate and inanimate beings which exist in the world for a very limited time. It might be said that the various types of Shinto belief in many *kami* work together toward the achievement of a higher harmony.

Next, concerning the nature of life, we find in Shinto several functional concepts of spirit as aspects of soul. According to some interpretations of Shinto mythology and historical teaching, the spirit found in both *kami* and human beings is made up of 'one spirit' and 'four souls'. The four souls – which are the turbulent, the tranquil, the propitious, and the miraculous – act together complementarily. Of the four, the tranquil and turbulent souls are sometimes used to explain an individual's mental condition. Apart from such psychological matters, however, ethical subjects such as good and evil can also be understood in terms of the operation of these souls. In this sense, both human sin and spiritual defilement have a common basis. As a result, any time that spiritual defilement is sensed, purification – called '*harae*' in Shinto ritualism – should be observed as the way to revitalize one's life within the social and bio-ecological system. Any object or being in the universe, whether it be animate or inanimate, exists in relation with others. We exist within a series of communal bodies at differing scales, from family to nation, and the harmonious interaction of these communities is very important to Shinto. It is here that we find the meaning of the 'imagined community' of Japan as the nation in Shinto, both in religious and political aspects, or alternately in mythological and modern senses.

Shinto and Japanese nationalism

Following the episode of the heavenly rock cave, the mythological account continues on a long and convoluted path to arrive at the foundation of Japan. In brief, the mythological origins of Japan are described as follows. Initially, 'terrestrial' deities exploited the land. After this, sovereignty over the land was transferred to the deities of 'celestial' genealogy, centring around Amaterasu's grandson Ninigi, who descended from heaven. He and his successors concluded ties of marriage with mountain and maritime *kami* clans of terrestrial lineage. Then Ninigi's great-grandson, the first Emperor Jinmu, subdued the central part of the country and founded the nation at a date corresponding in the western calendar to 660 BCE. At the time of his royal inauguration, the first emperor observed a *matsuri* as a priest to worship his ancestral *kami*.

This episode portrays the source of Japanese kingship as residing in the institution of an ancient theocracy – a charismatic priest-king – which was subsequently interpreted in the modern period as the sacred living symbol of Japanese national unification. Together with the political ideology generated from this, we can see here one of the basic concepts of Shinto, namely, that all human beings are descendants of the *kami*. In Shinto, human life is conceived in terms of community, never atomistically. All individuals share their lives with others within a community. Human life itself is given us by parents and ancestors, and one's mentality and personality are a product of the community in which one lives. One's existence, in relation to ancestors and posterity, to former generations and later generations, must be embodied in rituals for ancestral spirits. I am content with the notion of the simple mutuality of the living and the dead, that is, gratitude to ancestors and protection of descendants. I have no particular image of any afterlife beyond such spiritual connections, although the afterworld in Shinto tradition has been named and described in various ways.

As an 'imagined community', the Japanese nation is grasped in Shinto thought as a social unit comprised of individuals in correlative existence who are awakening to the divine mandate connecting past and future. Japanese national identity thus naturally comes to bear a kind of religious as well as secular significance. Here it is the ambiguity of nationalism, working both to subsume and to exclude, that emerges as the issue at stake in the case of Shinto. Occasionally, the shell of Japanese national identity works to inhibit the understanding of the overall universe from the perspective of Shinto belief. There now arises a significant question: Can or should Shinto be propagated beyond the consciousness of Japanese national identity, in the same way that Christianity broke through the provincialism of Mediterranean and European identity?

The actual diffusion of Shinto shrines throughout the world might not be necessary, but I believe that Shinto thought has the potential to contribute toward a pluralistic global society by turning its polytheistic characteristics to advantage. At the very least, Shinto should not be made light of as a political jumble or an anachronistic mode of thought about a divinely chosen people. If it is to become a notable religion today, Shinto will have to pierce through the geographical and cultural parochialism of the Japanese nation. Of course, we should also remember the fact that, even within Japan, quite a few people reject *kami* faith.

To seek out clues to the universal features of Shinto, however, further contemplation of the historical record is indispensable. In my doctoral thesis I examined the history of overseas Shinto shrines in Japanese colonies, particularly those established in colonized Korea and Taiwan, and focusing on thoughts and beliefs regarding the *kami* enshrined there (Suga 2004, 2010b). While these shrines were originally built and operated to respond to the religious needs of immigrants from mainland Japan, they were ultimately transformed into institutions that mediated Japan's cultural assimilation policy, including the so-called 'compulsory shrine worship' during the period of total war. Ultimately, the shrines could not survive the destruction of the Japanese colonial empire that accompanied Japan's defeat in World War II. Through an examination of this historical case of failure in universalizing Shinto, I discovered that there were very few instances in which colonial shrines were able to confront native religious cultures, whether through syncretization, competition or mere dialogue. That result was, of course, derived from the state policy that declared Shinto shrines to be nonreligious institutions and further demanded that any *kami* enshrined in a Shinto shrine be selected from the 'Pantheon of the Japanese Empire'. But it should be emphasized that even in the decades from the end of World War II to the present, very few academic works have looked at the potential of universalizing Shinto, including historical reflections on Shinto and Japanese expansionism beyond the vague term 'State Shinto'.

Given this situation, any interreligious dialogue regarding the philosophical elements of Shinto provides me with an invaluable opportunity for deepening my faith, since any deity or religious object has the potential to become *kami* if enshrined in a Shinto shrine. It is also important that Shinto has the theological resources and discernment to discover and acknowledge, across the world's divergent cultures, harmonious values as well as reverence towards things in nature. In light of the recent growth in public awareness of environmental issues, together with the resurgence of certain animistic belief-systems, it appears that when provided with a forum for interreligious dialogue Shintoists frequently emphasize faith in natural beings as Shinto's most characteristic feature.

The ecological aspect of Shinto belief – the harmonious *kami* way between human life and nature – is indeed a significant value to share with people of other religions, and even with atheists. As anyone may notice after visiting a Shinto shrine, the sanctuary of the shrine is nearly always surrounded by trees. The sacred forest or grove is called '*chinju no mori*', or 'woods of the local guardian shrine'. The vitality of green leaves, branches and trees is indispensable in capturing the enshrined *kami's* spiritual 'aura'. I too deeply feel the effects of this aura in helping to purify me spiritually whenever I set foot in the *chinju no mori*. In my view, however, the emphasis placed on such matters consists in a restriction to forms of appearance and their meaning (somewhat akin to discussions about what is represented by the height of the steeple of a Gothic cathedral) rather than delving into the theological issues themselves. Also worth noting is that ecological themes have featured prominently in accounts of 'traditional' Japanese life, as opposed to being viewed as the specifically religious preserve of Shinto.

Possibilities for Shinto

From my viewpoint, Shinto is a religion deserving of consideration in discussions on pluralism, as it has something of great value to bring to these discussions. There are, as we have seen, opposing opinions that focus on Shinto's historical and political ties with Japanese chauvinism, or at least nationalism. As can be easily imagined, this connection with nationalism may lead to a type of ethical particularism, according to which there are no (absolute or *prima facie*) moral principles or rules. It would be interesting to explore the relations between pluralism and ethical particularism. In the meantime it can be said that the emphasis on Japanese national identity in the modern period has tended to operate as a hindrance to Shinto's advocacy of universalism. In fact, in other areas, even the most basic research regarding Shinto and ethical particularism/universalism is lacking. Further research on the relation of Shinto to such philosophical issues is therefore necessary.

In looking at the case in support of Shinto, I would like to discuss an aspect of Shinto belief slightly different from the environmental connections and other elements usually emphasized in interreligious dialogues. In particular, I would like to confront the issue of Yasukuni belief or faith in the spirits of war dead as *kami*. As demonstrated by the fact that the Yasukuni Shrine has often been claimed to represent a secular national memorial rather than a religious institution, faith in the war dead *kami* bears affinities with governance under the modern nation-state system. One could draw parallels with the ties existing between historical monuments and cultural policies based on a secular, humanistic interpretation of national history. It must be admitted, nonetheless, that faith in the war dead *kami* developed along with Japanese militaristic ideology. Concerning this point, persistent criticism has been directed toward the Yasukuni Shrine since the end of World War II, based on its role in mobilizing the Japanese people to invade East Asian countries through the deification of war dead in the name of the sacred emperor. In short, critics claim that reverencing the war dead as *kami* represents a dangerous invention serving to sacralize state policy and national history.

Certainly one of the roots of Yasukuni faith must be seen as foreign to Shinto, originating instead in memorial services observed in modern states. Unlike such secular memorial services, however, the dead soldiers enshrined at Yasukuni were not merely memorialized by having their names inscribed on a secular monument. Rather, they were revered as supranormal *kami*. In spite of the claims of critics regarding the incompleteness of the separation of state and religion at Yasukuni, these critics frequently underestimate the religious significance of the apotheosis of war dead at the shrine. On the other hand, the same tendency can be observed in pro-Yasukuni advocates who demand official support from the state. But it is inconceivable that the reverencing of dead war spirits as *kami* could be either mere propaganda to mobilize people toward a harsh war front or a deception intended to appease bereaved families. Another fundamental element of Yasukuni faith is the religious combination of ancestor worship and the personality cult as found in early modern Japan and in prior periods, this being derived in part from the Confucian tradition.

I will now turn to the issue of the coexistence of beliefs in various *kami* in Shinto. In one respect, this characteristic is a reflection of the public morals of an agricultural society based on rice cultivation existing since ancient times. Such a community depended for its survival not only on unity amongst people but also on harmony amongst the elements of the earth. The members of these communities thus developed concepts and ritual systems to help their society flourish by working collaboratively and in support of one another. Compiled in the early eighth century, the Japanese mythologies, the initial forms of native reverence for the way of *kami*, or the religious bases for Shinto, were forged within the lifestyle and customs of the prehistoric age. And in my view, foreign religious ideas that have appeared in Japanese history, whether they be from Daoism, Confucianism, the multiple Buddhist schools that arrived from the Chinese continent and the Korean peninsula, or Christianity via the West, impacted Japanese society to their respective degrees but always in accordance with or against the religious basis of *kami* worship.

The modern reverence for the spirits of war dead as *kami* was also generated from this religious basis in Shinto. Subsequently, under the state administration of Shinto shrines, the upper structure erected upon that base was not to be religious but rather a secular monument in the same way as war memorials found in other countries.

On several occasions I have visited the Shrine of Remembrance in Melbourne, Australia, a nonreligious war memorial dedicated to the service by men and women from the state of Victoria. I was particularly impressed by the verse, "Greater love hath no man," from the Gospel of John 15:13, which is inscribed on the Stone of Remembrance, the marble slab at the centre of the shrine sanctuary. I do not intend here to simply advocate that the ideal of moral altruism is inherent in military service. Since coming into contact with the history and discussions that surround this Stone, originally called 'the Rock' and fashioned as a symbolic space for a kind of cenotaph or 'empty tomb', I have become increasingly aware of the differences between Yasukuni and the Shrine of Remembrance (Scates 2009: 132–135). But the existence of that simple religious verse at the very centre of a secular memorial implies something to me, suggesting another way of interpreting Yasukuni belief.

We as human beings have yet to overcome the folly of war. And memorializing the war dead of all nations and all wars is not something undertaken by any national government. At the same time, many memorial services dedicated to 'all war dead' have been observed by religious and civic groups. I admire such efforts, but do not agree with criticisms based on a smattering of knowledge about Shinto such as the following: "If you talk about sympathy for the war dead as a whole, why not memorialize former enemies in the Yasukuni shrine, too?" (Takahashi 2005:166). I suggest that we recognize that every death of a human being, including those on the battlefield, is personal and particular. According to Shinto belief, every *kami* may indicate a transcendental path toward a vague ultimacy, or a path from particularity to universality. As a result, I believe it to be neither intolerant nor one-sided to enshrine the war dead of a specific nation as *kami*. We pray for world peace to the particular *kami* of the Yasukuni shrine, and through them to the spirits of all war dead everywhere (Suga 2010a).

This transcendental route from the particular to the universal, as embedded in Shinto cosmology, may suggest a certain philosophical potential in Shinto. As noted earlier, we can deduce the presence of such a path even from beliefs that may in other ways be regarded as the product of narrow-minded chauvinism. In this chapter I have not examined the metaphysical aspects of Shinto but have considered the meta-philosophical conditions undergirding it. Whether despite or because of this fact, I hope that my comments may contribute to the future progress of interreligious dialogue.

Note

1 For historical research on Shinto written in English, see also Hardacre (2017), a thoroughgoing work recently published by the most esteemed scholar today in this field.

References

Gellner, E. 1983. *Nations and Nationalism*. Oxford: Basil Blackwell.
Hardacre, H. 1989. *Shinto and the State, 1868–1988*. Princeton, NJ: Princeton University Press.
Hardacre, H. 2017. *Shinto: A History*. New York: Oxford University Press.
Holtom, D. 1947. *Modern Japan and Shinto Nationalism: A Study of Present-Day Trends in Japanese Religions*, rev. ed. Chicago: University of Chicago Press.
Motoori, N. 1968. *Kojikiden*, vols. 1–11. Tokyo: Chikuma Shobo.
Scates, B. 2009. *A Place to Remember: A History of the Shrine of Remembrance*. Melbourne: Cambridge University Press.
Suga, K. 2004. *Nihon Tochika No Kaigai Jinja: Chosen Jingu, Taiwan Jinja to Saishin*. Tokyo: Kobundo.
Suga, K. 2010a. "Senshisha Saishi No Ba to Shiteno Jinja." In *Reikon Irei Kensho*, edited by K. D. K. K. S. Senta, 166–188. Tokyo: Kinseisha.
Suga, K. 2010b. "A Concept of 'Overseas Shinto Shrines': A Pantheistic Attempt by Ogasawara Shozo and Its Limitations." *Japanese Journal of Religious Studies* 37: 47–74.
Suzuki, D. 1959. *Zen and Japanese Culture*, 2nd ed. Princeton, NJ: Princeton University Press.
Takahashi, T. 2005. *Yasukuni Mondai*. Tokyo: Chikuma Shobo.
Ueda, K. 1991. *Shinto Shingaku Ronko*. Tokyo: Taimeido.

First Responses

5 Imran Aijaz

Introduction

In what follows, I will provide some brief replies to the Position Statements of each of the participants involved in this discussion. To better understand my replies, I would like to point out to the reader that the authors of the Position Statements were asked to present a discussion in the *philosophy of religion*. As David Stewart explains, this discipline is not to be confused with providing "a systematic statement of religious beliefs (which would be theology or dogmatics)"; rather, it is "a second-order activity focused on the fundamental issues of a given religion". The task of philosophy of religion is to "submit claims such as those made by religion to a *thoroughgoing rational investigation*" (Stewart 1980: 6; my emphasis). As such, in addition to providing an *explanation* of the core fundamental beliefs held by each participant, it was necessary to answer the question (as stipulated in the Position Statement guidelines provided by the editors): What *reasons*, if any, do you have for these beliefs? And yet, generally speaking, I found very little rational *argument* in support of the religious beliefs that were outlined in the Position Statements, even as I read very interesting and enlightening *expositions* of various religious perspectives. As a preliminary, generic response to my fellow participants, I would urge them not to lose sight of the nature of the discipline in which our discussion is being conducted. My specific replies to each of the participants follow.

Response to Isherwood: Radical incarnational Christianity

I am going to be rather critical of Isherwood's Position Statement. Before I discuss my criticisms, though, I would like to point out some areas of agreement between us. First, I have no trouble at all with feminist theology construed as the "notion that women are fully human", as Rosemary Radford Ruether, whom Isherwood cites, maintains (this volume: 49). I suspect most readers will agree with Isherwood here.

Second, there is no denying that androcentrism in Christianity (and in other religions such as Judaism and Islam) is partly a product of external influences (e.g., Hellenism) and (all-too) human interpretations of sacred texts. This point is especially important, I think, in contemporary discussions of women and Islam, since the Muslim faith is usually the first one to be brought under the spotlight when concerns are raised about the plight of women in religious surroundings. The Qur'an states that God created humanity from one soul and, from that soul, created its mate and dispersed from both many men and women (4:1). From man, woman was created so that man "might dwell in her" (7:189). From such Qur'anic references, many Muslim theologians have concluded that man was the original creation and womankind was created by God with the purpose of the pleasure and repose of man. For contemporary Muslim scholars dealing with the topic of women and Islam, it is important to ferret out and expose such theological interpretations and assumptions that underlie many unjust actions taken against women today, such as Saudi Arabia's prohibition on women driving.

A third area of agreement between Isherwood and myself concerns the importance of a theology that relates to vital *practical* issues in the world. A theology that focuses too much on the 'you will get your reward in heaven' answer is clearly inadequate in dealing with "crippling poverty and the pain, suffering and abuse that often comes with it" (Isherwood, this volume: 52). Again, I think this point is especially important for Muslim thinkers who tend to over-stress the role of the afterlife when discussing earthly affairs. The Qur'an states that this life is a test (2:214) and is "not but amusement and diversion; but the home of the Hereafter is best for those who fear Allah" (6:32). In a famous *hadith* (report), the Prophet Muhammad is reported to have said that you should "be in this world as if you are a stranger or wayfarer". Based on such sources, many Muslim theologians have crafted a picture of the world that strongly resonates with Mother Teresa's words, when she said: "In light of heaven, the worst suffering on earth, a life full of the most atrocious tortures on earth, will be seen to be no more serious than one night in an inconvenient hotel." The trouble with such a theological answer, as Isherwood notes, is that it is "not sufficient and . . . somewhat patronizing to people who clearly [understand] that their plight was created by human action and not divine dictate" (this volume: 52). It also calls into question the adequacy of the concept of God understood as an omnipotent, omniscient and omnibenevolent Creator (see, for example, Bishop and Perszyk 2011).

The central problem I have with Isherwood's Position Statement is that it lacks a clearly defined thesis or set of theses. She states in the opening paragraph that she will "navigate the question of the divine and the implications this may have in [her] life and beyond" and that she will "draw out the implications of each of these parts of [her] personal and professional identity and demonstrate the impact each has in the private and public arena" (49).

What counts as a "question of the divine"? What sort of implications are we talking about? Other than one explicit mention in her Position Statement, where she claims that she will "argue that there are heteropatriarchal assumptions underpinning the construction of religion and sexuality/gender which result in narrow and hierarchically driven narratives about both" (53), I failed to find what, precisely, Isherwood intended to argue about.

The absence of a clear thesis or set of theses further compounds a second problem I have with Isherwood's Position Statement: she presents a series of musings (often heavily anchored in what various authorities have to say) where the transition from one thought to another is all too quick and unclear, leaving the reader unsure as to what particular point (if any) she wants to make. For example, in just the first third of her chapter, the reader is given snippets on feminist theology, the history of androcentrism, a static view of revelation, radical incarnational theology, liberation theology, the construction of gender and sexuality, and heteropatriarchy!

What makes most of Isherwood's brief musings all the more difficult to understand and engage with are: (i) the obscurity of the language in which they are presented (mainly due to Isherwood's reliance on authors who are not known for their clarity of exposition, to put it mildly), and (ii) the lack of any real argument(s) accompanying them. I will give an example of each.

Isherwood makes the plausible point that gender is (at least partly) a construct, one that affects "power and significance in the world" (this volume: 54). So far, so good. She then dives into a discussion of Lacan that cries out for explanation and clarification. She writes: "For [Lacan] the Symbolic Order is what defines us as embodied persons" (54). What is this 'Symbolic Order'? Why is it an "Order of the Fathers" (54)? Or, as she says: "Sexual/gender difference ... is at the centre of the Symbolic Order, and the Phallus reigns supreme as the structuring principle" (54). Why is sexual/gender difference at the centre of the Symbolic Order? What, exactly, is *the* Phallus (with a capital 'P')? What is meant by a "structuring principle"? Such obscurity is all too familiar, I'm afraid, to readers of Lacan's work, along with some of the others mentioned by Isherwood, such as Irigaray and Butler (see Sokal and Bricmont 1999; Roney 2002). It is unfortunate that it plagues Isherwood's Position Statement, since it hampers her discussion of some rather important philosophical topics.

As an example of a segment in her Position Statement lacking any substantive argument(s), let me cite Isherwood's discussion of the allegedly "massive contribution offered by feminist theologies ... in the area of sexuality" (57). Here, she discusses thinkers who construe the notion of Christ as 'erotic power'. Two points here immediately place the burden of proof on those who wish to advocate such a claim: (i) it is an *atypical* claim, one that will not be held by the majority of Christians, or even Christian scholars for that matter; and (ii) it is an *unusual* claim, for the concept of the 'erotic' is usually taken to refer to a *state* of anticipation of sexuality or the arousal of *feelings* of sexual desire, neither of which can be reduced to, or treated as synonymous with, *a person*. So, what argument(s) are there for this idiosyncratic hermeneutic? Here is one that Isherwood attributes to Rita Brock:

> Brock believes that when speaking of Jesus as powerful, we have to be quite clear that this is erotic power; this is no abstract concept but is power deeply embedded in our very core. This kind of power is wild and cannot be controlled, and living at this level saves us from the sterility that comes from living by the head alone. *Eros* allows us to feel our deepest passions in all areas of life, and we are enjoined to reclaim it from the narrow sexual definition that has been used by patriarchal understanding.
> (this volume: 57)

But *why* must we understand *Christ's* power as erotic power? And why should power that is "wild and cannot be controlled" be understood as *erotic*, as opposed to sexual *mania*? Indeed, on the contrary, isn't there a level of *control* in the erotic that ties it conceptually to, say, seduction, and distinguishes it from, say, full-blown pornography? Isherwood provides no substantive argument here. If Brock and (by endorsement) Isherwood want to *revise* the traditional understanding of *eros*, that is fine, but they will have to proffer explanation and argument to defend this new understanding and, certainly, to defend its applicability to the notion of Christ. Care must also be taken not to subsequently *equivocate* on two different meanings of the 'erotic' in an attempt to justify all sorts of sexual lives and erotic practices by appealing to the Divine Nature.

Response to Suga: Shinto

Reading Koji Suga's Position Statement constituted my first real introduction to Shinto, a religion that I have previously only heard about. I did not find anything in his discussion that I disagreed with; indeed, there were several points of philosophical agreement that I will mention in my reply to him. All of these points are congruent with the sort of theistic philosophy of religion that I defended in my own Position Statement, perhaps even to the point of augmenting it.

The first philosophically interesting point I want to discuss is Suga's observation that, in Shinto, one sees "the possibility of religious practice without belief" (70). If he is right about this, then practitioners of Shinto provide *empirical* evidence confirming that one can engage in religious acts, such as prayer, without holding *beliefs* that are typically associated with them (e.g., the belief that there is a God, that God responds to sincere prayers, etc.). This empirical confirmation can be the starting point for arguments that religious belief is neither necessary nor sufficient for religious practice; since I am especially interested in *theistic* religious belief, I think Suga's insight here can be useful for those philosophers who argue that holding theistic *belief*, (e.g., the belief that God exists, that God is to be worshiped etc.), is neither necessary nor sufficient for *practical commitment* to theism.

Let's consider, first, whether holding theistic belief is necessary for practical commitment to theism. If followers of Shinto can engage in religious practice, such as praying at a shrine, without holding what we would consider to be requisite, correlative religious beliefs, then it seems at least feasible that one can engage in theistic religious practice without holding theistic beliefs. Indeed, one can appeal to cases that specifically pertain to theism, where individuals, say, go to church to pray, or fast during Ramadan, despite not holding beliefs like 'There is a God' or 'God wants me to fast during Ramadan'. These would be individuals who are doubters, skeptics, etc., but who have not altogether written off the plausibility of theism. Moreover, for such individuals, the so-called 'evidentialist objection' to theistic belief will not be insurmountable. In brief, this objection, stated in the form of an argument, runs as follows: theistic belief should not be held unless it is rational; theistic belief is rational only if there is sufficient evidence supporting it; there is insufficient evidence supporting theistic belief; therefore, theistic belief should not be held. The evidentialist objection is typically accompanied by the plausible, psychological point that beliefs are not directly under our control. One cannot directly will to believe in the truth of propositions like 'God exists' or 'God wants us to fast during Ramadan'. Therefore, the objection runs, what is needed is sufficient evidence for theistic belief, exposure to which will probably result in one forming theistic beliefs. If, however, theistic *belief* is not required for practical commitment to theism, then that allows for the possibility for those who doubt the truth of theism to circumvent the evidentialist objection. Perhaps such individuals are motivated by non-doxastic attitudes, such as hope. Or, it may be that, upon taking up certain forms of theistic practice – taking holy water and attending Mass, as suggested by Pascal, for instance – theistic belief arises *indirectly*, and despite the absence of sufficient evidence for theism.

It seems to me, then, that holding theistic belief is not necessary for practical commitment to theism. But is theistic belief *sufficient* for such a commitment? Clearly not. For if merely *holding* theistic belief was sufficient for practical commitment to theism, then Satan or his cohorts should be counted among the faithful. It is clear that Satan and his followers have plenty of beliefs about the existence and nature of God, but it is equally clear that they do not have *faith* (consider James 2:19: "You believe that there is one God. Good! Even the demons believe that and shudder"). As many theists will point out, what matters for faith is the appropriate *practical* response to God. Simply holding a number of beliefs about theism will not be enough.

Now, if holding theistic belief is neither necessary nor sufficient for practical commitment to theism, then perhaps theists should focus less on whether people have the 'right' beliefs about God and more on *other* factors that affect the value of theistic commitment – for example, whether theistic commitment is in accordance with correct *morality*. This particular point can be further strengthened by incorporating the kind of agnostic attitude that one finds in Shinto, as Suga explains, where one sees the universe "without any clear horizon of ultimate truth" (73). Given the 'religiously ambiguous' nature of the world, we shouldn't concern ourselves too much with trying to find out the truth about ultimate reality. Rather, more time should be invested in trying to figure out a common ethical code with which followers of different religions can agree. Many theists will agree with, or at least be sympathetic to, Suga's view that "an optimistic faith that can keep away evil by means of purification rituals offers a secure way to happiness" (73).

In sum, Suga's discussion of Shinto, "a religion deserving of consideration in discussions on pluralism" (78), provides several philosophically interesting points of reflection for those wishing to defend a theistic philosophy of religion from a pluralistic perspective.

Response to Drob: Mystical Judaism

Sanford Drob's Position Statement is to be commended for being the only one to *explicitly* mention, and attempt to deal with, the key questions that were stipulated in the editors' Position Statement guidelines (this volume: xiv–xv)! Here, I will restrict myself to some brief comments on his discussion of Mystical Judaism.

Towards the end of his statement, Drob explains that his "own predilection is for what J.N. Findlay referred to as a 'rational mysticism', in which mystical and theosophical insights are expressed, as far as possible, in rational terms" (45). I am curious to know what, precisely, this rational mysticism consists of and why it is to be preferred to the more traditional, theosophical tradition of the Kabbalah. Perhaps it is because, in attempting to stay away from rationalist Jewish philosophy of the sort articulated by Maimonides, which offers rational criteria and constraints, the esoteric approach struggles with the typical problems of subjectivism and relativism.

I found the most intriguing and fascinating part of Drob's Position Statement to be his discussion of *ha-achduth hashawaah* – the 'coincidence of opposites'. With this notion, as Drob explains, the Kabbalists held that *Ein-sof*, the infinite God, "unites within itself realities, attitudes and ideas that are opposed to or contradict one another" (37–38). Drob suggests how this idea can be taken further by pointing to "a philosophical program in which fundamental dichotomies and oppositions in thought are resolved only when we come to understand that these dichotomies represent interdependent as opposed to conflicting or contradictory ideas" (38). He explains:

> As we have seen, according to the thirteenth-century Kabbalist Azriel of Gernoa, there is a coincidence of opposites between faith and unbelief in our understanding of the divine. Atheism, by challenging the idols of dogmatic religion and theology and by opening the mind to alternative perspectives and interpretations, is to my way of thinking a necessary stage in the manifestation of divinity as the creative, open economy of thought and experience. There is a sense in which my own

understanding of God involves an atheization of theology and a spiritualization of atheism, as I identify divinity with the very values that often prompt an atheistic reaction towards religion.

(45)

Although his remarks here are brief, I think Drob touches on something that is very important but has thus far been neglected in contemporary philosophy of religion (most likely due to its paradoxical description) – the *religious* uses of *atheism*.

The first thing to point out, something that most traditional theists as well as Kabbalists agree on, is that there is a distinction between *God* and our *understanding (concept) of God*. From a Kabbalist perspective, this point can be argued for, and further supported, by availing oneself of some of the points of negative theology that Drob discusses (this volume, 33–34), as well as arguments for the conclusion that there is a distinction to be made between "language and the world, signifier and signified" (38).

Second, it is also agreed upon by most believers in God that there are at least some concepts of God that are inadequate, abominable and, indeed, idolatrous. Atheism can be a useful reference in helping religious theists to see which concepts of God are inadequate. In my view, one of the best examples of "[identifying] divinity with the very values that often prompt an atheistic reaction towards religion" is to be found in discussions on the problem of evil. In particular, a number of philosophers have argued that reflection on *certain kinds* of evils in our world (e.g., what Marilyn McCord Adams [2000] has called 'horrendous' evils) leads us to the conclusion that a certain *conception* of God is inadequate, given that we hold certain value commitments, such as the importance of being in right relationship with one another (see Bishop and Perszyk 2011). Is it really reasonable to believe, one might wonder, that an omnipotent, omniscient and omnibenevolent deity sustained the world while the Holocaust took place, given that one also believes that God, being loving, treats each human being as an end in himself or herself, to use Kant's expression? Furthermore, certain theistic responses to the problem of evil, especially those that resort to constructing *theodicies*, often betray value commitments that are regarded as antithetical to values typically held by theists, such as utilitarian ethical standards. God is held to have a morally *sufficient* reason in permitting or even causing evil in order to bring about greater goods that somehow depend upon its existence. Now, it may very well be that some evil, *e*, being logically connected to a greater good, *g*, provides a *necessary* condition for God to permit or cause it. If one is anti-utilitarian, however, and holds that God himself is not a utilitarian, then it would not be the case that *e*'s logical connection to *g* constitutes a *sufficient* condition for God to permit or cause *e*.

In sum, those who are exploring the religious uses of atheism (see, for example, Westphal 1998) would do well to explore further the Kabbalistic concept of *ha-achduth hashawaah*, since it provides a religious context in which some criticism of religion from atheists, secularists, etc., can be taken seriously.

References

Adams, M. M. 2000. *Horrendous Evils and the Goodness of God*. Ithaca, NY: Cornell University Press.

Bishop, J. and K. Perszyk. 2011. "The Normatively Relativised Logical Argument From Evil." *International Journal for Philosophy of Religion* 70: 109–126.

Roney, S. K. 2002. "Postmodernist Prose and George Orwell." *Academic Questions* 15, no. 2: 13–23.

Sokal, A. and J. Bricmont. 1999. *Fashionable Nonsense: Postmodern Intellectuals' Abuse of Science*. New York: Picador.

Stewart, D. 1980. *Exploring the Philosophy of Religion*. Englewood Cliffs, NJ: Prentice-Hall.

Westphal, M. 1998. *Suspicion and Faith: The Religious Uses of Modern Atheism*. New York: Fordham University Press.

6 Sanford L. Drob

Response to Isherwood: Radical incarnational Christianity

My first reactions to Lisa Isherwood's splendid and rich chapter on 'Radical incarnational Christianity' and 'body theology' are personal and psychological, rather than theological. I will begin by relating two brief personal anecdotes. Years ago when I was an undergraduate, I served as a research assistant to the late Paul Edwards, who was then a professor of philosophy at New York University and had earlier served as the editor of the *Encyclopedia of Philosophy*. Edwards, who was born in Austria, knew and had been deeply impacted by Wilhelm Reich, and although Edwards was not trained in medicine or psychology, he was apparently willing to dabble in the techniques of Reichian psychotherapy. Edwards explained to me that, according to Reich, the neurotic complexes which Freud had conceived of in largely psychological terms were actually encoded in the 'muscular armour' of the body, and that body work, in addition to psychological analysis, was necessary in order to release one from their grip. Edwards had come to know me quite well, and he concluded that I had a great deal of neurotic tension in my eyes and forehead. During one of our discussions, he requested permission to run his hands gently along my brow, and in the course of this I was amazed to find tears running down my cheeks, tears the origin of which I had only a faint understanding.

Years later, when I was going through a personal crisis related to a divorce, I entered psychotherapy with a therapist who practiced a form of bio-energetic psychotherapy. She told me that I was *living in my head* and that it was important for me to plant my feet firmly on the ground and feel the energy coursing through my body while I spoke. This turned out to be a critical moment in my therapy, one that moved me from my 'head' into my body and feelings, and enabled me to do much productive psychological work. Isherwood's chapter reminded me of these experiences and the great impact they had on me, but it also caused me to reflect how much, in spite of them, I continue to live in my head and to participate in what Isherwood refers to as "the exaltation of the intellect".

There is no doubt that passion and intimacy are a very significant part of the theological story. Reason alone will never result in a lived awareness of the divine, our fellow humans or even ourselves. Bodily emotions are the chief vehicle through which we arrive at the majority of values (loving-kindness, compassion, beauty, gratitude, pleasure and even wisdom) that figure into any 'I-thou' encounter. I realize that I can all too easily forget that I am an embodied being and that without the passion of my body, my intellect would have no direction and my life no genuine meaning. Further, I am under no illusion that what Isherwood calls 'the wild and the uncontrolled' can be avoided; to live a creative, meaningful life means to at least sometimes open oneself to chaos.

Yet a part of me still wants to justify this preference for the intellect. Reflecting on the matter, I do believe that it is our intellect that is the source of our highest achievements and which makes us "a little lower than the angels" (Hebrews 2:7). I should add that I am in full agreement with the view that intellectual discourse, and the symbolic order in general, is not an exclusively masculine or patriarchal affair. It seems to me that the relegation of the symbolic to the masculine and the bodily to the feminine simply reflects a long-standing prejudice, one that must be overcome in our age.

Isherwood suggests that an "embodied subjectivity" is at the heart of knowing and that *absolute rationality*, which has been the norm within a "patriarchal mythology", must be overcome. This is certainly an idea worth meditating upon. My only hesitation stems from my concern that any abandonment of reason as the criterion for knowledge leaves us at the mercy of the irrational and poses a great danger. My study of (and great ambivalence towards) C.G. Jung has reinforced this point of view (Drob 2010, 2012). Jung (perhaps for different reasons than Isherwood) thought it important for western culture to overcome its prejudice in favouring reason over passion. Jung, like Isherwood, held that there was a non-rational power that was "wild and cannot be controlled", and his celebration of the irrational resulted in an important renewed interest in mythological experience and its relevance to both psychology and theology. However, it also unfortunately resulted in his positive estimation of National Socialism, which he saw as embodying the mythic, irrational forces of the Germanic spirit.[1] To be fair, Isherwood's call for an awareness of feminine erotic power is very different from the mythological (perhaps masculine) passion that Jung saw in the Germanic myths, but I have come to mistrust all calls for displacing reason as an ultimate basis for either knowledge or action. The possibility that this is a patriarchal prejudice is something that I am certainly willing to consider. However, as a psychologist who for three decades has worked on a daily basis with accused and convicted criminals (male and female, gay and straight), I have come to see that the passions unmitigated by reason can wreak havoc on soul and world. I believe that a balance must be struck between *logos* and *eros*, reason and passion, *with reason serving as the ultimate guide*. Indeed, in my view, it is reason rather than passion that prompts us to relinquish our prejudices and open ourselves to a God of justice.

There is so much in Isherwood's chapter with which I resonate, and I hardly know where to begin. The belief that women, gay people, transgender people and all who are simply 'different' must be given complete equality in our spiritual and secular communities, the idea that revelation is dynamic rather than static, the vision of Christ as a model for liberation rather than a saviour, the idea that the messianic Kingdom is one that is deeply planted on Earth, the critique of reification and institutionalization in religion, the view that theology cannot be separated from politics, and the vision that we cannot determine the nature or manner of God except through negotiating significant issues involving values and sexual difference are among the many ideas in Isherwood's chapter that command attention and assent.

Finally, as a Jew, I have always struggled with my relationship to Jesus, who in many Jewish circles is regarded as an almost unspeakable *apikoris* (heretic), but who has always struck me as an important Jewish prophet who had little, if anything, to do with the institutionalized version of Christianity that resulted in such things as the papacy and the Spanish Inquisition. I was struck by Isherwood's discussion of Jesus as a saviour and hero, and her claim that both of these positions tend to disable his followers. This very issue was taken up in some detail by Jung in his recently rediscovered and published *Red Book* (2009), and his view is one that impresses me as quite simple but profound: Jung urges us to view Jesus neither as a saviour nor as a hero but as one who went his own way and teaches us to do the same. It is gratifying then to see the contributors to this volume, Lisa Isherwood among them, taking their own philosophical or religious path.

Response to Suga: Shinto

Koji Suga's chapter on Shinto is the personal witness of a Shinto scholar and priest struggling to understand his own tradition. Suga readily acknowledges some of the difficulties that make others regard Shinto as either tainted with imperialistic Japanese nationalism or as a nonreligious, cultural practice. Yet, as he suggests, Shinto has much to commend itself: its emphasis upon spiritual and physical purity, its embeddedness within a simple and wonderful aesthetic tradition, its concern for nature and the environment, and its emphasis on prayer without specific metaphysical beliefs are among its great strengths. In fact, the last of these traits, which makes Shinto a religious tradition that is saddled neither with scripture nor mandatory theology, has enabled Suga to embrace those beliefs that have recommended themselves to his heart, reason and soul without having to answer to a limiting authority. As I pointed out in my chapter on Jewish mysticism, this feature of doctrinal flexibility is also evident in Judaism, which has traditionally placed far greater emphasis upon conformity of behaviour and practice than it has to any set of theological beliefs or doctrines. Yet Shinto appears to be far more radical than normative Judaism in its distance from metaphysics and theology. Whereas Judaism certainly holds that belief in a single unnameable God is a minimal commitment, Shinto – at least on Suga's reading – is compatible with polytheism, agnosticism and even atheism. For these reasons, the practitioner of Shinto appears to be in an excellent position to develop his or her beliefs in a pluralistic, open-minded manner that is in accord with contemporary developments in philosophy, psychology and natural science. The capacity to do this strikes me as the greatest challenge for today's theologians within the traditional monotheistic faiths.

Indeed, there is something very honest and even liberating about "the possibility", as Suga puts it, "of religious practice without belief" (this volume: 70). Many individuals find it easier to pray and to partake in religious ritual than they do to testify to matters of belief and faith. The possibility and even necessity for prayer is something that I believe is essential to the human spirit, and I am of the view that prayer is and should be available to all those in need of it, regardless of their affiliation or theology. While I am willing to acknowledge that there may indeed be atheists in foxholes, there are many individuals with no particular religious convictions who will find themselves turning to prayer under dire circumstances. Prayer as a psychological phenomenon cannot be limited to those who have definite ideas about where and to whom prayers are directed and if and how they will be answered. Again, in my own tradition, we have the example of Mordecai Kaplan, the founder of the Reconstructionist movement in Judaism, who denied the existence of a supernatural God but still believed that the traditions of the Jewish people, including the tradition of worship and prayer, had an important place in the life of the Jewish people.

Suga's heartfelt Position Statement raises important questions and provides us with an example of an author whose modest claims about his own religious tradition provide his writing with great spiritual power. I am moved by many things in Suga's chapter, but one thing that I find particularly intriguing is the description of Shinto as providing "an interpretation of the universe without any clear horizon of ultimate truth, while the possibilities to access it would be found in each occasion" (73). This idea, that religion and theology can be invented anew at each spiritual moment or encounter, is extremely powerful. As a psychologist, I am reminded of the notion advanced by Wilfred Bion (1967) that each psychoanalytic session should begin without memory, desire or understanding in order to best permit the emergence of the analysand's unconscious. Such an open economy of experience seems to me to be one, if not the highest, manifestation of the divine spirit.

Response to Aijaz: Sunni Islam

Imran Aijaz works from the premise that, while two inconsistent positions cannot both be rationally compelling, they may each be rationally defensible. This leads to the notion that one can be an adherent of a particular religious faith and still hold that others have good reason to adhere to faiths that differ from one's own or even to adhere to no religious faith at all. Much of Aijaz's Position Statement is devoted to an interesting discussion of the familiar philosophical arguments for the existence of God (arguments that are certainly not specific to Islam) and to a review of the less familiar arguments that claim to support the divine origin of the Qur'an. He holds that these philosophical arguments, while not absolutely compelling, provide good reasons for his own religious beliefs.

While I strongly support the application of reason to religion and theology and hold that reason must be the ultimate arbiter in matters of moral conflict, I have never found the classical arguments for the existence of God particularly compelling. For example, the argument from design has been thrown into grave doubt by the theory of natural selection. With regard to Aijaz's Leibnizian formulation of the cosmological argument, where he holds that "If the universe has an explanation of its existence, that explanation is God" (this volume: 6), I have never been persuaded that there must be an explanation for the cosmos as a whole. Further, to my mind, invoking 'God' is no explanation at all, as this immediately raises the question, 'From whence God?' Again, while Aijaz recognizes that reasonable people may not be persuaded by theistic arguments, he holds that such arguments may nonetheless serve as a foundation for religious belief.

Turning to rational arguments for the foundation of Islam, the claim that the Qur'an is a miracle may be persuasive to believers, but it is not, in my view, persuasive for *rational reasons*. I would make the same point regarding the divine origin of the Torah. Even if the Qur'an (or the Torah) were inimitable, this could hardly prove its miraculous nature. The same argument could be used to prove the divine nature of works by Shakespeare or even James Joyce. I am not familiar enough with the Qur'an to speak specifically about it, but with respect to the Jewish Bible, while I am deeply moved by its narrative, imagery and literary power, I am in agreement with the suggestion in the Zohar, the *locus classicus* of Jewish mysticism, that if the Torah says what it superficially appears to be saying, "we could write a better Torah ourselves, using our own words". Certainly we could produce one that was less celebratory of violence and more in accord with the values that we, as Jews, claim to be our 'Torah values' today. More on this a bit later.

Aijaz asks us to consider the 'argument from parity', that is, the contention that the reliance on others' religious experiences as a basis for our faith in God is analogous to relying on others' normal perceptual experiences for our information about the world. However, we rely on others' perceptions of objects and events in the world because they do not differ in kind from our own. Everyone believes in and has experiences of material objects and events, but not everyone has experiences of God and other heavenly occurrences. People who claim to experience God directly may have some reason to believe in the divine, but the grounds for their religious beliefs are of a very different sort from the grounds we typically have for believing that there is a chair or a tree. It is only in the latter case that the observer can point to the objects of his experience and have them confirmed by virtually anyone. With regard to the reliance upon others as a basis for religious faith, there is also an asymmetry between past and present. Why do we trust the experiences of the prophets of old while we mainly regard today's 'prophets' as either hucksters or madmen? The opposite, by the way, is true with regard to normal perceptual experiences. There we often hold contemporary observations (e.g., of the craters on the moon) to be far more accurate than observations remote in time.

I believe that the argument from 'parity' works a bit better for so-called scientific objects than it does for objects of the everyday world. After all, very few of us have seen an electron or a black hole. However, I am personally inclined to dismiss this argument as well. The reasons for positing an invisible electron involve a very large matrix of objectively observable data placed in the context of a theory or theories that have predictive power of mathematical precision. The reasons for positing God in the face of human experience are much less specific and clear.

In my view, the best arguments in favour of religious faith (or at least religious interest) involve the notion that there is an irreducible spiritual dimension to human life. Just as there are material, aesthetic and moral dimensions that point to material, aesthetic and axiological objects (though even this is debated), there is a spiritual dimension that at least seems to point to or *intend* spiritual objects, and perhaps even an 'Absolute' spiritual centre – a centre which, whether it exists or not, is very significant for human life and experience. Here I am not relying on the experience of prophetic others, nor am I relying exclusively on my own experience but rather (as per William James) on the phenomenology of human religious experience in general. I believe that the various rational arguments for the existence of God – such as the appeal to a creator-God as a first cause, the apparent design of the universe and improbability of intelligent life, the inspirational power of scripture, the apparent miraculous in history and individual lives – all point to the spiritual dimension of our experience. However, I also believe that attempts to rationalize these experiences and cast them in a logical argument may remove them from that experience and thus remove them from the very foundation of spirituality. I believe that a similar thing occurs when we move from our undoubted (and extremely important) *experience* of free will to philosophical or scientific efforts to rationalize or prove the *existence* of free will in the face of a science that is clearly deterministic in its assumptions.

From where does the spiritual dimension of experience arise? I would here only hazard the guess that it arises from a number of different areas of human experience, among which are: the awe and wonder that there is anything at all; the magnificence of nature; the great potential of humankind; the experience of consciousness and free will; the transcendence afforded by experience of the human arts, literature and scripture; the possibilities of reason; the magnificence of mathematics; and the great conversation that results in the dialectic of the human spirit. I see spirituality as growing out of an awareness of a spiritual dimension of experience that, like the aesthetic and moral dimensions of experience, is not simply the product of rational argumentation. Kant's famous claim to the effect that two things caused him awe and wonder, "the starry skies above and the moral law within", comes close to expressing what I believe to be some of the sources of religious interest and the spiritual life.

I want to return now to the argument, initially propounded by Hick and raised again by Aijaz, that the universe is *religiously ambiguous* and that both naturalistic and religious views are in principle complete, leaving no data unaccounted for. In my view, this is an extremely interesting possibility, provided that religious accounts of the universe, like their scientific counterparts, are subject to change and indeed to *paradigmatic shifts* in response to new experiences and to internal tensions within religious theory. The problem with the analogy is that the major faith-based traditions, at least for many of their more orthodox adherents, are mired in the religious equivalent of Aristotelian science and have failed to develop in a manner commensurate with developments in modern thought. The result is that religion has, for many, been saddled with ideas accepted on the basis of religious authority that are simply untenable in light of progress in both the natural and human sciences, and even, I might say, progress in the moral sciences. Religion, of course, has the problem of 'authority', a problem that is much less salient for naturalism. While scientists, too, can get stuck in an old 'paradigm', science as a whole has shown itself willing to reject an old idea in light of such considerations as evidence, parsimony and practicality. The theories of the four elements, bodily humours and the ether are all in the scrap-bin of history, while religion, in many instances, struggles to maintain creationism, the biblical version of the origin of the earth, etc.

If one purpose of religion is to provide a complete and consistent account of the world that is on an equal footing with naturalism, it must do a better job with the problem of authority than it has in the past. Perhaps the scientific attitude to authority is too radical for theology to adopt as its own, as it is often the case that scientists engage their past only as a historical subject. Theology (and religion in general) is better served by following the lead of philosophy, which recognizes the significance (epistemological and otherwise) of its history, and dialogues with it but refuses to be bound by it. An example of this kind of engagement from my own faith tradition is found in the period of the Talmud, a fertile intellectual era when the rabbis debated and essentially completely recast Judaism in response to then-contemporary life and events. Unfortunately, this process generally came to a halt for normative Judaism in the Middle Ages, and efforts to restart it have resulted in division within the Jewish world. Furthermore, as I am about to explain, this process is not without its own considerable cost.

These considerations raise questions regarding the survival of traditional cultural and religious forms in the face of the liberal, ecumenical and universal thinking that is amply illustrated in several of the contributions to this volume, not the least of which is my own. As one moves towards a liberalized open economy of thought, recognizes the value inherent in other faiths and philosophies, and regards one's own traditions as affording spiritual opportunities rather than sacred obligations, there is an inevitable dilution and even fading-away of religious and cultural differences. I see this as an inevitable result of the massive exchange of information and ideas that is characteristic of the contemporary world, and it is both welcome and melancholy. One thing is for certain: it is a process that we have yet to fully understand and work through. A possible reaction to this process, one that I understand but do not recommend, is to shore up orthodoxy in the face of the spiritual and philosophical globalization we read about in these pages.

Note

1 The issue of Jung's purported anti-Semitism and pro-Nazism is very complex. I devote a long chapter to it in my book, *Kabbalistic Visions: C. G. Jung and Jewish Mysticism* (2010). Here I will cite one example of Jung's demotion of reason in his evaluation of National Socialism. In a 1935 lecture at the Tavistock Clinic in London, Jung stated regarding the Nazis: "When I am in Germany, I believe it myself, I understand it all, I know it has to be as it is. One cannot resist it. It gets you below the belt and not in your mind, your brain just counts for nothing, your sympathetic system is gripped. It is a power that fascinates people from within, it is the collective unconscious which is activated. . . . We cannot be children about it, having intellectual and reasonable ideas and saying: this should not be" (Jung 1977: 164, para. 372).

References

Bion, W. R. 1967. "Notes on Memory and Desire." *Psychoanalytic Forum* 2: 279–281.
Drob, S. 2010. *Kabbalistic Visions: C. G. Jung and Jewish Mysticism*. New Orleans: Spring Journal Books.
Drob, S. 2012. *Reading the Red Book: An Interpretive Guide to C. G. Jung's Liber Novus*. New Orleans: Spring Journal Books.
Jung, C. G. 1977. "The Tavistock Lectures." In *The Collected Works, Vol. 18: The Symbolic Life*, edited by H. Read, M. Fordham, and G. Adler, 1–182. London: Routledge & Kegan Paul.
Jung, C. G. 2009. *The Red Book – Liber Novus*, edited by S. Shamdasani, translated by M. Kyburz, J. Peck, and S. Shamdasani. New York: W. W. Norton & Co.

7 Lisa Isherwood

Response to Suga: Shinto

Koji Suga opens his Position Statement with an important and challenging question: Is Shinto a religion? While Shinto includes rituals and the worship of unique spiritual beings, it does not have a canon of scripture but rather draws from folk tales and mythological stories. From a feminist perspective, the lack of a canon of scripture and the use of mythological material raise interesting questions. Feminist biblical scholarship has questioned whether the absence or sidelining of women in the canon amounts to revelation, tradition or patriarchy, and as such it has developed a *hermeneutic of suspicion* (Schüssler Fiorenza 1983) that acknowledges the absences in scripture. In its early conception, these absences were women, but as time has gone on the same method has been used to identify gaps in terms of race, class and sexual orientation. The hermeneutic also involves *creative actualization*, which means that with sufficient multidisciplinary research the gaps may be populated by those left out from the canon or those silenced by the way in which the canon has been written. This, of course, has meant a much more flexible approach to scripture itself, which ceases to be the unchangeable word of God and becomes a record of how men have understood their religious history. It may therefore be possible to say that folk and mythological tales are as legitimate as any in telling the story of human history.

Further, the absence of a fixed set of beliefs does not in the view of feminist and other liberation theologies imply that something is not a religion. Appeal to orthopraxis rather than orthodoxy has been a large part of liberation theologies, since people have been galvanized around what needs to be done in society more than what one's co-worker for justice believes in terms of systematics. It is of course true that there needs to be a common understanding that social justice is a goal, but this is embedded in many belief-systems and many values that could not be viewed as religious or theological.

It is interesting to see how Shinto was embedded as a nationalistic practice with appeal to honoured ancestors and war heroes. This play between nationalism and religious practice is obviously found in Christian history and is still found today in some forms of Christianity, such as that of fundamentalists in the United States. Brock and Parker (2008) demonstrate graphically how Christianity after the first thousand years changed from a religion concerned with love of the world, by which they mean justice and beauty, into one concerned with making warriors for Christ in order to spread imperial power. They show how this trajectory has continued in the United States and the devastating consequences it showers on the rest of the world. It is also interesting to note that these warriors for Christ did and do in some sense become the honoured ancestors. Certainly soldiers from the USA or UK who now invade, some may say illegally, the soil of other countries are referred to as 'heroes', and the country is believed to owe them a debt. Those who survive are also to be honoured, even in retail outlets, where they are meant to receive preferential treatment. It is perhaps a step too far to suggest that the honoured hero has a crucial part to play in advanced capitalism – or is it? I would be interested to know how, if at all, the Shinto ancestors relate to the economy.

What grabs my feminist heart is the way in which Allied forces at the end of World War II worked to abolish Shinto shrines, seeing them as lying at the centre of Japanese racism and nationalism. Yet those same Allies had made no attempt (nor make any attempt) to curb the racism and Nazi-like nationalism at the heart of much American Christian fundamentalism (Ruether 2007). Ruether argues that, historically and ideologically, America views itself as an 'elect nation', the 'Promised Land' whose task it is to overcome all other powers and spread redemption in the form of democracy throughout the world. The imperial delusion and double standard are plain to see. It would be interesting to know if Shinto has a counter to this imperial attitude in others, having attempted to overcome these connections in its own practice.

The term 'agnostic pantheism' strikes me forcibly when Suga describes the idea of there being no supernatural creation outside the universe, no clear horizons of ultimate truth, while there are endless possibilities to access it in each occasion of life and a goddess and imperial ancestor at the centre. This leads in Suga's opinion to incompleteness in the theological realm, something which he finds appealing. There is much here that appears to intersect with polydoxy (Keller 2003) and the exploration of the multiple (Schneider 2008) that some feminist theologians are attempting. It is interesting that they would not call their work 'agnostic', although they may say it is pantheistic, but in any case they would still claim that it lies within the realm of Christian theology. The wider horizons and incompleteness spoken of by Suga, which lead him away from the idea of conversion to that of 'moulting', would be recognized by many feminist theologians working in the process and quantum aspects of the discipline. Within this area, the idea is not to convert people to one set of beliefs but rather to awaken to a greater sense of relationality between all animate and inanimate beings on the planet, understanding that all have the same divine energy within them. I suppose this is what makes such an approach 'theistic', even if a face cannot be put to that divine energy – an energy that makes co-emerging subjects of us all rather than being able to make objects out of those we consider to be lower than us, so that there is no 'lower' and 'higher' but only an outpouring of dynamic creative energy in multiple forms (Isherwood, in Isherwood and Bellchambers 2010: 121–136). This has major implications for the way in which we are able to understand our relationship with nature and, by extension, with the resources of nature, which can no longer simply be understood as there to be used and abused by humans. It would be interesting to know how Shinto situates itself in relation to sustainable development and cyborg issues, where animal parts are used to save or enhance human life.

It would also be interesting to know if the placing of a goddess and an imperial ancestor at the centre of an otherwise open horizon has any implications for gender relations within Shinto or for continued imperial aspirations, be they through military power or economic control. Certainly within Christianity the male deity has had serious gender consequences over the centuries.

Response to Aijaz: Sunni Islam

As a feminist theologian I found this chapter particularly interesting, given that it uses as its basis two strands that have undergone change in the hands of feminist theology: religious texts and arguments for the existence of God. The latter has long since been replaced with a different sort of question, one that asks what belief in God does in the world in terms of what kind of political, economic and social system it lends itself to. The creation of a just, equal and inclusive society is considered to be the mark of a society that has worked through a number of issues raised by religions across diverse periods and cultures, issues which are bound therefore to carry within them vestiges of those earlier times and societies which stand in need of reevaluation in light of present-day ethics and understandings. For example, Hampson (1996) suggests that Christianity needs to move forward morally in terms of equality issues, as it is lagging behind the best of secular society. She acknowledges that the early founding fathers of Christianity may not have fully engaged with the equality of women, but this she considers to be an indisputable good of the modern world, and for churches to deny women full access through religious orders is now indefensible. Ruether (1983) holds the same position, stressing that to believe in a God who wishes full equality to be denied to any race, colour, creed, sex or gender is a blasphemy. She is clear: any belief that stands in the way of the full flourishing and equality of any person has to be discarded. I think this shows that many feminist theologians are more concerned with the outcomes in society of belief in God rather than arguments for the existence of God. In their eyes, all those arguments would come to nothing if the God found to exist oversaw an unjust and unequal society. Although the two questions are not quite the same – one may feel it necessary to argue for the existence of God before debating what that God stands for – feminist theologians tend to concentrate on the practical outcomes of belief, given that those who believe God is a God of hierarchy and exclusion may be little moved by arguments or proofs. The feminist approach to the question of God's existence is perhaps therefore one that understands the question in more psychological than philosophical terms and so takes the limitations of philosophical argumentation as one of its presuppositions.

On another matter regarding theistic proofs, the appeal to 'religious experience' in some of these proofs (as in John Hick's case for the reality of God) poses interesting questions for feminist theologians, given that our insistence on women's experience as a valid starting point for the construction of theology has been hotly disputed in Christian circles. This leads me to ask: Whose experience are we talking about, and who decides what is acceptable or not?

The second point of interest is the notion of Scripture as a 'miracle', and its role in proving that Islam is a valid religion. I am assuming that even if this were the case, it is open to many interpretations, and just as in Christianity, I suppose there are those who believe it is only their interpretation that is correct. I find the weight placed on the Qur'an to uphold the validity of the entire religion astonishing, and I wonder if this is still a widely held belief. This also raises the issue as to what extent may the text be challenged if it has such a central role.

Feminist biblical scholars have been challenging the Bible for many years now, beginning with Elisabeth Cady Stanton in the nineteenth century and her creation of the Women's Bible. This was a project to remove sexist and racist texts from the Bible, as well as texts that involved violence to women. Perhaps the best known approach in twentieth-century feminist thought has been Elisabeth Schüssler Fiorenza's (1983) 'hermeneutic of suspicion'. As the name of this approach suggests, Schüssler Fiorenza scrutinizes each text with a suspicious eye, identifying androcentrism, emphasizing the absence of women or their thoughts and 'creatively actualizing', where this involves putting women back in the picture, that is, writing them into the biblical narrative. This obviously involves a multidisciplinary approach, since women cannot simply be inserted into texts without a real understanding of how life may have been and what clues there may be in the absences and traces. A good example of this is the discovery of the Corinthian women prophets, a search that was prompted by the Apostle Paul's command for women to stay silent in church (1 Corinthians 14: 34–35). Rather than assuming that Paul meant 'do not gossip', the question was posed as to what the women may have been saying. This led to an interdisciplinary investigation of women in the period and what their concerns may have been, as well as examining Christian documents of the time to look for other gaps that may shed light on women's lives – this, in the end, has led to a wonderful creative actualization of the lives of these women prophets.

Schüssler Fiorenza is not willing to abandon the power potential that lies in women remembering their own heritage. She argues that to abandon our history – particularly our authentic history within biblical religion – is to give in to oppression, since it is oppression that deprives people of their history (1983: xix). Scripture is therefore not necessarily regarded as a 'miracle', and indeed many fundamentalist Christians would view this approach as lacking in respect towards the word of God. However, Schüssler Fiorenza and others take a contrary stance, regarding this mining of the texts as proclaiming faith in the religion itself, as opposed to faith in those who have transmitted it through interpretation.

One of the tasks of contemporary feminist scholarship is to extract the 'content' of the message from its patriarchal 'form'. This requires a critique of the prevailing patriarchal culture as much as it requires textual analysis. Women have suffered under patriarchy, and because of this they wonder if the texts that perpetuate such suffering can really be 'divine absolutes'. This question is translated by feminist biblical scholars into research that discloses the texts not as absolutes but as faith responses – therefore, not as archetypes but as prototypes. This is a major shift in scholarship, as it opens up the possibility that Scripture can be transformed, thereby also transforming our models of faith and community (Schüssler Fiorenza 1983: 33). Feminist biblical scholarship does not only enable us to 'find the women' in Christian beginnings but also to locate the power struggles behind the texts. They were struggles that women lost, but searching and finding them can be an empowering experience for contemporary women.

Women of colour have also been recovering their own history, both as historical fact and as biblical narrative, which has led to some challenging readings. For example, women of colour who sit with the Syrophoenician woman (Mark 7:24–30) understand Jesus to be exhibiting sexism and racism – the references to dogs can be less easily spiritualized when such words of abuse are part of one's everyday life. Hagar has also been claimed as a woman who highlights the myth of global sisterhood: she is doubly abused, both as a surrogate and as a scapegoat, and the story highlights that Sarah is not her ally (Genesis 16:1–16, 21:9–21).

In my view, the two foregoing approaches are interlinked: if one is less interested in arguments for the existence of God and more concerned with the kind of society that belief in God creates, it would seem reasonable that texts that develop out of certain ideas about God could be held up to scrutiny if they appear to offer interpretations that create prejudice, inequality and even genocide – all of which in certain hands the Bible has done. I would like to know if any such approach has been adopted by Muslim women, and whether Aijaz considers that such an approach to the Qur'an is ever possible or desirable? If possible, what might the implications be for the Qur'an as a validation of Islam?

I would also like to know if Islamic scholars have set about a similar task to that outlined in the work of Hick, and if so, why did the author not appeal to them in his Position Statement? If they have not, what are the reasons for this? Do they not consider such arguments important? If a similar task has been undertaken, it might find points of connection with some feminist theology.

Response to Drob: Mystical Judaism

The opening statement of Drob's chapter, where it is maintained that Judaism is a practice rather than a belief-system, would resonate with the emphasis that feminist theology places on orthopraxis rather than orthodoxy. However, the way in which Kabbalah is then described seems to go way beyond simple orthopraxis and instead appears prescriptive.

As a first question to the author, I would like to ask whether there has been a feminist analysis of Kabbalah as there has been of Christian mysticism, where it was discovered that, despite certain claims being made about equality, the understanding of what may or may not count as mysticism was male-defined. Would the author consider the question of whether Kabbalah is male-defined a legitimate question?

Contemporary feminist scholars have also discovered that many of their fore-sisters who have been called mystics appeared to play with gender identification, both in terms of changing gender for Christ and having Christ change gender for them – the latter can be seen in the visions of Catherine of Sienna, who desires Christ as a female lover and has her wishes fulfilled. Michael Warner (2004: 221) states that "religion makes available a language of ecstasy, a horizon of significance within which transgressions against the normal order of the world and the boundaries of self *can be seen as good things*" (emphasis in original). Reading with certain eyes opens up a Christian mystical history that is full of ecstatic transgressions against the norm, and I wonder if Kabbalistic practices open the norms in such a way in order to experience more completely the fullness of being human. I understand experiencing the full range of gender as more complete humanness, following Judith Butler's notion that once we have a gender script prescribed to us we are cut off from the potential of at least half our humanity. This loss may have implications for the next point I am taking up from the chapter.

One point that finds resonance in feminist theology is the completion of creation and the divine through human action. If I understood the chapter correctly, this completion lies in extracting the divine light from the husks and reassembling and repairing the broken values. This is perhaps where we part company, as feminist theology does not postulate any kind of 'Fall', that is to say, the disassembling of a once-ordered universe. We have been suspicious of this notion due to the weight that has been placed on women within the Christian understanding of the once-perfect, now-fallen creation. Due to its intersection with the new cosmology (an emerging scientific view which questions static, perfect order and considers the way in which the universe is grounded in chaos and paradoxes), feminist theology has in some instances moved even further from beliefs in perfect origins, Falls and final harmonies. That is not to say that process is not envisaged, but endless possibilities have replaced perfect endings. I would be interested to know if endless possibilities could be part of a Kabbalistic understanding of the divine and the world. Do we have to remain connected with the values that were once destined to fill the cosmic void or can we break free? Do the broken vessels always signal lack of freedom? I am also fascinated by the notion of the Celestial Father and Mother reuniting in erotic union once the values are repaired. Is this understood as a form of celestial complementarity where opposites are united? If so, then feminist theology might pose some questions about this view, or is it that the x and not-x of other forms of Kabbalistic thought are also at play here? Mention of feminine and masculine aspects of God, while being a move forward from the fully male God of Christianity, still carries some elements of defined natures which has historically led to unequal treatment – is this the case here? The author mentions that Jung found inspiration in Kabbalistic thought, but as we know his notion of male and female archetypes, as well as the anima and animus, have met with much criticism from contemporary feminist psychologists.

In the new cosmology, the notion of endless possibilities is also connected with the idea of paradoxes as being central to what it is to be human and indeed for what it is for the universe to exist. I find it fascinating that Kabbalistic thought speaks of the union of contradictions as the basis even of the nature of God and certainly the nature of humankind. In the new cosmology, this allows an embrace of chaos as a creative – even divine – activity. I wonder to what extent this is the case in Kabbalistic thought, given that this seems to be in opposition to its view that if one single letter is not correctly transcribed, then the whole world is destroyed. This, perhaps, is yet another paradox.

The connection between the divine speech and the creation of the world is one that Christian feminist theologians have taken to task, contending that the utterance of a male divinity in a disembodied way spoken as a command has been at the root of many of the problems of Christianity. Contemporary feminist scholars wish to move back beyond the Logos of John's Gospel to the divine Sophia, which they understand as more co-creative and empowering (Johnson 1994). Sophia permeates all that is and does not dwell above in a commanding position but rather emerges as humans awaken to full mutuality through love. This places the notion of the creative word of God in a rather different light and replaces the signified and the signifier with co-emerging subjects.

Much feminist work has been done on how language constructs reality and where women need to look for other forms of language (Irigaray 1985). To repeat parts of my initial chapter: for Lacan, the Symbolic Order is what defines us as embodied persons and, following Freud, he makes it difficult for women to find a place at all in this Order of the fathers, since the acquisition of language is utterly important and Lacan claims that women have no language of their own. There is no way to resolve this situation within the world of the Symbolic Order, and Lacan urges women to find their own economy beyond that of the phallus. This can be done through female sexual pleasure (*jouissance*), but it is never likely to be achieved, since it is beyond the phallic and therefore beyond language and meaning. Irigaray highlights this dilemma by suggesting that there can be no subjectivity until women find a place in culture, since such belonging gives psychic leverage to our personhood. For Irigaray, this can begin with the body: we can find a language when our genital lips meet and speak. She also feels that we have to find a language of the divine – in fact, the two processes are not entirely distinct. It is a matter of great urgency that we find a language because, if we do not, then we simply repeat the same history through an inability to think otherwise. Both Butler (1990) and Braidotti (1994) challenge the Lacanian notion that women are outside language. Butler suggests that woman is in process and so not a finally defined other who can be placed outside. She is a body becoming. This is a language of its own, a language of materiality. And Braidotti speaks of figurations that are politically informed accounts of alternative subjectivity. While she does acknowledge that we, as women, have no mother tongue, we do have linguistic sites from which we both see and fail to see. For this reason, we need to be nomads, taking no position or identity as permanent but rather trespassing and transgressing, making coalitions and interconnections beyond boxes. No language – but we do have bodies, and these bodies can be radically subversive of culture when they find their voice beyond the fixed language and meaning of the master discourses.

This raises a question for both Kabbalah and feminist theology about which actually comes first: language, or the experience and mediating significance of language? Feminist scholarship has raised the issues of who defines what words mean and who has the power to insert meaning into language – and perhaps we both agree that in the face of the chaotic, changing, ever-unfolding nature of that which we call 'divine', there are no words but only relations or relationality. Could a Kabbalist accept this?

Conclusion: Position restatement

As outlined in my Position Statement, my core belief is that all animate and even inanimate beings are entangled in what we call 'the divine', the energy that is all-in-all, as spoken of in Paul's First Letter to the Corinthians (12:4–6), which does not permit any separation between persons, things and the divine. There are certainly differences, but the same divine energy pulsates through all. As a Christian theologian, this presents some issues in relation to the way the life and death of Jesus have been traditionally portrayed and understood in theological terms. The Incarnation and life of Jesus become the focus for those who begin their theology from the place where I do, rather than starting from or focusing on Jesus' death and resurrection. Further, the Incarnation is not understood as a once-and-for-all event but rather as a breaking into reality of an alternative way of living that is available to all.

The place of reason is also reexamined from a feminist-body theological position. Reason has been that which Christianity has claimed women do not have, being the more physical and less rational side of the complementarity scheme. Of course, feminist thinkers have more recently examined this claim and turned it on its head, seeing 'pure reason' as a product of a divided mind and body and therefore capable of providing only one side of the total picture. Knowing becomes more than a brain activity associated with pure reason and is viewed rather as an embodied experience. Therefore, the reasons behind belief become embodied ways of knowing rather than purely rational ways of thinking. The appeal to somatics is perfectly in line with an incarnational religion but still somewhat out of step with western philosophical reason – although in certain areas the gap is becoming narrower. Feminist theologians remain painfully aware that impeccable reason has often led to unthinkable actions, both by individuals and by societies, and as a consequence they give emphasis to embodied knowing. This, in their view, leads to more mutual ways of considering action, where all parties affected by the relevant actions are involved in the process of deciding what will happen. This approach, so unfamiliar to churches and governments, allows for the consequences of actions on the bodies of others to be taken seriously.

Although I suspect the outcomes may be quite different, an interesting point of contact between a number of these chapters and feminist theology is that feminist theology cannot in itself claim to be a religion, since it is applied to many religions worldwide. Feminist theology does have some core 'beliefs', but these have more to do with hoped-for outcomes in the lives of women than with matters of systematic theology. These visions, however, may affect the systematic or theoretical aspects of a given religion once the feminist practitioner or theologian applies them to the core beliefs of the religion. With its roots in liberation theology, feminist theology tends to be more concerned with orthopraxis then orthodoxy (Isherwood 1999). As such, it is less concerned with whether people believe the same things and more interested in whether people work for justice and the full humanity of women and men. This will assume various forms in different settings and thus requires diverse approaches, and it is the bodies of women and men that decide these matters. Are these bodies freer, more liberated and less tortured in the conditions and societies in which they are situated? These are the issues of ultimate concern to feminist theologians, rather than questions of belief.

References

Braidotti, R. 1994. *Nomadic Subjects: Embodiment and Sexual Difference in Contemporary Feminist Theory*. New York: Columbia University Press.
Brock, R. and R. Parker. 2008. *Saving Paradise: How Christianity Traded Love of the World for Crucifixion and Empire*. Boston, MA: Beacon Press.
Butler, J. 1990. *Gender Trouble: Feminism and the Subversion of Gender*. London: Routledge.
Hampson, D. 1996. *Swallowing a Fishbone: Feminist Theologians Debate Christianity*. London: SPCK.
Irigaray, L. 1985. *This Sex Which Is Not One*, translated by C. Porter and C. Burke. Ithaca, NY: Cornell University Press.

Isherwood, L. 1999. *Liberating Christ*. Cleveland: Pilgrim Press.
Isherwood, L. and E. Bellchambers (eds.). 2010. *Through Us, With Us, In Us: Relational Theologies in the Twenty First Century*. London: SCM Press.
Johnson, E. 1994. *She Who Is: The Mystery of God in Feminist Theological Discourse*. New York: Crossroad.
Keller, C. 2003. *Face of the Deep: A Theology of Becoming*. London: Routledge.
Ruether, R. R. 1983. *Sexism and God Talk*. London: SCM Press.
Ruether, R. R. 2007. *America, Amerikkka: Elect Nation and Imperial Violence*. London: Equinox.
Schneider, L. 2008. *Beyond Monotheism: A Theology of Multiplicity*. London: Routledge.
Schüssler Fiorenza, E. 1983. *In Memory of Her*. London: SCM Press.
Warner, M. 2004. "Tongues Untied: Memoirs of a Pentecostal Boyhood." In *Curiouser: On the Queerness of Children*, edited by S. Bruhm and N. Hurley, 215–224. Minneapolis: University of Minnesota Press.

8 Koji Suga

First of all, I would like to express my appreciation to all my co-participants in these dialogues. I am delighted to have received my colleagues' Position Statements; they have prompted me to realize that I have very little knowledge about other faiths outside of Shinto.

My first and general question to the other participants is: What in your personal lives led you to your current religious beliefs and faith? Did any particular experiences play a role in shaping your view of the world?

It seems that among us I am the only one who refers to their private family background and to their personal history of growing up in a religious context. I understand that my Position Statement differs significantly in comparison with the trajectories of the other Position Statements, but my hope is that this line of dialogue will allow me to further explore the question with which I began: Is Shinto a religion worthy of consideration from a philosophical perspective?

As I mentioned in my opening paper, I call the evolution of my faith an experience of 'moulting' rather than one of 'conversion' or 'proselytism'. This is connected with my view of religious faith as a 'way of life' despite any diversions *en route*. Along the way, I have tried to recognize other people's faith (tolerance) and have attempted to understand their perspectives (empathy). Rather than focusing on the doctrines of established religious groups, my focus has been on listening to personal narratives so as to experience an affinity with believers.

In order to be open in this way, to understand and to empathize, I draw on the 'way' of *Shinto*, literally 'the way of *kami*', where '*kami*' refers to deities exhibiting supranormal vitality and character. In East Asian languages, words corresponding to 'way' include *michi* or *do* in Japanese, *kil* in Korean and *dao* (or *tao*) in Chinese, all represented by the same Chinese character. (Each of these three variants has the meaning of 'route', 'method' and 'style of manner', echoing the meanings of the English word 'way'.) Variations among these languages should not be overlooked. Nevertheless, these terms are commonly employed in the foregoing languages to encompass both religious and nonreligious realms, such as *dotoku* (morality, literally 'the way of virtue') and *Judo* (literally 'the gentle way') in Japanese. A 'way' may consist in specific practices, teachings, faiths, forms, disciplines and experiences which have been, are and will be followed by people. In other words, the term 'way' can be conceived as a collective noun comprising specific deeds and values. My understanding of 'way' has been influenced by the idea of 'the experience of way' suggested by Yo Hamada, a Japanese scholar who employs this in combination with the notion of 'interreligious experience' in order to examine multi-religious encounters. Hamada defends the potential of this notion in integrating religious matters from the private realm and ethical matters from the public realm, so that these are conceived in terms of the single sphere of 'way' as they were originally in East Asian culture before the introduction of the concept of 'religion' from the West (see Hamada 2005: 206–221).

I will develop the concept of 'way' in accordance with my own Shinto faith (Hamada himself does not belong to any particular religious community). In Confucian usage, the *Dao* refers to the 'way' of ethical teachings that humans should follow, as laid down by sages and others. In Daoism, the *Dao* is the unproduced producer from which all appearances derive, and the primordial source of order; to live in accord with the *Dao* constitutes the 'way' to realize the natural order.

These Chinese cases aside, in coming to the 'way' or *michi* in Shinto, again I reference the works of Norinaga Motoori. In short, Motoori asserted that the original, simple and plain way of *kami* is neither the 'way' of nature in Daoism nor the artificial, elaborated 'way' of Confucianism and Buddhism. It is, rather, the 'way' of the sun-goddess, the imperial ancestral *kami* Amaterasu, while she inherited that 'way' from preceding deities with the grace of *musuhi* ('spiritual produce'). According to Motoori, this original 'way' must be revealed in reductive fashion by eliminating the philosophical influences of foreign 'ways', such as those of Confucianism, Buddhism and Daoism, from present life in Japan.

Motoori's case is based upon the following points. The foregoing foreign 'ways' of morality are human inventions and were introduced to Japan after the age of *kami*, along with the eclipse of the original 'way' of *kami*. Thus, during the ancient age of *kami* there was no positive and verbalized system of moral virtues in communal life; there was not even any necessity for the word 'way', since all could perceive the object intuitively in the proper manner. On the other hand, the human-derived 'ways' of Confucian and Buddhist teachings and the naturalist 'way' of Daoist morality would prevail by means of the providence of deities whenever they were required by people. Therefore, even these other 'ways' must be the way of *kami*. Although admitting the conventional popularity of other 'ways' in Japanese society, including syncretic ones with Shinto, and the existence of other 'ways' for people in other countries, Motoori nonetheless argued for the excellence of the original 'way' of *kami* (Motoori 1989: 49–63).

I depart from Motoori's view regarding the supremacy of the way of *kami*. I attempt to utilize his interpretation of the way of *kami* not as an expression of self-affirmation but as a vehicle to understand other people's faiths. Applying the concept of 'way' conceived both singularly and collectively is beneficial, in my view, for identifying commonalities between faiths and thus deepening mutual understanding. Of course, great care must be taken to avoid any undue ethnocentrism. Motoori's work (I note that it was produced in eighteenth-century Japan under the seclusion policy) obviously reinforced Japaneseness. More than a century later, we can see that his claims regarding the superiority of the Japanese 'way' of *kami* fed the ultra-nationalistic interpretation of Shinto under the total war regime. The classification of 'way' as a political-religious ethos with a common or universal character throughout East Asia would strike many nowadays as controversial, partly since this recalls Japanese expansionism. Indeed, the first four aircraft units of the *Kamikaze* ('divine wind') operation took their names from Motoori's well-known *waka* poem about the Japanese spirit: "If I am asked about the meaning of *yamato-gokoro* ('Japanese spirit'), I will answer that it is the blossoms of mountain cherry trees shining in the rising sun."

There are, of course, positive ethical dimensions to Motoori's figuration of Shinto that are discernible today. A certain calm acceptance of fate, or *amor fati*, and an emphasis on the significance of communal life were apparent in the aftermath of the 2011 earthquake and tsunami. In the devastated towns, the affected populace was unobtrusively engaged in reconstruction without seeking to defy its fate but with hope in the future. Indeed, there was not one riot and no plundering in the stricken area, and people even continued to display awe and gratitude towards the sea. Here we can observe a general feeling of veneration and reverence directed to unspecified *kami*, beings who possess extraordinary and surpassing abilities and virtues. Such a response to a great calamity indicates a kind of openness to diversity, difference and conflict, and even acceptance of the presence of evil.

The English word 'faith' is used as an uncountable noun when it refers to one's religious beliefs, and it is used as a countable noun when it refers to a particular religion. In line with the term's resonances with 'way', I regard 'faith' as more like an uncountable than a countable noun: yes, I assuredly have faith in Shinto, the way of *kami*, but at the same time I would like to recognize and be recognized by other religious and even nonreligious groups. In looking for common grounds and experiences, this being akin to a sharing of 'ways', I pose to my dialogue partners another general question in addition to the first: What concrete experiences have you had which have led you into conversation with other religious faiths?

Supplement to Position Statement

As mentioned in my Position Statement, my beliefs are reinforced by the fact that people are usually seen in Shinto shrines praying without obvious consciousness of some belief in a divine object. In fact, while it has its own sense of value, a Shinto shrine is open to everyone, including the irreligious or atheist. No one is refused in principle (the exception being the Grand

Shrine of Ise, the highest ranked Shinto shrine housing Amaterasu, which had at one time refused entry to Buddhist monks into its precincts). The Shinto shrine's inclusiveness is indicative of the possibility that everyone who visits a shrine shares not a set of beliefs but a 'way'.

I hold that 'way', thus understood, potentially points to something common abiding in any and all religions. The term 'way' is therefore not to be restricted to that which is learned empirically by following particular practical rules or disciplines. Rather, I would like to suggest a more expansive conception of 'way' so that it allows for people with mutually incompatible beliefs or positions to nonetheless share a 'way'. As this indicates, however, more precision may be required in delineating the meaning and contours of 'way'.

Furthermore, it seems that my agnostic disposition (that we cannot know the ultimate origin and cause of the universe) differentiates itself from the other participants' positions. I suspend belief in a positive image of a single essential unity behind the diversity of appearances. As Wittgenstein once stated: "*Wovon man nicht sprechen kann, darüber muß man schweigen*" ("Whereof one cannot speak, thereof one must be silent"). What I seek to do, therefore, is to learn more about other traditions so as to determine whether I can overcome my agnosticism, while at the same time going beyond contemporary Shinto research, which limits itself to historical or social phenomena based on a naïve realism. Despite Motoori's great influence on modern Shinto thought, I sought in my Position Statement to refer as minimally as possible to his work without neglecting his ethical conclusions so as to concentrate on the modern period of Shinto that arose after Motoori's time. As a result, I focused on the Yasukuni Shrine (a shrine that commemorates individuals in the service of the Japanese Empire), which did not exist in Motoori's age and is the most controversial aspect of Shinto worship today. I now, therefore, seek to supplement in certain ways my initial Position Statement.

With some reserve, Motoori sought the ultimate cause of the universe in the single identity of two of the first three Shinto deities in the universe, Takamimusuhi and Kamimuzsuhi, which he posited as the origin of the divine grace, *musuhi*. Another outstanding Kokugaku scholar in the generation following Motoori, Atsutane Hirata (1776–1843), held that another deity, Ame-no-minakanushi, must be the creator-God (Hirata 1887: 1–16). Hitherto, there existed the popular view, especially among Confucian Shintoists, that attributed the universal origin to the deity Kuni-no-tokotachi. Kenji Ueda's discussion of beliefs in unknowable noumena beyond the universe refused any monist tendency in Shinto. This discussion, on which my argument is based, was a result of his examination of these interpretations from his fundamental standpoint on polytheism (Ueda 1986: 143–164).

From a different viewpoint, a well-known Japanese ethicist, Tetsuro Watsuji (1889–1960), remarked that the *kami* described in Japanese ancient mythology are "not the deities conceived as the Absolute *noematically*, but the deities as pathways through which the *noetic* Absolute represents itself" (Watsuji 1962: 44; translation mine). My own view, that every *kami* may signal a transcendental path toward a vague ultimacy, could be seen as reflecting Watsuji's view, though also requiring further examination. Watsuji's remark was embedded in a profound philosophical context, including a discussion of Motoori's account of 'way'; nonetheless, his remark (originally made during World War II) could lead to only one conclusion: the divine significance of Japanese imperialism. What is clearly required, therefore, is further development of the philosophical dimension of Shinto. Thus, to construct an inclusivist multi-faith perspective as resonating with 'way', I retain my agnostic disposition while echoing Hume's famous statement towards the end of *The Natural History of Religion*: "The whole is a riddle, an ænigma, an inexplicable mystery. Doubt, uncertainty, suspence of judgment appear the only result of our most accurate scrutiny, concerning this subject" (1998: 185).

Response to Aijaz: Sunni Islam

In his Position Statement, Imran Aijaz discusses the rational justification of Islamic belief, where the constitution of the religion of Islam is said to lie along three axes: (i) practice, (ii) faith, and (iii) the perfection of faith. Aijaz states that, "Preceding (i) and (iii) is (ii); Islamic practice stems from faith, and the perfection of faith requires that one have faith in the first place" (4). Thus, the aim and nature of Aijaz's chapter are quite different from mine. Nevertheless, I appreciated the clarity and argumentative force of his chapter, and in what follows I will make some comments and pose some questions by way of response.

Referencing Joshua Golding's distinction between a position that is 'rationally compelling' and one that is 'rationally defensible', Aijaz develops his defence of Islamic belief from considerations such as the following:

> [I]t is possible for two inconsistent positions to each be rationally defensible (for different people). It is possible, then, that a person who subscribes to a religious position such as Islamic theism can maintain that this position is rationally defensible while allowing that positions that are different from, and perhaps even inconsistent with, it are also rationally defensible.
>
> (5; italics removed)

If we were to put the matter in terms of 'way', we could say that inconsistent positions or beliefs could share a 'way' when they are rationally defensible. The remainder of Aijaz's chapter consists in a demonstration of the position that Islamic belief is rationally defensible, and I tentatively accept his argument. Thus, despite my skepticism as to whether Shinto belief is rationally defensible (it has been increasingly reinterpreted as 'rationally compelling' in the course of Japanese modernization and the construction of a national identity), I can at least hope to share a 'way' with the author.

I would also like to explore how Aijaz understands the relationship between a text and its interpretation, given his argument for the stylistic inimitability of the Qur'an. This is not a question about techniques, of course, but rather concerns the universality of the particular figures and forms in the Islamic faith as developed by the Prophet and the Qur'an. In other words, is there any special and rationally defensible meaning in the fact that the Qur'an was written in Arabic during a specific point in history? Again, this is not a skeptical criticism but a question about how the ultimate truth of a 'way' expressed in a particular language could be rationally defensible. Otherwise, it seems that Aijaz's view implies some variety of religious exclusivism.

Aijaz also discusses what Swinburne calls 'the principle of credulity' and mentions that "a person will be open to accepting another's report of religious experience only if the religious beliefs to which they point are judged by that person as being possibly true" (this volume: 19). This is quite important in terms of how to share a 'way'. Aijaz goes on to quote John Hick's view, drawn from William James' essay "The Will to Believe", as consisting in "an argument for our right to trust our own religious experience and to be prompted by it to trust that of the great religious figures" (this volume: 21). My question to Aijaz is: Do you think the phrase 'great religious figures' in this context may be replaced with 'ancestors' in their collective voice? I ask this because, for Shinto, the original 'way' of *kami* is essentially the 'way' of our ancestors.

Aijaz also rightly refers to ethics (as part of his criticism of Hick). However, I believe that an emphasis on ethics should be supplemented by a consideration of the political realm as well as religious systems, a point underlined by the relation between Shinto and modern nationalism. Concerning the connection between religious life and politics, especially within a 'way', it would be interesting to learn how Aijaz judges the view that those who perish in war die as martyrs (a view sometimes found in modern Shinto, as I mentioned in my Position Statement), and the possibility of reconciliation in God between former allies and enemies.

Response to Isherwood: Radical incarnational Christianity

In light of my rudimentary knowledge of feminist theology, I would like to pose some basic questions that have to do with Isherwood's views on the relation between the approach and aims of traditional Christianity and those of radical theology.

To begin with, does Isherwood seek to establish a new, liberal interpretation of Christianity, or does she think that Christian theology constitutes one of the irreplaceable 'ways' of achieving liberation? Which of these is her main goal? Further, does Isherwood hold that liberation can be promoted and attained not only by way of radical Christianity but also through other religions and secular movements? Also, does the main task of her radical theology consist in being a counter-discourse within traditional Christian societies?

In the case of modern Shinto and Japanese modernization, the idea of the 'good wife and wise mother' is very common. However, I regard Shinto's history as containing features which may be critically appropriated to contribute to the reformation of gender stereotypes, such as the existence of high-ranked priestesses (elected from the Imperial Household) in important shrines up until the medieval period, thus distinguishing these more radical elements from hyper-masculinized modernism.

It seems that the Christology that Isherwood calls 'radical incarnational theology' holds the key to understanding her emphasis on liberation and transformation:

> Incarnation tells us that our bodies are our homes, that is to say our divine/human desiring dwelling places; therefore our Christological journey is home to the fullness of our incarnation, the co-redemptive, co-creative reality of our fleshly heaven. It is a Christology based on a gospel picture of empowerment, not servitude, and finds inspiration in the life of Jesus and not salvation through the death of Jesus.
> (this volume: 51–52)

Given that Isherwood promotes inclusivism, how does she negotiate her inclusivism with her Christology? This question recalls my inquiry into the relation between particular forms of belief and their purported universality. Is Jesus' Incarnation a singularity in our space-time? I too find a 'way' in Jesus' life, but if his death was not an act of universal redemption, what is his unique significance for people beyond Christian cultures? Isherwood's position, therefore, may be 'rationally defensible' but not necessarily 'rationally compelling' (to borrow from Aijaz's terminology).

I was interested in Isherwood's discussion of sexuality and the erotic, though I could not clearly fathom the nuances and implications of her argument. These matters would, of course, be central to 'body theology', so further exploration would be welcome, particularly as a Shinto scholar, given the Kokugaku scholars' admiration of unpretentiousness in Japanese mythological episodes. Differentiating themselves from Confucian asceticism, Motoori and several Kokugaku scholars appreciated the direct, unsophisticated but accurate descriptions of sexuality in Japanese mytho-historical documents as part of the original 'way of *kami*'. In Shinto, the importance of sexual desire for the human being is generally interpreted merely as a source for procreation, thus losing the richness and sensibility found in artistic representations of eroticism in Japanese culture.

Turning from bodily concerns to cosmological ones, I found the following passage in Isherwood's chapter particularly intriguing:

> Body, feminist and liberation theology compelled me to engage with the question of the new cosmology and theology as a way to further investigate identity and notions of divinity hitherto contained and controlled within the Christian understanding of the One All-Powerful God. This led to an investigation of the Deep, which is the very ground of who we are, though. . . the Deep does not offer a fixed identity relying on and embedded in the One. It is a Deep situated in the cosmos itself that gives the lie to *creatio ex nihilo* and opens before us the God who is of intimate/infinite entanglements.
>
> (63)

On this view, 'the Deep' is the ultimate ground of our being; somewhat similarly, on my conception of Shinto, the ultimate origin or cause of the universe remains vague and dim, like the original chaos or abyss in mythology which contains the potential cosmos within itself.

Isherwood goes on to state: "The cosmos did not emerge from Platonic forms but rather from *tehomic* chaos; there was no blueprint but instead the glorious outpourings of surprise and novelty" (65–66). Here we come across an ecological interpretation of the biblical *tehom* (the deep or abyss) that is quite attractive to me. I recall that the term '*tehom*' had also attracted me from before my 'moulting' by nihilism, so I probably have been influenced by such cosmogonic ideas and interpretations without being aware of them. At present, however, I would conceive the *tehom* not as the chaos preceding the cosmos but as the absence of any clear horizon of ultimate truth. My own concern, now, is to seek a path from *tehom* to the form of 'body theology' encapsulated in Shinto discussions.

Response to Drob: Mystical Judaism

I have long desired to learn about Kabbalistic Judaism, and so I greatly enjoyed Sanford Drob's chapter. I responded to much of the latter half of the chapter with a sense of *déjà vu*. This uncanny feeling may be accounted for by the fact that there are close parallels between Kabbalistic Judaism and postmodern philosophical currents, particularly in terms of the acknowledgement of a multiplicity of perspectives and interpretations, and of the view that language helps to construct reality. It is interesting to note, however, that both Kabbalistic Judaism and postmodern thought tend to neglect, or not draw inspiration from, the periods of the Renaissance and the Enlightenment.

The focus of Drob's chapter is the theosophical Kabbalah of Isaac Luria. While the nature of the Lurianic theosophical system in the history of Kabbalah is clearly explicated, I would have liked more detail about the social circumstances in which the Lurianic system was generated, since (as Drob points out) it "serves not only as a foundation for a contemporary Jewish theology but anticipates the thought of later western thinkers" outside of Jewish mysticism (28). This relates, once again, to the conundrum between particular forms and their purported universality.

The Kabbalist notions of '*Ein-sof*', conceived as "everything and nothing... the beginning and end of all existence", "the origin of and completed by the finite world and humanity" (28, 29) and *ha-achduth hashawaah* or *coincidentia oppositorum* bear certain similarities to the *Dao* in Daoism and *taiji* in Confucianism. Like the notion of *Ein-sof*, the concepts of the *taiji* and the *Dao* express the supreme ultimate state, or the highest conceivable principle from which existence flows and which creates a set of opposite forces, yin and yang. In light of such correspondences, I wonder whether Kabbalist writers make use of metaphorical expressions such as 'way' in reference to *Ein-sof*.

I also wonder how the origin of the one-way direction of time or the so-called 'arrow of time' is explicated in the processes of creation as outlined in Kabbalist thought. According to Drob, *Tzimtzum, Adam Kadmon, sefirot, Otiyot Yesod*, etc., are the events and symbols which represent the phases of creation in time. It seems, further, that these stages of creation are followed by the 'Breaking of the Vessels' in human history, which is symbolized in such biblical events as the expulsion from Eden, the death of the kings of Edom, the Flood, and the destruction of the Temple in Jerusalem. Obviously these events are neither retroactive nor reversible, while *Ein-sof*, as the antecedent condition of the beginning and the end, could be interpreted as the principle of circulation and even of eternal return. But then wherein lies the origin of the one-way direction of time?

Drob states that the Breaking of the Vessels brought about the current condition of the various worlds:

> As a result of the Breaking of the Vessels, the worlds are not comprised of the organized combinations of divine values that were originally destined to fill the cosmic void, but rather of the displaced, broken and now meaningless values that are symbolized in the figure of the husks and the disordered letters. It is the individual's divinely appointed task to extract (*Birur*) the sparks of divine light from the husks that are encountered in one's life journey and in the process reassemble, repair and restore the broken values and meanings.
>
> (this volume: 30)

This is perhaps an anticipation of the 'anthropic principle', understood as the view that the character of the physical universe must be compatible with the conscious life of human beings. If any one of the numerous cosmological constants and parameters whose numerical values determined the course of the universe was even slightly different or altered, the human beings who observe the universe would not exist. In Kabbalist thought, as described by Drob, it is the individual's task after the 'Breaking of the Vessels' to extract the sparks of the divine light in order to restore the broken values and meanings. Here we notice that human activities, including observations of the cosmos which are aimed at restoring the original values and meanings, already seem to take precedence over divine revelation in the mid-sixteenth century (at the time of Isaac Luria). This is confirmed when Drob states elsewhere: "If representation is the 'Big Bang' that sunders the One into a multitude of finite entities and ideas, the realization of *coincidentia oppositorum* is our means of 'listening to the echo' of the original Unity" (42).

Drob also remarks:

> The Kabbalists, as is typical of mystics in other traditions, were loath to define God or the Absolute in anything but 'negative theological' terms, and this posture provided them with a degree of freedom to experiment with ideas about the ultimate nature of things, something which would have been more difficult within the framework of normative Judaism. The Kabbalists described *Ein-sof* as that about which nothing can be said or known, and some of them went so far as to hold that the proper mode of apprehending the divine is through 'unknowing' or 'forgetting'.
>
> (this volume: 33–34)

I find myself in agreement with the position expressed in the final sentence, especially with the emphasis on forgetfulness. I see the mode of 'forgetting' to apprehend the divine as another expression for eschewing commitment to the Absolute, preferring instead a vague or merely hypothetical truth. In line with this, it seems that the Lurianic system has resonances with the contemporary process of secularization:

> [O]n the Lurianic view the divine cannot properly be conceptualized as a being or entity but is rather identified with the very process of creative inquiry, open-mindedness and the taking of multiple perspectives that is stimulated by an interest in (and a failure to circumscribe) ultimates and which takes its concrete form in intellectual, spiritual and artistic endeavour.
>
> (Drob, this volume: 34)

Again, a fuller picture of the social conditions surrounding Luria's thought would have helped in better understanding its meaning and place in intellectual history. Also, Drob's view of atheism ("There is a sense in which my own understanding of God involves an atheization of theology and a spiritualization of atheism"), much like Azriel of Gerona's conception of *Ein-sof* (as the foundation of both belief and unbelief), provides me with the impetus to share a 'way' with atheists also.

Drob moreover, and rightly in my view, reinforces the intimate connection between language and the world, as rooted in the Talmud. This idea has been one of the major currents in modern western philosophical thought, which, as Drob mentions, has given great attention to the relation between 'representing' and 'represented', between 'signifier' and 'signified'. In Shinto, the notion of *kotodama* ('soul of word') refers to the spiritual power contained within words. But while people usually consider the works of Japanese *waka* poetry as the result of *kotodama*'s graces (practicing *waka* is also regarded as a 'way'), the basic or mystic connections between language and world have never been construed in a sophisticated way akin to other Shinto ideas and practices, including ritual action and its theological interpretation.

References

Hamada, Y. 2005. *Kyoson no Tetsugaku*. Tokyo: Kobundo.
Hirata, A. 1887. *Koshiden*, vol. 1. Digital Library of the Meiji Era, the National Diet Library. http://kindai.ndl.go.jp/info:ndljp/pid/772139.
Hume, D. 1998. *Principal Writings on Religion*, edited by J. C. A. Gaskin. Oxford: Oxford University Press.
Motoori, N. 1989. *Naobi no mitama*. Tokyo: Chikuma Shobo.
Ueda, K. 1986. *Shinto shingaku*. Tokyo: Kobundo.
Watsuji, T. 1962. *Sonno shiso to sono dento*. Tokyo: Iwanami Shoten.

Second Responses

9 Imran Aijaz

Introduction

Before responding to the first set of replies proffered by my fellow participants in our multi-faith dialogues, it will be useful, I think, to once again be very clear about (what I have understood to be) the main aim behind our discussion. In our initial Position Statements, in addition to providing an *explanation* of our core fundamental beliefs about religion, we were asked by the editors to give *reasons* for holding them. This particular way of asking for an account of one's beliefs about religion is important, for it allows us to avoid getting confused about the question 'What reasons, if any, do you have for your religious beliefs?' (as stated in the Position Statement guidelines provided by the editors). The request for 'reasons' here is *not* for a historical account of the set of causes that led one to hold one's beliefs about religion, such as upbringing, exposure to various cultural and religious practices, etc.; *that* would fall under 'explanation'. Rather, it is a request for *argument* that supports the *rationality* of holding these beliefs.

In my own Position Statement, I sought to provide such an argument in support of the rationality of holding Islamic belief; that is, an argument attempting to show that Islamic belief is a *rationally defensible* position. Recall some features of a position that is rationally defensible: (i) argument can be given to support it; (ii) criticisms of, and objections to, the argument can be rebutted; and (iii) not all rational beings will be compelled to accept it. A position that *any* rational being ought to adopt is *rationally compelling*. Clearly, then, to offer a position as rationally defensible is to make a more modest claim about its rationality than claiming that it is rationally compelling.

As I maintained in my initial Position Statement, I do not think that there are any successful arguments to show that Islamic belief is rationally compelling, despite traditional Islamic claims to the contrary. I explained how classical theistic arguments that are discussed in Islamic philosophical writings, such as cosmological and design arguments, can be rationally resisted by those who do not believe in their conclusions. The same goes for the primary argument that Muslims have given, and continue to give, in support of the prophethood of Muhammad; that is, the argument based on the Qur'an's alleged stylistic inimitability, which is said to prove the scripture's status as a miracle and Muhammad's claim to be a true Prophet of God.

An argument can, however, be given for the rational defensibility of Islamic belief. In my Position Statement, I gave an account and defence of the more general version of such an argument, as given by John Hick. In brief, Hick's argument aims to support the view that it is rational for us to trust our religious experiences, provided that certain conditions are met, in a world that is religiously ambiguous. I ended my Position Statement by noting some implications of my argument for the conclusion that Islamic belief is rationally defensible: (1) the argument can be applied, *mutatis mutandis*, to other religious positions and traditions, such that, for instance, holding Jewish and Christian beliefs is also rationally defensible; and (2) attempting to convince others of my own beliefs about religion is not particularly important.

So, how have my fellow participants responded to all this? In what follows, I will address the first set of replies from Koji Suga, Sanford Drob and Lisa Isherwood, with a principal focus on their replies to my Position Statement.

Response to Suga: Shinto

In his First Response, Suga asks these questions of his fellow participants: "What in your personal lives led you to your current religious beliefs and faith? Did any particular experiences play a role in shaping your view of the world?" (111). Now, answers to these questions may be interesting and important in certain contexts – for example, in aiding an anthropological exploration of the similarities between religious societies. If, however, our focus is on the *rationality* of religious belief, that is, exploring whether there are reasons in support of such belief, then it is hard to see how answers given to Suga's questions will be relevant. Now, Suga does think that answers to the questions that he poses will help him in figuring out whether Shinto is a religion worthy of consideration from a philosophical perspective (111). But, once again, it is hard to see without further explanation or argument how the connection can be made between the *origin* and *development* of religious belief and its being open to *philosophical scrutiny*.

In thinking about Suga's questions, it (re-)occurred to me that, speaking more generally, in many cases of interfaith dialogue participants do not focus all that much on matters related to the rationality of religious beliefs. Rather, there is a lot of talk of shared experiences and struggles, similarities in religious convictions, comparative analyses and the like, often seasoned with nice-sounding phrases like 'building bridges', 'unity in diversity', etc. Of course, there is nothing wrong with this and, indeed, it is commendable and much needed in the cultural and religious melting pot that our world has become. But discussing the rationality of religious belief is *at least as* important as discussing matters related to its sociological or anthropological aspects. I feel it necessary to stress this given how all too often these days we see acts of violence that rest on *religious* motivations. Just to cite one recent example, a woman belonging to the Ahmadiyya sect of Islam and her two granddaughters were murdered by a mob in Pakistan who accused her of blasphemy.[1] Since people who hold religious beliefs will typically also *act* on them – sometimes in ways that are questionable, immoral or downright horrific – it is critical that we scrutinize these beliefs and assess their rationality using our reason. Although I respond to him specifically in the next section, let me quote Sanford Drob's remarks (with which I agree wholeheartedly) about the important role that reason has to play in tempering the non-intellectual side of our nature:

> [A]ny abandonment of reason as the criterion for knowledge leaves us at the mercy of the irrational and poses a great danger . . . [P]assions unmitigated by reason can wreak havoc on soul and world. . . . [A] balance must be struck between *logos* and *eros*, reason and passion, *with reason serving as the ultimate guide*. . . . [I]t is reason rather than passion that prompts us to relinquish our prejudices and open ourselves to a God of justice.
>
> (this volume: 94; emphasis in original)

In thinking specifically about my own community, I feel that Muslims today especially should pay heed to Drob's remarks here, given how little attention is devoted in Islamic circles to discussions about the rationality of religious belief.

I turn now to some specific queries and comments from Suga regarding my Position Statement. He asks how I understand the relationship between a text and its interpretation in light of the argument for the inimitability of the Qur'an (p. 9). To be clear, this is not an argument that I endorse or believe to be successful, in light of the criticisms of it that I gave in my Position Statement. Suga asks: "[I]s there any special and rationally defensible meaning in the fact that the Qur'an was written in Arabic during a specific point in history?" (116). This question is not clear to me. If Suga is asking whether the Arabic text of the Qur'an – a seventh-century text – provides the basis for some sort of *argument* for the rationality of Islamic belief, then I would answer 'no'. I have already explained why I find the Islamic argument based on the Qur'an's alleged inimitability to be problematic. Part of my objection to the argument is that I think it is difficult to assess, in any objective sense, the aesthetic merits of the Islamic text. Suga wonders "how the ultimate truth of a 'way' expressed in a particular language can be rationally defensible" (116). Well, that depends on whether the beliefs that are part of this 'way' satisfy the conditions that are necessary for them to be rationally defensible. (I stated these conditions in my Position Statement and they are reiterated in the previous section of this reply.) Suga's remark that my view "implies some variety of religious exclusivism" (116) is confusing and seems to me to be misplaced, given that it is not accompanied by any further explanation.

Suga's last two remarks pertaining to my Position Statement concern Hick's argument for the rationality of religious belief. According to this argument, we are entitled to trust our religious experiences (provided certain conditions are met), some of which may be prompted by great religious figures. In thinking about Shinto, Suga asks whether the reference to great religious figures may be substituted with 'ancestors'. I see no reason why this would be an issue, since such substitution would leave the essence and logic of Hick's argument intact. In my Position Statement, I explained that Hick's argument can be strengthened by adding a moral criterion to ensure that whatever actions are influenced by holding religious beliefs are not ethically problematic. Suga agrees with this but feels that "an emphasis on ethics should be supplemented by a consideration of the political realm as well as religious systems" (116). I have no problem with this. Indeed, I think Suga's point applies especially to Islam – a religion that, according to many traditional Muslims, incorporates politics. Because of the political influence that a religion like Islam has, an ethical consideration of the permissibility of holding and acting on religious beliefs is very important. Suga asks how I judge "the view that those who perish in war die as martyrs" (116). The Qur'an states that those *who are slain in God's way (or fight for His cause)* will die as martyrs (see, e.g., 3:169–170, 9:111). So, not anyone who perishes in a war counts as a martyr. Of course, what, precisely, is meant by being 'slain in God's way' or 'fighting for God's cause' is open to debate, and it is here that rational reflection and ethical consideration are important. Finally, Suga wonders what I think of "the possibility of reconciliation in God between former allies and enemies" (116). I'm not sure what he is asking here. If Suga is asking about the possibility of reconciliation between people of different religious convictions by appealing to a shared belief in God, then I would say that this is indeed possible. Without further elaboration on Suga's part, however, I cannot comment further.

Response to Drob: Mystical Judaism

Drob's response to my Position Statement begins with a misunderstanding of my view regarding arguments aiming to show that Islamic belief is rationally compelling. He states that, on my view, "these philosophical arguments, while not absolutely compelling, provide good reasons for [my] own religious beliefs" (97). This is false. As I explained in my Position Statement, these arguments are not rationally compelling. I do not, however, think that they are worthless or have no evidential value in thinking about the rationality of Islamic belief. Nevertheless, nowhere in my Position Statement did I claim that they provide good reasons for Islamic belief. My defence of the rationality of Islamic belief – its *rational defensibility*, that is – is predicated on Hick's argument that it is rational for us to trust our religious experiences (given that certain conditions are met) in a religiously ambiguous world. I find it unnecessary, then, given the intent and purpose of my initial Position Statement, to address Drob's criticisms of the cosmological argument, design argument, and the Islamic argument based on the Qur'an's alleged stylistic inimitability.

I will, however, address Drob's criticism of the parity argument that I discussed in my Position Statement. The main thrust of this argument is that, since no noncircular justification is possible for both basic perceptual and religious (theistic) beliefs, religious (theistic) belief should be regarded just as rationally acceptable as ordinary perceptual belief. Given that this is the basic form of the argument, Drob's depiction of it as "the contention that the reliance on others' religious experiences as a basis for our faith in God is analogous to relying on others' normal perceptual experiences for our information about the world" is clearly incorrect (this volume: 97). The parity argument says nothing about whether we should or should not rely on other people's testimony about their experiences – religious or otherwise. In discussing whether we should accept other people's testimony of their experiences, what Drob seems to have in mind is something like Richard Swinburne's 'Principle of Testimony' – "the principle that (in the absence of special considerations) the experiences of others are (probably) as they report them" (Swinburne 2004: 322). Drob seems to think that, in the case of religious experiences, there are special considerations for doubting what subjects report. Essentially, these special considerations point out differences between our ordinary perceptual experiences and religious experiences: (1) not everyone has religious experiences (which are different in *kind* from ordinary perceptual experiences), and (2) "we trust the experiences of the prophets of old while mainly regarding today's 'prophets' as hucksters or madmen" (97–98). By way of response, let me say that (1) is indeed true. But how much does it tell against reports of religious experiences? I'm not sure that, in and of itself, (1) suffices to undermine reports of such experiences. We would have to consider a number of important factors, including (1), before judging the evidential value that reports of religious experiences have. Some of these factors include: (i) an overall assessment of the evidence that supports theism, (ii) the number of people reporting religious experiences, and (iii) the circumstances in which reports of religious experiences occur (e.g., changes in people's lifestyles). I should point out that 'ordinary' perceptual experiences are not universal either, and whether reports of these experiences should be accepted is something that we typically consider in light of other factors (e.g., reports of people who say that they are colour-blind).

What about (2)? I'm not sure who Drob has in mind when he says that, in the main, we regard prophets of old as real whereas the ones today are either hucksters or madmen. In any case, consider two replies to Drob's point. First, as I maintained in my Position Statement, a moral criterion can be added as a constraint on the sorts of actions one can take based on religious experiences. From the theistic standpoint, this move is certainly not *ad hoc*. As we read in Matthew 7:16: "By their fruits you will recognize them. Do people pick grapes from thorn bushes, or figs from thistles?" Based on such moral criteria, many Christians, for example, find themselves suspicious of preachers who have lavish lifestyles while claiming to be men of God and preaching the Gospel where it is said that "it is easier for a camel to go through the eye of a needle than for someone who is rich to enter the kingdom of God" (Matthew 19:24). Second, accepting some men as prophets while regarding others as frauds follows merely as a point of logic. If, for instance, I believe that Muhammad is a true Prophet of God and accept the Qur'anic teaching that he is the last of God's prophets (33:40), then I will regard as fraudulent those people who come after Muhammad and claim to be prophets of God.

In Drob's view, "the best arguments in favour of religious faith (or at least religious interest) involve the notion that there is an irreducible spiritual dimension to human life" (98). This dimension seems to point to spiritual objects or even an 'Absolute' spiritual centre (98). I think that Drob is correct in his estimation, and I would include this as a fact of religious experience in general, something that he acknowledges (98). Again, to be clear, I am not claiming that religious experiences provide the basis for an argument that either would show religious belief to be rationally compelling or could be used in attempts to rationally persuade those who lack religious belief. Rather, I only intend the appeal to religious experience as a strategy for showing that religious belief is rationally defensible.

In response to Hick's view that our universe is religiously ambiguous, a view that I also endorse, Drob writes that it is an extremely interesting possibility provided that "religious accounts of the universe, like their scientific counterparts, are subject to change and indeed to *paradigmatic shifts* in response to new experiences and to internal tensions within religious theory" (99; emphasis in original). Now, clearly, this is possible because a religious *account* of the universe is not exhausted by the thesis that *evidence for and against the existence of God is ambiguous*. A religious account of the universe will also include other religious beliefs and practices, the truth or appropriateness of which is independent of the ambiguity thesis. Consider a religious account of the universe which includes the belief that the earth is less than 10,000 years old and that adulterers must be stoned to death. A person who believes that the evidence for and against God's existence is ambiguous can quite consistently reject belief in Young Earth Creationism and the practice of stoning adulterers to death; there is strong evidence *against* Young Earth Creationism (no religious ambiguity here!), and it is simply immoral to brutally execute people for extramarital sexual relations. Drob points out that "the major faith-based traditions, at least for many of their more orthodox adherents . . . have failed to develop in a manner commensurate with developments in modern thought" (99). Although this point is irrelevant to the truth of the ambiguity thesis, let me say this. It isn't clear that religions have been quite as static in their outlook as Drob thinks. Many religious theists, for instance, now interpret Genesis differently in light of Darwin's findings. And religions are becoming more ecumenical in their outlook. Consider, for instance, the more inclusivist outlook on salvation as promulgated by the Second Vatican Council (*Lumen Gentium*, ch. 2).

Response to Isherwood: Radical incarnational Christianity

Isherwood's reply to my Position Statement consists mostly of further thoughts on feminist (Christian) theology. She begins by noting that two strands that feature in my Position Statement – religious texts and arguments for the existence of God – have undergone change in the hands of feminist theology (103). According to Isherwood, the principal concern in feminist theology is the political, economic and social *outcome* of holding religious (theistic) belief (103). An exploration of these outcomes is no doubt important, but it isn't clear to me that the agenda of feminist theology should take *precedence* over the philosophical enterprise of assessing the rational merits of theistic belief. Isherwood writes that, for feminist theologians, "all those arguments [for the existence of God] would come to nothing if the God found to exist oversaw an unjust and unequal society" (103). I'm not sure how to understand Isherwood here. Suppose that arguments for the existence of God succeeded in showing that belief in God is rationally compelling (as I stated several times before, I do not believe that this is the case, but I ask the reader to allow me this supposition for the sake of argument). Suppose, moreover, that there are additional arguments to show that this God prohibits homosexuality and considers it a violation of his commands. Clearly, the fact that I dislike or disagree with the conclusions of these arguments has no bearing on whether or not they are any good. In this regard, I fail to see how, without an examination of the arguments themselves, one can maintain that they amount to "nothing". But perhaps Isherwood's key claim is that those who believe in a "God of hierarchy and exclusion" will not be moved by arguments or proofs (104). Even if this is true, again, it has no bearing on whether or not the arguments in question are successful. Or maybe Isherwood thinks that discussing the merits of the arguments is futile, whatever their actual merit, if those who believe in a "God of hierarchy and exclusion" do not pay attention to them. I'm not sure that I believe this to be the case. For, surely, the main reason why many theists believe that homosexuality, for instance, is a sin is because they believe it to be *true* and will appeal to scriptural arguments to support their convictions. And, surely, one way to challenge their convictions if one disagreed with them is to criticize their arguments.

In reading Isherwood's description of feminist theology, I must say that I see instances of what in the context of philosophical and theological discussions I call 'dogmatic substitution'. The religious person who says, for example, that homosexuality is a sin and perversion of human nature is quickly dismissed as a dogmatic zealot who proclaims his theology with little to no rational reflection. But consider some of the phrases in Isherwood's discussion that similarly lack rational argument. She cites Rosemary Radford Ruether as saying that, "to believe in a God who wishes full equality to be denied to any race, colour, creed, sex or gender is a blasphemy" (this volume: 103). Or, again, "any belief that stands in the way of the full flourishing and equality of any person has to be discarded" (103). What is the supporting evidence for these assertions? Clearly, if taken at face value, these claims are false. Is it really blasphemous to believe in a God who wishes full equality to be denied to the creed of Satanists or that of the Islamic State of Iraq and the Levant (ISIS)? Consider also that *we* believe that Sharia Law, according to which thieves should have their hands amputated and apostates executed, should *not* be established in western society. Would Isherwood maintain that this belief be discarded, since it presumably prohibits certain Muslim fundamentalists from feeling that they are 'equal' and 'flourishing'?

Isherwood comments briefly on Hick's argument for the rationality of religious belief (which she misconstrues as a "case for the reality of God"). She asks "whose experience we are talking about, and who decides what is acceptable or not" (104). There is clearly no gender discrimination required or entailed by the logic of Hick's argument, if that is what Isherwood is getting at. Whether the religious experiences in question are acceptable will depend, in part, on whether they satisfy *moral* criteria, as I explained in my Position Statement.

In commenting on the argument from the Qur'an's 'inimitability' for its miraculousness, Isherwood states that she "find[s] the weight placed on the Qur'an to uphold the validity of the entire religion astonishing" and "wonder[s] if this is still a widely held belief" (104). If we are talking about orthodox Islam, then the answer is 'yes'. Belief in the inimitability and miraculousness of the Qur'an is prevalent among traditional Muslims. Isherwood asks to what extent the text of the Qur'an may be challenged (104). Specifically with reference to the 'inimitability' of the Qur'an, the text itself challenges those who doubt its message to produce a work like it (see, e.g., 17:88, 11:13, 2:23 and 10:38). As for challenges to the interpretation of the Qur'an based on the sorts of social justice issues that Isherwood mentions with respect to the Bible, these do exist but are perhaps not as well-known or prominent as the works of some of the feminist biblical scholars that Isherwood cites. Let me just mention two contemporary Muslim thinkers. In her work *The Veil and the Male Elite* (1992), the Moroccan feminist writer and sociologist Fatima Mernissi argues that Muslims from the seventh century onwards have misinterpreted and distorted the Qur'anic text, resulting in the exploitation and unfair treatment of women for centuries. Similarly, the American scholar of Islam Amina Wadud attempts a gender-inclusive reading of the Qur'anic text, distinguishing it from patriarchal interpretations, in her *Qur'an and Woman: Rereading the Sacred Text from a Woman's Perspective* (1999). What ramifications do such feminist interpretations have for "the Qur'an as a validation of Islam", as Isherwood asks (105)? It seems to me that a Muslim can accept the *authority* of the Qur'an and yet disagree about how to interpret its *content*. So, for instance, Muslims who adopt contrary interpretations of the Qur'an, such as patriarchal and feminist readings, can agree on the fact that the Qur'an is indeed a revelation from God, even if they are not entirely sure how to understand its contents and fail to come to a consensus on its interpretation.

In her closing remarks on my Position Statement, Isherwood asks whether Islamic scholars have developed philosophical perspectives or arguments of the sort that one finds in the works of John Hick (105). There are Muslim writers, both classical (e.g., al-Ghazali) and contemporary (e.g., Martin Lings, Seyyed Hossein Nasr, and those who follow the *philosophia perennis* of Rene Guenon), where one can find elements of Hick's perspective on religion. Why then did I not appeal to these authors in my Position Statement, as Isherwood asks? Quite simply because they were not required for the purposes of my discussion or arguments.

Note

1 "Ahmadi Woman and Children Killed After Pakistani Mob Torches Homes." *The Guardian*, 28 July 2014, http://www.theguardian.com/world/2014/jul/28/ahmadi-woman-children-killed-pakistan-mob-attack.

References

Mernissi, F. 1992. *The Veil and the Male Elite: A Feminist Interpretation of Women's Rights in Islam*. New York: Basic Books.

Swinburne, R. 2004. *The Existence of God*, 2nd ed. Oxford: Clarendon Press.

Wadud, A. 1999. *Qur'an and Woman: Rereading the Sacred Text From a Woman's Perspective*, 2nd ed. New York: Oxford University Press.

10 Sanford L. Drob

Response to Aijaz: Sunni Islam

Imran Aijaz asks for some specifics regarding "rational mysticism" and "why it is to be preferred to the more traditional, theosophical tradition of the Kabbalah" (this volume: 90). I do not think that this is a question of 'either/or'. My turning to *rational* mysticism grows out of my interest in determining the extent to which mystical and theosophical propositions, particularly those of the theosophical Kabbalah, are comprehensible in philosophical terms. My view is that mystical ideas (such as the coincidence of opposites, the identity of subject and object, and the essential unity of all things) have a rational as well as an intuitive content, and that this rational content both supports the mystical intuitions and, perhaps more significantly, places them within an ideational and dialogical context in which they are subject to critical examination. In this, I suppose, I am not very far from the approach to mysticism taken by Hegel, who subjected the ideas of Boehme and other Christian mystics to philosophical explication and critique.

Aijaz notes with approval my use of the coincidence of opposites, especially in connection with theism and atheism. Here I would again emphasize that, in my view, the significance of the coincidence of opposites goes beyond theology and is of crucial significance to other disciplines, including psychology and philosophy. Philosophers since Kant have recognized that the major quandaries in philosophy (e.g., free will versus determinism) result in opposing, seemingly contradictory, theses, each of which appear to be demonstrably true to the exclusion of their opposites. I believe that a rational reconstruction of the Kabbalistic view that the Absolute (*Ein-sof*) is a union or coincidence of all contradictions leads to the hypothesis that philosophical antinomies involve interdependent as opposed to mutually exclusive propositions.

For example, I believe that the contrast between naturalism and constructivism/idealism is one of interdependence rather than complete opposition. While on the one hand science regards the mind as a function of material processes that have evolved over time in a physical world (naturalism), the physical world is itself a construction of mind and language (constructivism/

idealism). We might say that while the mind is metaphysically dependent upon the natural world, the natural world is itself epistemically dependent on the mind. As put by the philosophers Hut and Shepard (1999):

> The standard approach [in natural science] builds upon an epistemologically weak foundation: what it takes for granted is a physical world containing physical brains composed of atoms, molecules, ions, electric fields, and so on. But what are directly given to any scientist are only the consciously experienced appearances (filled with 'qualia' and their relationships) that (on the basis of certain regularities and correlations) are interpreted as independently existing physical objects.
>
> (p. 307)

Indeed, it is a similar coincidence of opposites that can be discerned in the relationship between theism and atheism. While the world is thought by many theists to be the creation or manifestation of the unfathomable spirit or principle that produces it (God), this 'God' is clearly a human concept that evolves in the course of human experience, language and culture. This is one way of understanding the "union of faith and unbelief" suggested by the Jewish mystic Azriel (Scholem 1987: 441–442), or of the "divine and human perspectives" spoken of by Schneur Zalman of Lyadi (Elior 1993: 137–138).

To respond to another of Aijaz's points, I am indeed attempting to steer a middle course between, or rather embrace both, the rational tradition of Maimonides and the mystical tradition of Luria. As pointed out in my Position Statement, while my philosophical approach to the Kabbalah has antecedents in certain late medieval Kabbalists and the eighteenth- and nineteenth-century Chabad Hasidim, it is only in our time, when Kabbalistic ideas have entered the marketplace of scholarly discourse, that a philosophical Kabbalah can be more fully developed.

I agree with Aijaz that "[t]here are at least some concepts of God that are inadequate, abominable and, indeed, idolatrous" (91). In fact, I view the majority of conceptions of the deity (i.e., those that identify God as a quasi-empirical entity that creates, sustains, guides and controls the world) as idolatrous. In order to make my point, a point that underscores the value of at least a certain aspect of 'atheism' for theology, I will ask the reader to follow me in a brief thought experiment, one that can be conceived as a modern, computer-age version of Descartes' hypothesis of the evil and deceitful genius (Descartes [1647] 1996).

As the Oxford philosopher Nick Bostrom (2003) has pointed out, many philosophers today, as well as the majority of cognitive scientists, believe that it will only be a matter of time before human beings have created computers powerful enough to fully simulate consciousness and produce a 'matrix' within which fully functional, conscious, human-like entities interact in a simulated world and believe themselves to be alive and real. According to

Bostrom, if this is true then there is reason to suppose that we ourselves may be such beings, existing in an information matrix created by 'future' (presumably biological) humans who have decided to produce an ancestor simulation (or 'second life') for their amusement. For my purposes here, it is irrelevant whether such a matrix exists or is even scientifically plausible. What is relevant in our thought experiment is that the creator of such a simulation could well perform miracles, provide prophets with visions, take vengeance, destroy whole populations, issue commands and control this simulated world in any way he or she sees fit. It is obvious, however, that such a creator would not be 'God' in any but the most perverse and idolatrous of terms. Indeed, such a 'God' would be no more divine than a futuristic super-intelligent adolescent who controlled our simulated world much as today's children control the worlds in their video games. Unfortunately, the conception of God that emerges from much of scripture (and which is held to be God by so many religious adherents) comes uncomfortably close to the adolescent video game operator.

While I certainly do not hold to the view that we are currently living in a digital simulation, the logical possibility that we are and the potential impossibility of distinguishing a 'video game God' from a genuine one leads me to reject any notion of a controlling and commanding creator god. Such a 'video game God' would hardly be worthy of our worship and adoration (although, like an earthly potentate, he or she might well respond to our prayers!).

To my way of thinking, the only God worthy of our consideration is a God that embodies an eternal, incorrigible principle or set of principles – principles like wisdom, understanding, love and compassion – the sort of principles said by the Kabbalists to be embodied in the *sefirot*, the manifestations or archetypes of the Infinite, *Ein-sof*. God cannot be anything resembling an empirical being, regardless of that being's level of greatness and power, but must be closer to some principle or value to which all empirical beings – human, post-human, simulated and (apparently) God-like – are subject to. Perhaps, as I have argued in my Position Statement, the highest of these values is the open spirit of inquiry, experience and understanding that enables us to criticize, deconstruct and revise even our own conceptions of God, the world and ourselves. This to me is divine; the rest is in danger of becoming idolatry.

I would add, in passing, that the values that I believe are embodied in the Godhead are more objective than anything material or natural – and here I would again turn to the 'simulation argument' to support this view. On the hypothesis that we are living in a computer simulation, it becomes clear that the so-called physical constants of our universe – the speed of light, the atomic weight of lead and even Martin Rees' famous six numbers or constants that presumably define our universe (Rees 2000) – are essentially arbitrary and would have been *programmed into our matrix and could have conceivably been quite different*. We could live in a digital matrix in which these numbers were different and we would not be particularly troubled by this. Indeed, if scientists suddenly announced that it had been discovered that the speed of light was off by 10,000 miles per second, what difference would this make to our everyday (non-simulated) world? But consider the possibility that we resided in a world/matrix in which compassion to others was programed as an evil (or if it was discovered in our presumably non-simulated world that compassion and love were no longer values). What effect would it have on us if we were commanded to adhere to the 'good' by destroying all those different from us in belief or custom? This, I daresay, we could not abide. Indeed, the basic values that so many philosophers have argued are subjective additions to our objective natural world are, as I believe the simulation argument shows, more 'solid', more incorrigible, than virtually anything else, as they would (or should) hold in all worlds regardless of their material or digital nature. It is against such values that we must judge any world and any presumed God – including, to my mind, the God who destroyed humanity in the Flood and who permitted the Holocaust and other genocidal atrocities!

I recognize that there will be those who will hold that my approach is overly rationalistic, and I am certainly cognizant of the fact that there are irrational, intuitive and bodily aspects of humanity that must be considered in any full conception of spirituality. Indeed, I have struggled to express my reaction to the Holocaust, which took numerous members of my own family, in rational terms, and having been unable to do so, have turned to painting in order to do so (Drob 2013; cf. Drob 2014a). Nevertheless, I am deeply suspicious of any theology or ideology that places emotion, intuition or faith above reason. Indeed, in my view it was precisely the failure to follow reason, in the name of an irrational ideology, that was a prime cause of the Holocaust. It was precisely the failure to treat all human beings as an end in and for themselves that enabled (and enables) people to feel justified in the wholesale slaughter of those who were 'different' from themselves.

Response to Suga: Shinto

Koji Suga asks what in our personal lives has led to our current religious beliefs and faith? This is certainly an interesting and important question but not one that I can readily answer. Certain autobiographical details stand out for me: the fact that my mother lost six of her brothers and sisters in the Holocaust, along with numerous nieces and nephews, is one; that my paternal grandfather, a prominent New York rabbi, while vehemently denouncing the Holocaust maintained his faith throughout those dark years, is another. Another influence is to be traced to the fact that when I was a very small child my grandfather, Rabbi Max Drob, lifted me over his head and said to my father, "It skipped a generation," referring to the historical chain of rabbis in our family that had been broken only by my father's generation. (Although I did not enter the rabbinate, I feel that I have in some way fulfilled his prophecy!) That I had wonderful teachers, T. J. J. Altizer and J. N. Findlay, who were not Jews but who influenced me deeply and encouraged me to reflect upon the philosophical and theological foundations of my own heritage, was another critical influence. But, however moving and important, these 'influences' were in a sense superficialities. How one arrives at one's worldview is both a deep mystery and as plain as the day. When it becomes less than plain it then becomes time to reflect and perhaps shift. Such shifts have occurred throughout my life and will continue. To live in the spirit of open inquiry means to be subject to change.

It is interesting to me that Suga asks why it is that Kabbalistic Judaism has not drawn inspiration from the periods of the Renaissance and the Enlightenment. From a purely historical point of view, the religious communities within which the Kabbalah arose were largely insulated from these developments, but a certain cross-fertilization must have taken place. We know that certain Renaissance philosophers such as Marsilio Ficino and Giordano Bruno (de León-Jones 2004) became quite conversant with Kabbalistic ideas. As I pointed out in my Position Statement, it has also recently been argued that the Kabbalistic notion of *Tikkun ha-Olam*, the (quite humanistic) idea that humanity has a pivotal role in repairing the fault in creation, had a significant impact upon Leibniz and Locke (Coudert 1995, 1998). One can surmise that the influence went in both directions. Certainly my own attraction to the Lurianic metaphors of *shevirah* (rupture) and *tikkun* (repair) stems from their patent openness to transformation, not only of the world but our ideas about it.

With regard to the Renaissance, I would add another personal note. As a university student in New York I frequently wandered the halls of the Metropolitan Museum of Art, troubled by the fact that *all* of the medieval and Renaissance depictions of biblical events, including those of the 'Old Testament', were done from a Christian point of view. It had not yet occurred to me that the ban on graven images that for millennia had been taken so literally and so seriously would have prevented Jews from forming their own pictorial representations of the Bible. But even then I harboured the secret desire to create a 'Renaissance pictorial form' from a Jewish perspective. It has only been in the last few years that I have taken up this aspiration and allowed my interests in Jewish thought and painting to fuse in a series of images that are imbued with what I take to be the spirit of both Renaissance art and Kabbalistic theology (Drob 2013). Needless to say, I view the Kabbalah as a living tradition, one that grows through its encounter with various other forms of human experience.

With regard to Suga's question about the social conditions under which the Kabbalah – particularly the Lurianic Kabbalah – evolved, this was a theme that preoccupied the founder of modern Kabbalah scholarship, Gershom Scholem. Indeed, Scholem held that the very notions of *shevirah* and *tikkun* (the breaking of the vessels and their restoration), which I have just alluded to, reflected the condition of the Diaspora Jews, and most importantly their then-recent exile from Spain. For Scholem, the Kabbalistic symbols directly reflected the Jewish experience of exile and the fervent hope to be restored to and reintegrated with the land of Israel. Scholem even went so far as to hold that while the Lurianic metaphors had deep social and personal meaning for the Jews of the sixteenth century, they offer little in the way of theological or philosophical insight in the twentieth century. According to Scholem, the meaning of the *shevirah* is that "[n]othing remains in its proper place. Everything is somewhere else. But a being that is not in its proper place is in exile. Thus, since that primordial act, all being has been in exile, in need of being led back and redeemed" (Scholem 1965: 112). Scholem held that "[b]efore the judgment seat of rationalist theology such an idea may not have much to say for itself. But for the human experience of the Jews it was the most seductively powerful of symbols" (p. 113). This was because "[f]rom a historical point of view, Luria's myth constitutes a response to the expulsion of the Jews from Spain" (p. 110). While Scholem suggested the possibility that "the mighty symbols of Jewish life" might be understood as extreme instances "of human life pure and simple," he concluded that "[w]e can no longer fully perceive, I might say, 'live', the symbols of the Kabbalah without a considerable effort, if at all" (p. 117).

My own approach, and I assume the risks associated with it, is to de-emphasize the social context of the Kabbalistic metaphors and reflect upon them in connection with both other modes of historical (and contemporary) thought and the basic existential issues that underlie religion. To me, a symbol that suggests that "[n]othing remains in its proper place" and that "[e]verything is somewhere else" can be readily understood in philosophical, theological and psychological terms – through the ideas that all of reality is somehow broken, flawed and incomplete and that humanity is exiled from itself (existentialism), from its unconscious (Freud, Jung), from the products of its creative labour (Marx) and from nature. Further, these symbols strike me as vehicles through which we can grasp the apparently unbridgeable gulfs between our most fundamental concepts – freedom and necessity, mind and matter, good and evil, appearance and reality, theism and atheism, to highlight just a few of the basic problems in philosophy that illustrate the basic 'fault' in both our thinking and our world (Drob 2000: 324–326).

While this is generally overlooked, earlier generations of Kabbalistic and Hasidic thinkers took an essentially ahistorical approach to their 'subject'. For example, in adapting the Lurianic metaphors to the conditions of eighteenth-century Poland, the Chabad Hasidim did not consider the social conditions of Spain or Safed in centuries past but rather meditated upon and interpreted the texts and traditions that were then in their possession from their *then-contemporary point of view*. I believe that in trying to explain the Kabbalistic metaphors in terms of the social conditions of the Jews in sixteenth-century Spain and Safed, Scholem missed an opportunity to adequately grasp their deep philosophical and theological significance. My own work, of course, runs the risk of being anachronistic and historically inaccurate, but I assume that risk in the interest of spiritual and intellectual vitality.

The question raised by Suga regarding the directionality of time is an important one and has received renewed attention by contemporary physicists, some of whom suggest that the arrow of time is not reflective of the deep structure of the universe (Tegmark 2014). Judaism, like Christianity, is a historical religion, which holds that there is indeed a movement and direction in time leading to an eschatological end. For the most part, the Kabbalists adopted this framework, viewing themselves as attempting to hasten the advent of the Messiah. This historical point of view is evident even today in the Chabad Hasidic understanding of the late Rabbi Menachem Schneerson as a messianic figure. There are, however, interpretations of the Kabbalah reflecting a cyclical understanding of rupture and repair (Fackenheim 1982). Further, as I suggested in my Position Statement, there are intimations within the Kabbalistic sources that the entire sequence of apparently historical events that define *Ein-sof* is actually co-present in all times and in all things.

The Kabbalists certainly took what Suga might term an 'anthropic' view of the universe, although they didn't understand the universe in physical terms. For them, the essential constituents of the world were axiological rather than physical. Values for the Kabbalists were more real than matter, and indeed the material world was understood, at least in one sense, as the result of a distance or alienation from true, axiological being. With this, as I have already said, I am in complete accord. As I argued earlier, the idea that one should not wantonly destroy other sentient beings or thwart their desires – unlike, for example, the speed of light, or the atomic weight of what we call 'gold' – is something that must hold in all worlds, not just the particular one that we happen to find ourselves in. For the Kabbalists, the 'anthropic' cosmos is revealed in the fact that the deepest structure of the universe is made manifest most adequately through the consciousness and values of humanity.

Response to Isherwood: Radical incarnational Christianity

Lisa Isherwood refers to my assertion that Judaism is a practice rather than a belief-system. She indicates, however, that Kabbalah appears to go beyond practice and appears to be "prescriptive". I am confused by the word 'prescriptive' in this context. Certainly Judaism as a system of 613 Commandments is prescriptive in terms of behaviour but less so in terms of belief. The Kabbalah, at least as I have understood it, is certainly theoretical, but it is hardly prescriptive in the sense of a catechism or set of articles of faith. Firstly, the Kabbalah is advanced as an interpretation of normative Judaism that an individual of appropriate age and understanding can engage with but need not adopt in order to remain a committed, even Orthodox, Jew. In fact, there have historically been large segments within the Jewish community that reject Kabbalistic thought. Secondly, my entire understanding of the Kabbalah is that it paves the way for an open economy of thought in which all theoretical systems (including the Kabbalah itself), like everything else in the world, are subject to rupture and revision.

I very much appreciate Isherwood raising the issue of "transgressions against the norm" (this volume: 106). In fact, the Kabbalists throughout their history have been accused of transgressing normative Judaism, and in certain of their forms gave rise to so-called heretical points of view, including Sabbateanism and Frankism (Scholem 1973). The early Hasidim were (and in certain quarters continue to be) thought of as transgressors. Their meditative practices, their emendations of the prayer ritual, their belief that humanity is a partner with God in repairing the world and their near-deification of their rebbes were all regarded as transgressive. As I touched upon in my Position Statement, the Kabbalistic sources went so far as to suggest that just as God creates humanity, humanity is the creator of God – for example, in the process of writing about God in the Torah (Idel 1988: 188) – and this is certainly a view that transgresses normative Jewish theology. My own view is that transgression is a source, if not the main source, of human creativity and transformation (Drob 2012).

With regard to feminist interpretations of Kabbalah, there are many, and these interpretations typically draw upon the Kabbalistic view that the *Shekhinah* or feminine aspect of God has the most intimate connection with the world (Novick 1998; Patai [1967] 1990). However, there are also strains within the Kabbalah that are quite phallocentric, and the Kabbalah scholar Elliot Wolfson has gone so far as to say that the feminist reading of the Kabbalah is "a misreading that [he] readily endorse[s] as a human being but regrettably reject[s] as a historical scholar" (Wolfson 1998, quoted in Seidenberg n.d.). This is a complex topic, one that echoes the problem of phallocentrism within Judaism (and other religions) in general. Here I will simply state that since I understand the Kabbalistic notion of the *shevirah*, the breaking of the vessels, to apply to all things, including the Kabbalah itself, the sometimes pejorative attitudes towards women (and other segments of humanity, including all gentiles) that the Kabbalah absorbed from normative Judaism are among the vessels that are in need of rupture and rectification.

I understand Isherwood's concerns about the view of 'the Fall' that regards Eve and hence all women as responsible for the production of evil. There are certainly strains within the Kabbalah that reflect this prejudice. For example, while the *sefirah Chesed* (Kindness) is often identified with the male, the *sefirah Din*, Judgement, is linked to the female and is viewed as the origin of negativity and evil. That being said, and on the assumption that such blatant genderism is non-essential to the idea, I am reluctant to abandon the metaphor of a fallen or broken world in need of rectification and repair. (Certainly, it is not women who have placed us on the precipice of ecological disaster, but we are on that precipice nonetheless.) The cosmos may have never been a paradise, but I experience and understand it as broken now. That being said, I like Isherwood's notion of "endless possibilities" replacing the idea of "perfect endings" (this volume: 107). My own notion of the Messiah is in many ways in accord with the image of the messianic in the work of Jacques Derrida, who speaks of the messianic as the impossible unknown that we perpetually strive for but never reach (Derrida 1994). In the process, an indefinite if not infinite set of possibilities will be realized. We must, however, attempt to realize a future that is as much as possible in accord with the values that we know promote the welfare of all living creatures, as opposed to their harm and destruction.

I have already addressed the question of embodiment in my response to Isherwood's Position Statement. I continue to reflect upon my own linguistic and rational tendencies, if not prejudices. I am sure that my raising the possibility that we live in a computer-based simulation, even only as a thought experiment, will reinforce my readers' idea that I am a person who lives in the head at the expense of the body. This is indeed true, at least insofar as my intellectual life is concerned, and I believe that there is a sense in which this is a limitation endemic to expressing oneself in language. However, as a visual artist, I have been fascinated by and I daresay in love with the human body. My aesthetic interest in the human body coincides with Hegel's view that the depiction of the human form expresses the unity of spirit and matter (Hegel 1970: 113).

With regard to language, there is a certain linguistic predicament that all theorists must confront. Whether or not we think in words, we write and speak with them, and in the process we utilize words that are defined through a long chain of signifiers by other words. There is a certain sense in which our talk about God, values, etc., ends up being about other words as opposed to nature, the body, etc. Even my speaking about nature, body, etc., places these words within a matrix of linguistic signifiers, and I thus become imprisoned by them. I think it is this predicament that has contributed to the view, expressed by Kabbalists and postmodernists alike, that "there is nothing outside of the text", that all is language. While the predicament can be recognized within language and we can to a certain extent break out of the 'linguistic prison' through the use of new language (e.g., in poetry and metaphor) or through the resignification of old language, there is a sense in which it can only be resolved outside of language, through forms of silent, bodily or other nonlinguistic experience and, in my view, through art.

I would think it tragic, however, if as a result of the history of male domination in philosophy and theology, or as a result of readings of Freud or Lacan (or the Kabbalah!), women feel that they cannot enter into and find a significant place within rational philosophical or theological discourse, even while having done so with respect to so many other institutions within society. I am not so sure that the idea of abandoning language altogether in favour of the body is a wise one, but perhaps this requires considerably more thought, or if not thought, some other kind of experience. With regard to gender, I have abandoned language in my engagement with the figure of Hypatia in several of my paintings, a figure whom I believe represents both the possibility and the brutal suppression of the intellectual female (Drob 2014b).

References

Bostrom, N. 2003. "Are You Living in a Computer Simulation?" *Philosophical Quarterly* 53, no. 211: 243–255.
Coudert, A. 1995. *Leibniz and the Kabbalah*. New York: Springer-Verlag.
Coudert, A. 1998. *The Impact of the Kabbalah in the Seventeenth Century: The Life and Thought of Francis Mercury van Helmont (1614–1698)*. Boston, MA: Brill Academic Publishers.
de León-Jones, K. S. 2004. *Giordano Bruno and the Kabbalah: Prophets, Magicians, and Rabbis*. Lincoln, NE: Bison Books.
Derrida, J. 1994. *Specters of Marx: The State of the Debt, the Work of Mourning, and the New International*, translated by P. Kamuf. London: Routledge.
Descartes, R. [1647] 1996. *Meditations on First Philosophy: With Selections From the Objections and Replies*, revised ed., edited by J. Cottingham. Cambridge: Cambridge University Press.
Drob, S. 2000. *Symbols of the Kabbalah: Philosophical and Psychological Perspectives*. Northvale, NJ: Jason Aronson.
Drob, S. 2012. "Transgression and Transformation: Is Psychoanalysis a Dangerous Method?" *Talking Cures* 10, no. 1: 1–6.
Drob, S. 2013. "The (In)humanity Triptych: Are We Left Now With a Useless God: Images and Thoughts on Human Destructiveness and Suffering." *Talking Cures* 11, no. 1: 1, 6, 11, 12.
Drob, S. 2014a. *The (In)humanity Triptych* (blog). Accessed November 2014. http://inhumanitytriptych.blogspot.com/.
Drob, S. 2014b. *Hypatia of Alexandria* (blog). Accessed November 2014. http://hypatiapainting.blogspot.com/
Elior, R. 1993. *The Paradoxical Ascent to God: The Kabbalistic Theosophy of Habad Hasidism*, translated by J. M. Green. Albany, NY: State University of New York.
Fackenheim, E. 1982. *To Mend the World*. New York: Schocken.
Hegel, G. W. F. 1970. *On Art, Religion, Philosophy: Introductory Lectures to the Realm of Absolute Spirit*, edited by J. G. Gray. New York: Harper & Row.
Hut, P. and R. N. Shepard. 1999. "Turning 'the Hard Problem' Upside Down and Sideways." In *Explaining Consciousness: The Hard Problem*, edited by J. Shear, 305–322. Cambridge, MA: The MIT Press.
Idel, M. 1988. *Kabbalah: New Perspectives*. New Haven, CT: Yale University Press.
Novick, L. 1998. *On the Wings of Shekhinah: Rediscovering Judaism's Divine Feminine*. Wheaton, IL: Quest Books.
Patai, R. [1967] 1990. *The Hebrew Goddess*. Detroit: Wayne State University Press.
Rees, M. 2000. *Just Six Numbers*. New York: Basic Books.
Scholem, G. 1965. *On the Kabbalah and Its Symbolism*, translated by R. Manheim. New York: Schocken.
Scholem, G. 1973. *Sabbatai Sevi: The Mystical Messiah*, translated by R. J. Zwi Werblowski. Princeton, NJ: Princeton University Press.

Scholem, G. 1987. *Origins of the Kabbalah*, translated by R. J. Zwi Werblowski. Princeton, NJ: Princeton University Press.

Seidenberg, D. (n.d.). "The Divine Feminine in Kabbalah: An Example of Jewish Renewal." *My Jewish Learning*. Accessed November 2014. http://www.myjewishlearning.com/beliefs/Theology/Kabbalah_and_Mysticism/Modern_Times/Mysticism_Renewed/Jewish_Renewal.shtml.

Tegmark, M. 2014. *Our Mathematical Universe: My Quest for the Ultimate Nature of Reality*. New York: Alfred A. Knopf.

Wolfson, E. 1998. "The Mirror of Nature in Medieval Mysticism." Paper presented at the Judaism and the Natural World conference, February 22–24, Harvard, MA.

11 Lisa Isherwood

I would like to thank the respondents for such thought-provoking chapters. This is a fascinating dialogue, and I feel excited that we are able to do this. I would like to clarify at the start that my position does not lie within what is normally called 'liberal' Christianity but drifts more towards the radical side and thus is best thought of as a 'radical incarnational' approach.

Response to Suga: Shinto

I found Suga's development of the concept of 'way' very interesting, especially since it is formulated by someone who refers to himself as an agnostic, as this suggests to me, perhaps wrongly, that the 'way' is not a prescribed or predetermined way at all. If this is the case, then it resonates slightly with some Latin American feminist theologians who refer to the 'walk', which is a journey one takes with comrades in the struggle, whatever that may be in the moment, and is not prescribed but rather develops in the walking itself (see Althaus-Reid 2004: 30–43). This is also an idea which has been taken up by Asian feminist theologians, who once again understand it as a walk of solidarity that one takes with those committed to the flourishing of all in a just society. The importance of this idea is that actions, ideas and beliefs manifest themselves as the 'walk' progresses. Every step, set of actions and so on brings to light greater understanding of what is needed, and this in turn affects the following steps. Many who follow this way of feminist liberation action do not have a set of religious beliefs, while others do. What they hold in common is the commitment to a future that can be changed by human relational activity and openness to where the path leads. This, of course, is a practical consequence of the view, upheld in process theology, that there is no preordained ultimate end and, in terms of Christianity, no perfect past from which we fell. There is, though, a god who is ever-present in the process, not directing it but rather animating it.

Turning now to Suga's direct questions and comments about my position, the aim of feminist theology – like the work of most liberation theologians – is to help bring about a more inclusive, just and relational society. Those who feel that a biblical basis for this commitment is necessary find it in the

Hebrew Scriptures, where the God of liberation is evident throughout, and in the work of Jesus, who included the outcasts and the lowly in what has been named the 'discipleship of equals'. It can be argued, then, that there is a solid foundation for liberation from social injustice at the heart of Christian understandings. Of course, society is not static, and so how one understands work for justice also changes. Christianity itself has changed its doctrinal stance on many occasions, with today's heresy being tomorrow's orthodoxy. Feminist theologians, then, are not looking for a new religion but rather another movement in doctrinal understanding that engages with the different in society. This is not to say that doctrine is at the mercy of whim but rather that as our understanding develops and we observe society engaging in more complex modes of oppression, a response should be offered by Christian theology. An example of what we mean by this can be given in terms of women who, in their theology, continue to labour under Aristotelian understandings of the sexes. This has laid the foundations for a Thomist-inspired theology regarding women, which still acts as a barrier in many cases towards the theological recognition of the full humanity of women. It is now well known that women are not biologically inferior, and so theology must reform its underlying assumption if it is not to remain incompatible with contemporary scientific and progressive ideas about gender.

Feminist theologies do not claim that Christianity is the only way to bring about liberation, and indeed Christianity's sad history suggests it has not been wonderful at this. As my earlier mention of 'the walk' suggests, feminist theologians never ask questions about orthodoxy of any kind but are more interested in orthopraxis, and so those of all religions and none are understood to be capable of commitment to justice-seeking. Feminist theologians engaged in formal interreligious dialogue have found themselves involved in joint social projects rather than in debates over doctrine.

The question about Christology and inclusion is an interesting one and the place where most interreligious dialogue falls flat, since for many Christians the once and for all redemptive power of Christ is the end of the matter. For feminist theologians, however, the matter is quite different. We have no interest in the conversion of others or in putting forward a case for the superiority of Christianity. We are content to work within our theology in order to make it more inclusive and world-changing. Christology for feminist theologians concerns the birthright of all, not just the man Jesus. This is where the understanding of *dunamis* as the power that enlivens everything is central. It is a concept found in Mark's Gospel, where it is contrasted with *exousia*, 'power over'. *Dunamis* is raw, erotic power, in the sense that it enlivens and draws us towards each other and the world. This is the power that feminist theology has suggested enabled the man Jesus to become a Christ. In the writings of Paul we are told that it is Jesus who is risen and who has become the Christ. There is no space here to discuss what feminist theologians understand by 'resurrection', but suffice it to say that it is not considered a literal rising of the body. In short, we move away from an understanding of Jesus as the one and only saviour towards a more inclusive understanding – inclusive of all human life and even, it has recently been suggested, of all life (see Isherwood 2010). Further, we move from the uniqueness of Jesus' actions to a commitment from all to serve justice in the way he did. When Suga asks what significance Jesus would have for people living in non-Christian cultures, I would suggest very little, as such people would find within their own religions similar calls for justice-seeking. Feminist theology is concerned with awakening Christians to their own message of liberation and to working with others in pursuing the goals of justice-seeking and liberation. There is no interest, as already mentioned, in claiming uniqueness for Christianity.

I am not sure what clarification Suga seeks regarding my discussion in my Position Statement of sexuality and the erotic. The main point that feminist theology makes in this regard is that Christianity has controlled sexuality and investigated all manner of questions relating to it, but all the while taking the male body as the norm. This control, it is suggested, has been the result of a fear of the body and, more importantly, of a concomitant fear of people who are at ease in their skin and how they may then use their embodied lives to pursue justice and liberation beyond what the churches and their political alliances have deemed appropriate. Sociologists have demonstrated how a society can be controlled and even understood through the sexual taboos it employs and especially by means of the restrictions and boundaries it places on the female body. An appreciation of this is therefore one of the many things that are necessary if one desires a freer and more just society. Perhaps it is the word 'erotic' that causes confusion. This is not to be seen in purely sexual terms. It is the dynamic energy that those reading Mark's Gospel conceived as *dunamis* – the energy that enlivens all things, and which in feminist theology is connected with the divine. Those working in feminist body theology encourage women to connect with *dunamis*, the erotic power, in order to have more authentic experiences of themselves in their skins, not only by way of sexuality but via all aspects of their embodied lives. Such connection, it is hoped, will free women, and men, from the constructions placed upon their bodies that do not allow for the fullness of liberation and a more authentic form of life.

Suga turns in his discussion from bodily concerns to cosmological ones, but feminist theologies propose not so much a turn of this sort but rather a moving deeper, since our bodies are made from the material of the cosmos itself. From my perspective, issues of cosmology form the next logical step when practicing what is known as 'body theology', particularly given that most religions make some cosmological commitments in their stories of origins. Once again, placing human genesis in the Deep rather than in a supernatural act of creation opens the horizons of human action; it also opens human and nonhuman relationality. Suga is quite right: this brings into question any notion of ultimate truth, but only as an abstract and controlling ideal, an ideal that in Christianity has often harmed individuals and nations. It does, however, place us in a very different relationship with the world and all that is in it. It requires a more mindful existence of seeking justice in all actions and not simply following preordained rules, many of which – in the case of Christianity – were laid down centuries ago and do not speak to our condition here and now.

Response to Drob: Mystical Judaism

I found the personal reflections at the beginning of Drob's response fascinating and moving. Of course, they also resonated with my own position about the importance of the body and being situated in it if we are to move forward in liberation. This is not simply because in so many ways we are captive within our constructed bodies, captive to our own image of ourselves and the thoughts of others about our embodiment, but also because it is the raw energy, *dunamis*, that can release those chains and open up wider horizons. It is the claim of feminist theologies that *dunamis* in the life of Jesus enabled him to see people and himself beyond the constructions of his society and religion, and thus to open new ways of being, new horizons. While on the subject of Jesus, I am sure he could be seen as a heretic precisely because he opened these new ways of seeing persons and things. This is not because Judaism had it all wrong and Christianity has it all right. Rather, it is due to Jesus' grounded way of living and the way in which he would perceive things which posed a challenge to the people of his day and remains so to those of our day, even those who claim to follow him. I too hold that Jesus is not a saviour or hero and, in this respect at least, I concur with Jung (even if there are many other areas where I disagree with him). In my view, any conception of 'going our own way' would need to be grounded in *dunamis* and be relational also – not simply 'doing it my way', but certainly free of predetermined oppressive structures in both society and theology. I am entirely in agreement with Drob that the Jewish man whom Christians claim so much for would be as heretical in the eyes of the church throughout history as he has been seen to be by his own religion of origin. Most churches, inquisitions and crusades would have little place for him, since his way of opening new horizons would shake their sense of power and importance.

Drob's argument for reason is of course sound, and perhaps what I am questioning is what we consider reason to be and how we consider it to be acquired. My view is that 'reason', when it refers purely to the analytical powers and activities of the brain, can be and has been dangerous. We can, I believe, reason ourselves into most positions. I certainly do not wish to take a position that plays down the intellect. After all, women have for so long been told they don't have any that such a position would be counterproductive from a feminist perspective. I wish to argue for a full-bodied way of coming to rational decisions, one that takes into account the embodied experience of more than the powerful. Perhaps I even wish to acknowledge that the brain, and therefore the power of rationality, is part of the body and should not dominate the decision-making process. Historically, this domination has sprung from the dualistic attitudes we work under and, in proposing that full embodiment can play a part in intellectual decisions, feminist theology is hoping to heal the rupture of body from mind that has been so damaging in the lives of people – on a personal level but also in the wider religious and political realm. Feminist theology has recently begun to engage with somatic psychology as a way to begin to unpack more of the innate 'knowing' of people. I certainly take the warning in Drob's chapter regarding Jung and Nazism and the associated drive for the spirit of a people, one that I understand is underway in Norway with a reclaiming of the old myths, leading in some cases to very right-wing ways of thinking. However, I do feel there is much about the individual in relation, the I-Thou relation, that can be enriched through body knowing. Such embodied knowing, furthermore, could and should impact on politics and religion. Perhaps naively, I hope that it is the 'in relation' part of this experience that would enable a wider vista than 'me and mine' to be at play, since relationality (as understood in feminist theologies) is universal.

The opening towards chaos suggested in some recent theology may be a frightening thought, but in a sense it is opening to the very foundations of our embodied being. I think there is much work to be done on the role of chaos in feminist theology, once again because women have so often been relegated to that realm in a quite negative way. However, the way in which Christianity has often equated chaos with darkness and by extension evil has been, I would suggest, very damaging to the psyche of many Christians, who have felt compelled to hide any less than perfect feelings and to appear in control of their emotions and desires – any lack of control often being seen as bordering on chaos and loss of salvation. Perhaps the point is too strongly made for those who sit within the middle of various traditions, but I feel it is not too strong a suggestion for those of a fundamentalist bent.

Response to Aijaz: Sunni Islam

To restate my position, I am a theologian who takes lived experience to be of the utmost importance in understanding what people call 'God'. This is because I am a member of an incarnational religion that takes as its starting point the enfleshed nature of its God. As a feminist theologian, I then understand all matters to do with the lives of people, personal and public, to be matters that reveal to us the God we say we believe in. As Aijaz concedes, religion has not simply been a matter of direct divine revelation but has been subject to all-too-human forces; within Christianity these have been the work of male hierarchies. Therefore, matters of God have become entangled with matters of human (male) power and definitions, women having been categorized in terms of second-class humanity by male interpretations of scripture and formulations of doctrine. The impact on the lives of women over 2,000 years has been immense, and these are the implications of male-constructed ideas of the divine that I addressed in my Position Statement. Further, as pointed out in some of my responses to the other chapters, my starting point results in slightly different ways of viewing what may be classed as traditional religious questions. Perhaps this could be seen in the approach to scripture that I outlined in response to Aijaz, where I showed that feminist theologians believe it is necessary to test scripture next to lived experience and social justice rather than simply accepting scripture as a miraculous communication from God. In this respect, questions of the divine extend from the construction of gender and sexuality to the use of scripture, ethics, ritual and doctrine, and also the ways in which we allow ourselves to image God.

Perhaps Aijaz will now be able to revisit my responses to colleagues with a clearer understanding of my position, and this in turn might help to meet the second problem he raises with my Position Statement. However, I have to say that the practice of referencing academic colleagues in an academic paper does not strike me as particularly problematic. I do not agree with Aijaz that the use of Lacan, Braidotti and Irigaray clouds any issues I am discussing. They are indeed central to matters of gender and religion/culture and have offered constructive insights into patriarchal systems. Aijiz seems to be familiar with Lacan and so knows well that the Symbolic Order is that which has been the foundation of western culture for generations based on the Phallus – that is, the definitions and positions formulated by males and their hierarchies that place all others within those hierarchies. Further, as we know, this order is one that even defines what words we use and what they mean and is thus the structuring principle of our worlds, since words, as Kristeva demonstrates (dare I mention Kristeva?), create reality if they are embedded in cultures and are thus spoken often enough. The words, ideas and assumptions traditionally used about women in relation to the divine have been negative and disempowering. Why pointing this out should cause problems I do not quite understand. It follows that women within this world of male construction have found it hard to 'find a voice' and so have begun to speak from a different place, that of embodied experience, in order to find the words to challenge the wall of patriarchy. The point that seems to have been missed, then, is that with no access to language that is based in male experience, women have to find another way. This other way is through the body, and the body can become a place of alternative subjectivity as opposed to the objectivity imposed on it by the male gaze, male language and so on. As part of the process, the female body needs to resist any fixed position within the male hierarchies, and so a nomadic existence might be a valid and preferable position to take.

Aijaz's next concern seems to be based upon a misreading of the concept of erotic power as set out in my Position Statement. That coupling it with the concept of Christ is atypical seems neither here nor there; one supposes it would be atypical since feminist analysis of scripture is a relatively recent approach. Do other Christian scholars have to agree? Of course not. Although many feminist scholars would not agree with the view that women, simply because of their physical make-up, should not be permitted to enter the ordained ministry, this has not stopped church theologians from putting forward such a view and the consequences being lived out in the lives of women. Aijaz, further, completely misunderstands what is meant by erotic power in feminist theology. Erotic power, as previously noted, is *dunamis*, the often-repeated word of Jesus in Mark's Gospel that refers to the divine birthright of all – the power that dwells in us as the divine spark of which Augustine spoke and that draws us out to others and the world. *Dunamis* is a very important aspect of feminist theology, as it speaks powerfully about claiming one's own divine-human nature and living authentically from it. Jesus in Mark's Gospel considers this to be the power that overcomes all attempts to dominate and which denies our own will to exert power over others. *Dunamis* is a power that increases in the sharing and the connecting. While erotic power is not exclusively understood as a sexual power within feminist theology and thus has nothing whatsoever to do with sexual anticipation and arousal, it has been spoken of within feminist sexual ethics as a significant element in women's reclamation of their bodies from a set of sexual expectations laid upon them by churches and enacted upon them by Christian men. This has placed much more agency in the lives of people and freed them from a top-down set of rules about their embodied pursuit of holy lives. It is also a concept that has been taken up by many male theologians involved in sexual ethics as a more grounded starting point for the development of a sexual ethics based upon an incarnational religion (Goss 1994).

As to why we should speak of Christ's power as erotic, the answer is to be found in feminist biblical scholarship, which has identified that Jesus himself speaks of this *dunamis*, this raw dynamism, this *eros* for life and liberation. This also perhaps answers Aijaz's question about sexual mania. It is clear from the gospel accounts that Jesus was in the grip not of a sexual mania but of a dynamic power that could not be controlled even by immense political power and, as the gospel accounts suggest, not even by death itself. In much of my previous work I have indeed developed the case in support of the conception of the 'erotic Christ' drawing upon feminist biblical scholarship, and I sought to lay this out clearly in my initial Position Statement. The dialogues we are engaging in here are, on my understanding, predicated on the assumption that many of our background views, such as the broadly feminist position I work from, would be recognized as having been elaborated and defended in scholarly fashion in previous works and thus are not in need of full exposition here within the limited space allowed.

Aijaz declares that care must be taken with the concept of *dunamis* as this may "justify all sorts of sexual lives and erotic practices" (this volume: 88). Once again, this evinces a misunderstanding of the concept itself. Yes, this concept certainly can underpin arguments for the acceptance of loving and mutual homosexual relationships, since this power to be drawn to others and to love them passionately for the good of each other and, further, for the good of the community at large is not confined to any particular manifestation of human living. The importance here lies in the love extending beyond selfish gratification to engagement with the community in which one lives; this applies to heterosexual love as well. The very nature of *dunamis* is justice-seeking and it is grounded in mutual relationality, and so when applied in the sexual realm, far from leading to abuse, it demands equality and respect. Those who accept that this power is open to all and might form the very basis of a liberation theology would not wish to police physical expression that is founded upon mutual relationality. This, one would argue, has been what patriarchal religions have done over the centuries: they have prescribed what is allowed and not allowed in loving relationships and, as suggested already, this has often weighed heavily on the bodies of women. It has been a way of course to control society and to place very firm boundaries surrounding insiders and outsiders and, as such, a way to disempower people psychologically and socially. The use of *dunamis* in the discourses surrounding sexual ethics is a way, feminists claim, of overcoming these power-laden directives that lead to alienation within our own skins and also within society. Aijaz's statement that feminists should take care not to "equivocate on two different meanings of the 'erotic'" seems to miss the point. We are clear that it is *dunamis* that underpins justice-seeking sexuality. As mentioned, we view sexuality in a wider frame than simply personal pleasure, and it is this biblical concept of *dunamis* to which we refer and not the more secular understanding.

I am grateful to Aijaz for highlighting, in his response to my position, the very problem to which feminists have often wanted to draw attention. Other colleagues are presented as advancing philosophically interesting points, while this feminist professor of theology is described as offering "a series of musings" (87). I think this clearly shows how the voices of women in theology have been received and why such a reception needs to be urgently addressed.

Conclusion

This dialogue has been fascinating and enriching, and I thank my colleagues. I, like Drob, am pleased to see colleagues taking their own path in terms of understanding their traditions and am very encouraged that in some cases this means an emphasis on walking the path rather than setting in stone doctrines and dogmas. I value the dialogue about reason and rationality and the ways in which the foundations of faith and religion are understood. I would value the opportunity for greater dialogue on the role of chaos in the development of a religious life and further discussion on how colleagues actually view the role of the body in its entirety, not just the brain, in the practice of theology. A small regret is that when I posed questions to certain colleagues on the role of women within their traditions, I received no response. Obviously I find this an important area of research, and it is difficult to know how to read the silence from respected academics.

References

Althaus-Reid, M. 2004. *From Feminist Theology to Indecent Theology*. London: SCM Press.
Goss, R. 1994. *Jesus Acted Up: A Gay and Lesbian Manifesto*. New York: Harper Collins.
Isherwood, L. 2010. "Wanderings in the Cosmic Garden." In *Through Us, With Us, In Us: Relational Theologies in the Twenty-First Century*, edited by L. Isherwood and E. Bellchambers, 121–136. London: SCM Press.

12 Koji Suga

In their in-depth First Responses, the other participants have generously understood Shinto as a religion worthy of consideration and have displayed an interest in some points of commonality I outlined in my Position Statement. I am concerned, however, that these observations of commonality between Shinto and other religions are due not so much to general features inherent in Shinto but to an interpretation of Shinto I had put forward, influenced by my orientation towards multi-religious philosophical investigations. Indeed, my respondents' comments have helped me to see the paucity and inadequacy of philosophical discussion on Shinto by Shintoists, myself included. It is apparent that further discussion would be helpful regarding the universalistic aspects, if any, in the philosophical thought of Shinto. In this Second Response, therefore, I will first seek to reply to common comments and queries, and I will then turn to other questions while also trying to extend my discussion.

The possibility of religious practice without belief

The first matter I would like to discuss relates to the possibility of religious practice without belief, a notion that is integral to my perspective on Shinto. Aijaz and Drob both discuss this possibility in their responses.

In his discussion, Aijaz sets out to show that "religious belief is neither necessary nor sufficient for religious practice" (88), where this entails that religious belief is not necessary and not sufficient for making a practical commitment to theism. I am supposing, of course, that Aijaz is employing the term 'theism' to refer to the kind of monotheism that is in accordance with his own faith. We might, however, expand the extension of the term so that it also encompasses polytheism. Given that Shinto, as far as it is a religion in the sense we have discussed so far, clearly has a polytheistic dimension, I think Aijaz's examination of the relations between theistic belief and practical commitment to theism may also be applied to religions such as Shinto. Particularly suggestive is Aijaz's view that the possibility of theistic practice is open even to those who doubt the truth of theism or to individuals motivated by nondoxastic attitudes such as hope. At least one moral this might give rise to, as far as Shinto scholarship is concerned, is that it would be advisable for Shinto scholars to take leave of their enthusiasm for rational verification (of, e.g., historical documents) and give greater attention to the conditions which make it possible to engage in a religious form of life.

Aijaz emphasizes that holding theistic beliefs is not merely not necessary for practical commitment to theism but also not sufficient for such a commitment. This strikes me as entirely correct, for as Aijaz explains, Satan and his cohorts have beliefs about God, but they never have faith in God. Aijaz concludes from this that theists should focus less on trying to determine whether they possess the right or true beliefs about God or ultimate reality and more on factors that impinge upon the value of theistic commitment, such as whether theistic commitment is in accordance with correct morality.

As we have already seen, according to the well-accepted definition of '*kami*' by Norinaga Motoori in the eighteenth century, all spiritual beings that lie behind any awe-inspiring phenomena – whether these beings are good or evil – are to be considered '*kami*'. Here, beyond good and evil, there exists no relation like that between God and Satan. In that case, where can we locate a place for justice among the intricate relations between *kami* and human beings and *kami* and others, including other *kami*? It seems that in this context the word 'justice' may be replaced by the notion of 'correct morality', following Aijaz's expression.

We also find in Shinto mythology a tendency to a form of relativism. Even the heavenly sun-goddess Amaterasu, described as the most sacred one among *kami*, seems to engage in worship directed to anonymous *kami*. Susanoo's rampage involves the obstruction of her preparation for such worship, so it drives his sister to hide in the heavenly rock cave. Therefore, his rampage is regarded with extreme seriousness as blasphemy, but blasphemy against what? This episode suggests that in Shinto a *kami*, whose nature lies beyond good and evil, may also have practical commitments to polytheism.

In the Shinto pantheon, a *kami* that is the object of worship may also in some cases become one who worships other *kami*. Tetsuro Watsuji examined such mythological relations between worshiping and worshiped deities and the priority accorded to the sacred power exercised through ritual over the existence of the object of worship. His remark, cited in my First Response, that the *kami* described in Shinto mythology are "not the deities conceived as the Absolute *noematically*, but the deities as pathways through which the *noetic* Absolute represents itself", formed the conclusion of his studies. Like Aijaz, I take the religious relativity or ambiguity of the world as motivating us to focus less on securing true beliefs about ultimate reality and more on involvement in practices, such as rituals and worship, which carve out pathways in accordance with a common morality.

Now, what kind of morality should form the standard for evaluating polytheistic commitment in Shinto? The relativistic implications of Shinto's polytheistic nature become even more complicated once we take into account the *kami*-nature within human personalities resulting from their being descendants of ancestral *kami*. In line with the views of modern Shinto theologians such as Kenji Ueda, it might be held that the 'collective will' of a particular community constitutes the key to determining the 'correct morality'. For example, the heavenly festival by which Amaterasu is lured from her cave would be regarded as expressing the correct morality given that the festival is in accordance with the collective will of the heavenly *kami*, a will formed at the conclusion of the divine conference held to decide how to attract Amaterasu from the cave. And what Susanoo's rampage infringes upon must also be the collective will of *kami* to honour the dignity of the pantheon containing these *kami* themselves.

Taking the discussion of 'collective will' further, in Japan at least the absence of a self-consciously held faith is clearly compensated by the normative customary codes of the individual's community. In terms of self-awareness, those who visit a shrine and pray are perhaps doing nothing more than observing an ancestral or communal tradition, as opposed to acting out an internalized form of religion produced by their own beliefs as Shintoists. On the surface, however, we cannot distinguish the former and latter cases merely by observing someone's ritual behaviour. Any doxastic issues, such as conflicts requiring Pascal's gambit, are not in evidence here. This must be true to some degree in other religious cultures in East Asia, where there exists a ritual system of worshiping ancestral spirits.

As a matter of course, Shintoists tend to assume a communitarian perspective rooted in rural communities which they regard as 'traditional'. From such a perspective, so far as expressing and enhancing social harmony in a peaceful way are concerned, it makes little difference whether an individual visits a shrine merely as a matter of custom or as an expression of personal faith. On the other hand, modern Shinto history includes episodes where a clear discrepancy appears between tacit and compulsory 'custom'. I refer here to the cultural conflict experienced by indigenous peoples of Japan's overseas colonies due to the practice of so-called 'compulsory Shinto shrine worship'. This practice appeared in the 1930s and early '40s as an element of Imperial Japan's cultural assimilation policy during the period of total war. In this instance, the system of general mobilization under the total war regime throughout the Japanese Empire was imposed as a normative community code for colonized people.

From one perspective, this case could be interpreted as one involving the separation of religion and state in line with the notion of religious freedom in the modern nation. The question arises in this context as to why practices of worship previously recognized as 'spontaneous', even under Japanese colonial rule, had come to be viewed as 'compulsory'. Who defines such practices as 'compulsory'? Of course, the reason for employing the term 'compulsory' in this instance is based on the assumption that what was an everyday custom on the Japanese side must have appeared foreign to the colonized people. As a historical fact, however, the problem of so-called 'compulsory worship' in the colonies occurred mainly as a conflict between Christian believers and Japanese state officials. These incidents of conflict took place mainly between Christians who didn't want to commit blasphemy by worshiping at a shrine and secular Japanese officials who wanted nothing more than to increase the number of shrine visitors as concrete evidence of the success of their mobilization policies.

As was argued by Emile Durkheim, our experience of the sacred is a function of social solidarity, and this can be seen in the history of Shinto. However, in today's individualist cultures any religious behaviour – including the worshiping of *kami* at a Shinto shrine – must be the outcome of some internal feeling, irrespective of whether this is an expression of the individual's faith or a product of the community's customs. On the other hand, we know that the reverse also holds in some cases, especially in educational situations, where collective participation in rituals is thought to generate and encourage personal belief. Parents frequently take their children to church or temple, but this is never considered 'compulsory worship'.

As an issue of personal religious freedom, we should of course distinguish cases of 'correct morality' as defined within a family from the public morality imposed by a governmental administrative unit, though both can be regarded as the individual's 'community'. Nevertheless, for some reason in Taiwan (though not particularly in Korea) a considerable proportion of older people born and educated under Japanese colonial rule feel an affinity for Shinto shrines. I have often heard the voices of elders speaking to that effect, together with recollections about their earlier lives as 'Japanese'. In Suga (2009) I investigated the case of a female shaman among such Taiwanese and sought to analyze some of the psychological intricacies about the former colonial subjects' feelings about Shinto shrines. Almost twenty years ago I served as an assistant priest on occasions of Shinto ritual in Taiwan that were revived by an elderly Taiwanese man who had been appointed a Shinto priest in the colonial period and went to war as a Japanese soldier. Of course, among the Taiwanese there might also be many people who possess uncomfortable memories about Shinto shrine worship. Since these elders are passing away with the years, such case studies about their precious experiences are becoming increasingly difficult. But as there are several Shinto shrines in the Hawaiian Islands that have never been administered by Japan and are mainly managed by ethnic Japanese people living in Hawaii, I hope to engage in further research about them from a slightly different perspective. This will in effect constitute an inquiry into the possibility and nature of Shinto beyond the influence of Imperial Japan or outside the customary codes of the Japanese community as a 'religion'.

In any case, are elders in the former colonized areas still affected by the morality they learned under the spiritual rule of Imperial Japan? An affirmative answer would be given at least by the political activists who want to censure the harshness of Japanese imperial rule. In this case, what remains of the subjectivity of these people and their feelings about their nationality after Japan's defeat, or their reminiscences of the past? This is as much a political issue as it is a religious one, and here again the 'correct morality' must be understood through the lens of the 'collective will' representing the reverence of the community as a whole towards the *kami*. But what are the criteria for determining the conditions underlying the 'collective will', assuming that this is a will formed in a noncompulsory or noncoercive way? Given, moreover, the dimension of polytheistic relativism in Shinto and the openness of the community, as exhibited in its allowance for practice without belief, discussion of the case of Shinto will require greater consideration of the conditions for knowing the 'correct morality' as opposed to engaging in analyses of theism. Since current-day Shinto advocates a harmonious way of realizing both communal and individual life, we Shintoists must reflect more deeply upon the conditions for attaining without compulsion the 'collective will'. In fact, in contemporary Japan, shrine Shintoists are sometimes criticized by liberals for attaching greater importance to the preservation of customary codes than to defending religious freedom for individuals.

Like Aijaz, who is concerned with showing that belief in God is neither necessary nor sufficient for making a practical religious commitment, Drob also emphasizes the possibility of making such commitment without explicitly subscribing to any religious beliefs or theology. In his First Response, Drob writes:

> Many individuals find it easier to pray and to partake in religious ritual than they do to testify to matters of belief and faith. The possibility and even necessity for prayer is something that I believe is essential to the human spirit . . . Prayer as a psychological phenomenon cannot be limited to those who have definite ideas about where and to whom prayers are directed and if and how they will be answered
>
> (96)

I entirely agree with these views. Indeed, prayer and ritual can be seen as a medium for communication between human beings and divine beings, one that exists beyond (or within) the plane of ordinary human relationships. Also, unlike cases of testifying or creedal confession, in prayer and ritual the divine object need not be directly specified.

How do matters look in the case of Shinto? The use of euphemism, including honorific expressions, is encountered quite frequently in the Japanese language. In Shinto prayers, called *norito* and composed even today in an archaic style modeled after tenth-century Japanese vocabulary and grammar, ritualistic euphemisms are found far more frequently than they are in ordinary language. However, without exception, at the beginning of every *norito* the name or names of *kami* expected to receive the prayer are directly stated, including those cases expressed collectively as "the kami enshrined in . . ." (here the name is provided of the shrine where the *norito* is recited). The origin of this practice is said to lie in ancient magico-religious beliefs about the power of calling a name. To call a *kami* by its name enhances the religious power of the priest who chants the *norito*, thus ensuring a response or reward from the *kami*. The practice also has some connection with the fact that, as archaeological researches show, in the pre-historical period it was common to set up a temporary ritual site at every occasion of *matsuri*, before the appearance of established Shinto shrines in each area.

This appears incompatible with the possibility I have defended of religious practice without belief in Shinto. In each *norito*, however, the importance of what is specified is grounded in the sites and conditions of the ritual prayer. The *kami* to whom a prayer is directed are specified among the indefinite pantheon just at the moment when *norito* is chanted at a particular time and place. Any site of *matsuri* worship, including fixed sites such as shrines, is understood as an interface between human beings and some providential other.

Every *kami* in Shinto, again, may indicate a transcendental path from each particular occasion toward a vague yet ultimate reality or universality. In my understanding, a human being's communication through prayer carves out such a transcendental path, even if the existence of the counterpart of such communication – the *kami* – is not recognized clearly, or in other words does not form the object of belief. This propensity to prayer, as Drob states, can be seen as something inherent in the human spirit.

Drob points out that, unlike Judaism, Shinto seems compatible with polytheism, agnosticism and even atheism, and he also refers to the Shinto practitioner's capacity "to develop his or her beliefs in a pluralistic, open-minded manner that is in accord with contemporary developments in philosophy, psychology and natural science" (this volume: 96). Drob's comments reflect an understanding of what Shinto is, or at least an expectation of what it could become, that is shared by both myself and a certain group of Shintoists today who would like Shinto to advance in academic fields besides historical studies.

The American religious scholar Floyd H. Ross (1965) has characterized the Shinto approach to morality in terms of 'situational ethics'. In doing so Ross was only seeking to account for Shinto's positive tendency to contribute towards communal development under given social conditions, but from another viewpoint the label of 'situational ethics' may give the impression of an opportunistic approach to morality. I realize again the importance for Shintoists to explore the conditions mediating between knowing the 'collective will' of a community at a specific time and place and the general religious freedom of individuals.

My thinking here also resonates to some degree with Isherwood's recognition of the possibility of religious practice without a fixed set of beliefs. As she states, "Appeal to orthopraxis rather than orthodoxy has been a large part of liberation theologies, since people have been galvanized around what needs to be done in society more than what one's co-worker for justice believes in terms of systematics" (this volume: 101). Isherwood then turns to the important question of the historical connection between Shinto and nationalism, a matter I will discuss later.

Agnostic pantheism and other topics

In order to take advantage of plural perspectives in the open-minded manner recommended by Drob, the principle of freedom must be followed when practicing Shinto. Of course, the 'traditions' of the community, particularly the customs of the Japanese people, must be the starting point in this process and should be respected. However, too great an adherence to these traditions (how moderation and excess in this context are to be identified constitutes a further difficulty) for the sake of developing a 'correct morality' would reduce Shinto to a form of ethnocentrism, as has happened in the past. We should take care regarding this point, and I would see this as going some way towards answering Isherwood's concern as to how Shinto might counter 'imperial attitudes' in others.

Now, following his suggestion about theistic commitment in accordance with correct morality, Aijaz also comments on my discussion of Shinto's agnostic aspect, citing my interpretation of the universe in the Shinto manner as "without the clear horizon of ultimate truth." Regarding my further statement that "the possibilities to access such truth would be found in each occasion", other participants expressed interest in the category of 'agnostic pantheism' as a descriptor of my own stance.

In sympathy with such agnosticism, Aijaz states: "Given the 'religiously ambiguous' nature of the world, we shouldn't concern ourselves too much with trying to find out the truth about ultimate reality. Rather, more time should be invested in trying to figure out a common ethical code with which followers of different religions can agree" (this volume: 90). The search for a common ethical code is clearly an important and essential function of interreligious dialogue.

Referencing his background in psychology, Drob responds to my hermeneutical method of renouncing any "clear horizon of ultimate truth" by noting: "This idea, that religion and theology can be invented anew at each spiritual moment or encounter, is extremely powerful" (96). I am encouraged by this to take a further step toward looking for what it is that is held in common by the various religious traditions. It is possible, I hold, at every spiritual moment or encounter with the other to develop anew religious views and theologies that are faithful to the other. This might be adopted as one way, if not the 'way', by which to delineate the 'collective will' of the human community, including therein both religious and nonreligious people.

The Shinto theologian I often reference, Kenji Ueda, was also a psychologist, though in Shinto studies it is historical rather than psychological approaches that are accorded priority. Although not a specialist in psychology, I judge that psychological approaches will take on greater prominence in future Shinto studies. This will be necessary in order to further interreligious dialogue amongst established religious organizations, and in particular to deepen and expand the common ground between the multi-layered beliefs of diverse individuals and groups. My view here is of course related to what I had proposed at the beginning of my First Response regarding the concept of 'way' as a category by means of which to uncover and understand commonly shared features between religions. Without wishing to repeat what I had previously stated, it may be worth reinforcing the point that since at each spiritual moment we are on the 'way', the 'way' is something we can share.

The idea of 'agnostic pantheism', Isherwood states, appeals to her feminist thinking. Given the connections Isherwood draws with feminist work on 'polydoxy' and 'multiplicity', work that is sometimes undertaken from a pantheistic perspective but rarely from an agnostic one, I was initially led to question the appropriateness of my use of the qualifier 'agnostic'. On further reflection, however, I regard the 'agnostic' label as capturing well an important dimension of Shinto, at least as I understand it. At the same time, various distinct views might be identified as lying within the bounds of 'agnosticism', including the personal or subjective view that 'I am unsure (or do not know) whether any deities exist', and the bolder claim that no one knows (or could possibly know) whether any deities exist. While I do not wish to rule out the possibility that someone might come to know of the existence of some deity, my own stance as a Shinto practitioner is that my beliefs about *kami* are just that – beliefs, not knowledge.

I was impressed with Isherwood's statement that, "the idea is not to convert people to one set of beliefs but rather to awaken to a greater sense of relationality between all animate and inanimate beings on the planet, understanding that all have the same divine energy within them" (this volume: 102). Such a view is in accord with the Mahayana Buddhist teaching about the Buddha nature and specifically the view found in the Mahayana *Mahaparinirvana Sutra* concerning the possibility that all sentient beings may attain Buddhahood. This teaching had an immense impact in East Asian Buddhism; and in medieval Japan, together with the philosophy of Original Enlightenment (*hongaku*) which asserts that the Buddha nature dwells in all beings, this teaching developed to include the concept of the attainment of Buddhahood by trees, plants, land and earth. I suspect that the ancient Japanese concept of *kami*, employed as a way of conceiving existence in terms of 'relationality', played an important part in the formation of this teaching. But in order to precisely identify the interactions between Shinto and Buddhism in Japanese religious history, further investigation on the connections between the idea of relationality and Shinto would be required. The relational conception of reality, Isherwood goes on to say, also has "major implications for the way in which we are able to understand our relationship with nature and, by extension, with the resources of nature, which can no longer simply be understood as there to be used and abused by humans" (103). This prompts Isherwood to ask about Shinto and sustainability, but unfortunately the Shinto community has thus far engaged in little philosophical attention on issues to do with ecology and sustainable development.

Isherwood also raises concerns about honouring soldiers and ancestors. Historically, of course, the veneration of great persons in Shinto derived from certain aspects of the tradition relating to ancestral spirit worship. Some scholars contend that the worship of the spirits of war dead in Shinto could be interpreted as a modern variant of propitiating vengeful ghosts, but I do not agree. For instance, I see it as essential to the practice of Shinto in the Yasukuni shrine that it be believed that the spirit of each human being after death becomes a part of *kami*, that is, a part of the community of 'ancestors'. Advocates for the Yasukuni shrine after World War II, such as Sen'yukai (the veteran's comrade society) and Izokukai (the war-bereaved association), thus hold that the past political achievements of the Japanese military are compatible with honouring the war dead. Without wishing to deny the possibility that underlying these beliefs some important theological aspects in the notion of *kami* could be uncovered, it might be better instead to see such political views in terms of jingoism (Suga 2013). At any rate, the practices of mourning the dead, honouring dead persons and displaying reverence towards dead spirits as *kami* constitute a complicated structure in the worshiping life of the Yasukuni Shrine, and research on this remains inadequate.

Finally, I would like to briefly introduce a unique Shintoist, Shozo Ogasawara (1892–1970), and the failure of his attempt to make shrine Shinto a universal religion. Ogasawara was a non-official Shinto activist in Imperial Japan, working mainly on the affairs of overseas shrines. Hoping to establish Shinto shrines throughout the world, he held that "in Shinto shrines, *kami* are the subject and buildings are the object", and the material aspects of Shinto (e.g., its shrines and priestly garments) as well as any special vocabulary and prayer rituals were considered by him as mere objects. These are objects that could, in his view, be altered or replaced in any way so long as the *kami* are enshrined in them as subjects (Suga 2010). This idea was clearly influenced by universally oriented Christian churches, based on the faith that God is the subject and the universe is the object in creation. In a polytheistic way, Ogasawara held that the omnipresence of the pantheon in the world corresponded to the position of the subject in the shrines. He also considered his religious mission of establishing overseas Shinto shrines as a critique of the opinion that 'Shinto shrines are historical monuments', a view that was officially advocated by the Japanese government at that time.

However, I detect here a fatal inconsistency in Ogasawara's thought. While criticizing the 'shrine as monument' view in mainland Japan, he relied upon the international popularity of historical memorials to establish shrines overseas. He had already retreated from his pantheistic ideal to the realm of commemoration of historical persons in the perspective of modern nation-states. But if all the conventional symbolism were taken away, what would be left to distinguish Shinto shrines from more ordinary historical monuments? In this respect Ogasawara was influenced by the state administration of Shinto shrines, which had no specific concept of the generic category of *kami* except as a collection of deities distinguished by the formalization of set standards of symbolism in conventional Shinto shrines.

Despite Ogasawara's wishes, it must be noted that no colonial shrines within the imperial sphere survived after the collapse of the Japanese Empire. Such historical and irreversible failure, the annihilation of several thousand overseas Shinto shrines, makes it vital that theological and philosophical reflection is brought to bear on Shinto faith, so that Shinto may be regarded as a worthy 'religion' in the world today.

References

Ross, F. H. 1965. *Shinto: The Way of Japan*. Boston, MA: Beacon Press.

Suga, K. 2009. "Jinja atochi to mitama okuri." In *Gendai shukyo 2009*, edited by Kokusai shukyo kenkyusho, 285–303. Tokyo: Akiyama shoten.

Suga, K. 2010. "A Concept of 'Overseas Shinto Shrines': A Pantheistic Attempt by Ogasawara Shozo and Its Limitations." *Japanese Journal of Religious Studies* 37: 47–74.

Suga, K. 2013. " 'Kokka ni yoru senbotsushairei' toiu mondai settei." In *Shokon to irei no keifu*, edited by Center for Promotion of Excellence in Research and Education at Kokugakuin University, 296–331. Tokyo: Kinseisha.

Index

Abba (Celestial Father) 31, 33
absolute rationality 56, 94
Adam Kadmon (Primordial Man) 29, 31, 32, 36, 46
Afghanistan: US invasion 23
agape 57
agnosticism 114
agnostic pantheism 73–6, 102, 160–1
Ahmadiyya Islam 127
al-Ghazali 133
al-Rummani 13–14
Althaus Reid, Marcella 59
Altizer, T. J. J. 138
Amaterasu-o-mikami 73, 74–5, 76, 155
Ame-no-minakanushi 114
androcentrism 86
anorexia 60
anthropic principle 119–20
anthropomorphism 36
arrow of time 119, 140
atheism: Kabbalistic view of 45, 120; religious uses of 91–2; and theism 135
Atsutane Hirata 114
axiology: and divinity in Kabbalah 36–8, 140
Ayin (Absolute/nothingness) 27, 34, 38
Azriel of Gerona 26–7, 29, 38, 40, 45, 135

beauty: and redemption 32
Berry, Thomas 64
Binah (Intelligence/Reasoning/ Understanding) 36
bio-energetic psychotherapy 93
Bion, Wilfred 96
Birur (Extraction) 30–1
body theology 60–3, 117, 147
Bostrom, Nick 135–6

Boullata, Issa J. 10
Braidotti, R. 55–6, 108, 150
Brock, Rita 51, 57
Bruno, Giardano 138
Buddha nature 161
Buddhism: idea of impermanence 75; in Japan 71
Bush, George W. 22–3
Butler, Judith 55, 56–7, 106, 108

Carlyle, Thomas 12
Catherine of Sienna 106
Celestial Mother and Father 31, 33, 107
Chabad Hasidim 135, 139
Chabad-Lubavitch Hasidism 27
chaos 64, 65–6, 94, 106, 107, 118, 149
Chasidim 37, 38
Chesed (Kindness) 29, 31, 32, 36, 141
chinju no mori 78
Chochmah (Wisdom) 36
Christ: as erotic power 57–8
Christian fundamentalism: diet rhetoric 60, 62; racism and nationalism in United States 102; and scripture 105
Christianity: androcentric bias 49, 86; and equality 103; and imperialism 102
Christian mysticism 106
Christology: and inclusion 146–7
coincidentia oppositorum/coincidence of opposites 29, 35, 37–8, 41–4, 134–5
compassion: and redemption 32
consciousness: and the material world 41
Corinthian women prophets 104
cosmic evolution 65

cosmological argument for theism 6–7, 97
cosmology: new cosmology 63–6, 106, 107, 118
Coudert, Allison 33
credulity, principle of 17–18, 19–20, 21–2, 116

Da'at (Knowledge) 31, 36
Dan, Joseph 26
Daoism 112, 119
Dao/the Way 112, 119
Dawkins, Richard 8–9
Deep, the 63, 118, 147
demonic possession 8, 9
Derrida, Jacques 26, 28, 39, 40, 41, 142
Descartes, René 135
design argument for theism 7–9, 97
designoid objects 8–9
Din (Judgement) 32, 36, 141
Divine Image: creation of man in 43–4
divinity: and axiology in Kabbalah 36–8, 140; feminist theological approach to 149–50; lived awareness of 94; Lurianic conception 33–5, 120; nature of 136
dogmatic substitution 132
Douglas, Mary 62
dualism 49
dunamis 146, 147, 148, 151–2
Durkheim, Emile 157

eating, politics of 60–3
Edwards, Paul 93
Ein-sof (the Infinite): apprehension of 27; evolution of 31; nature of 26, 28–9, 32, 33–5, 37–8; representation of 42–3; similarity to the Dao 119; as unity of opposites 42–3, 134
Elias, Norbert 61
Elior, Rachel 26
embodied knowing 148–9
embodied subjectivity 56, 94
Enlightenment 25, 118, 138
environmental philosophy 65
equality 103
erotic power of Christ 57–8, 87–8, 146, 150–1
ethical particularism: and pluralism 79
Eucharist meal 60–1, 63

evil, problem of 91
existence of God: design argument 7–9, 97; Leibnizian cosmological argument 6–7, 97
exousia 146
experiential theology 62

Fall, the 57, 106, 141–2
feminist biblical scholarship: hermeneutic of suspicion 101, 104; and transformation of scripture 105
feminist liberation theology 50, 54, 59
feminist theology 49–52, 85; aim 145–6, 147; application of 109; and arguments for God's existence 103–4, 131; on construction of gender and sexuality 53–4; and embodied subjectivity 56; and the 'Fall' 106; God's existence, approach to 103–4; orthopraxis over orthodoxy 101, 106, 146; and practical outcomes of belief 103–4, 131; and queer theory 58–9; recovery of the erotic 57–8, 87–8; on resurrection 146–7; on women's sexuality 57, 59–60
Ficino, Marsilio 138
Findlay, J. N. 37, 138
Five Pillars of Islam 14
folk tales 68, 101
Foundational Letters doctrine 30
Frankism 141
Freud, Sigmund 26, 28, 93
fundamentalist Protestant diet industry 60, 62

Galation baptismal formula 56
Gellner, Ernest 73
gender: Curia's rejection of term 56
gender/sexuality: construction of 52–5, 56, 87
Gevurah (Power) 32, 36
Gibbon, Edward 12
God: idolatrous conceptions of 135–6; personal relationship with 46; 'video game God' 136
Gokoku Shrine, Tochigi Prefecture 71–2
Golding, Joshua 5, 115
Graetz, Heinrich 26
Grand Shrine of Ise 113–14
Guenon, Rene 133

ha-achdut hashawaah (coincidence of opposites) 26, 29, 35, 37–8, 41–4, 90–2
hadith 3
Hadith of Gabriel 3–5
halakha (Jewish law) 25, 45
Hamada, Yo 112
Hasidism 25, 26, 27, 31, 45, 141
hatsumode/first worship 70
Haught, John F. 65
Hawaii: practice of Shinto 157
Hegel, G. W. F. 26, 28, 134, 142
Hellwig, Monica 63
Helmont, Jan Baptist von 33
Heraclitus 75
hermeneutic of suspicion 101, 104
Heyward, Carter 57, 58
Hick, John 15–21, 22, 23, 104, 126, 128, 133
Holocaust 91, 137
Holtom, Daniel C. 69
Horowitz, Aaron Halevi 35
human form: depiction of 142
Hume, D. 115

Idel, Moshe 26, 39
i'jaz 11, 12, 13
Imma (Celestial Mother) 31, 33
imperialism: and Christianity 102
Incarnation 108, 117
intellectual discourse 94
interfaith dialogue: feminist theologians in 146; and philosophical scruity of beliefs 126–7
Iraq: US invasion 23
Irigaray, L. 55, 108, 150
Islam: Ahmadiyya sect 127; and politics 128; and women 86; *see also* Sunni Islam
Izokukau 162

James, William 21
Japan: cultural assimilation policy 77–8, 156; nationalism and Shinto 69, 72–3, 76–8, 101, 102, 113; racism 69, 102
Jeffreys, Sheila 58–9
Jesus: as Jewish prophet 95; as savour and hero 50–1, 95; *see also* Christ
Jewish Bible 97
Jewish identity 25
Jewish mysticism *see* Kabbalah
Jinmu, Japanese Emperor 76

Judaism: ban on graven images 138; belief and practice 25; doctrinal flexibility 95; feminine ideas 50; phallocentrism 141; *see also* Kabbalah
Jung, C. G. 26, 28, 43–4, 94, 95, 100n1, 107

Kabbalah: coincidentia oppositorum 29, 35, 37–8, 41–4; Divine Image 43–4; divinity, nature of 33–5, 120; divinity and axiology 35–8; 'echo' of the absolute 42–3, 120; feminist interpretations 141; guiding principles 26–7, 35, 42; influence of Renaissance and Enlightenment 138; logic of Lurianic symbols 32–3; Luria's theosophical system 27, 28–32, 118–19, 139; New Kabbalah 27, 38, 45, 46; origin and history 27–8; personal relationship with the divine 46; as rational mysticism 44–5; scorn of 25–6; social context of development 138–9; status within Jewish community 140–1; study of 25–6; as theosophical system for all 26; transgressions against normative Judaism 141; word and thing, distinction between 38–41, 91
Kamimuzsuhi 114
kami-nature 156; naming in prayer 158–9
kami/spiritual beings 68, 69–70; in ancient mythology 114–15; and correct morality 155; definition 75, 155; divinity of 74; generation of 74–5; war dead as 71–2, 79, 80–1, 162; worship by kami of other kami 155
Kant, Immanuel 99
Kaplan, Mordecai 96
Keller, Catherine 63, 64, 65
Kellipot (Husks) 30, 34
Kierkegaard, Søren 72
Kojiki 68
Kokugau (National Learning) school 75
Koperski, Jeffrey 7, 8
kotodama/soul of word 121
Kristeva: Julia 150
Kuni-no-tokotachi 114

Lacan, Jacques 54–5, 87, 107–8, 150
Laden, Osama Bin 22

language: women as outside of 54–5, 107–8, 142–3, 150; and the world 38–41, 121
Last Supper 63
Leaman, Oliver 13, 14
Leibniz, Gottfried 33, 34, 138
Leibnizian cosmological argument 6–7
liberation theology 52, 59, 66, 86, 101
Lings, Martin 133
Locke, John 33, 138
Lorde, Audre 57
Luria, Isaac 26, 28, 31, 37, 38, 135
Lurianic Kabbalah: logic of symbols 32–3; theosophical system 27, 28–32

Mahayana Buddhism 161
Maimonides 90, 135
Malchuth (Kingdom) 32, 37
Marxism 52
matsuri/festive worship 68, 75, 159
Matt, Daniel 26
Mernissi, Fatima 132
messianic, the 142
Morton, Nelle 62
Moses 27
Moses De Leon 27
Motoori Norinaga 75, 112, 113, 114
Muhammad, prophethood of: and Qu'ran's miracle status 9–15; as rationally defensible 23
musuhi/spiritual producer 75, 114
mysticism 33; Christian mysticism 106; rational mysticism 44–5, 90, 134; *see also* Kabbalah
mythology: legitimacy 101

Nasr, Seyyed Hossein 133
nationalism: and religious practice 101–2; and Shinto in Japan 69, 72–3, 76–8, 101, 102, 113
naturalism: versus constructivism/idealism 134–5
natural theology step 7
nature: relationship to 103
Nazi Germany: Jung's view of 44, 94
Neoplatonism 49
Netzach (Endurance) 36, 37
new cosmology 63–6, 106, 107, 118
New Kabbalah 27, 38, 45, 46
Nielsen, Kai 22
Nietzsche, Friedrich 72
Nihon shoki 68

Ninigi 76
norito/prayers 159

Ogasawara, Shozo 162–3
open economy: of thought and experience 33, 35–6, 45, 96, 100, 141
Or Ein-sof (light of the Infinite) 29, 31
Original Enlightenment/hongaku 161
orthopraxis: over orthodoxy 101, 106, 146, 159
Otiyot Yesod (Primordial Letters) 29, 30, 35

panta rheii/everything flows 75
paradoxes 107
parity argument 16–17, 97–8, 129
Partzufim (Visages) 31
Pascal's Wager Argument 15
passion: fear of 57; and reason 94, 127
patriarchal ideology: and sexual inequality 53–4
Penelhum, Terence 16
phallocentrism 53–4, 87, 108, 141
philosophy of religion 85
Pickthall, Marmaduke 12
Plumwood, Val 64–5
pluralism 90; and ethical particularism 79
polydoxy 102
postmodernism 35, 118
prayer: and belief 70, 88, 96; and ritual 158
process theology 145
prophets: authenticity of 98, 129–30; women as 104
proselytization 45–6
purity: in Shinto 68

queer theory 58–9
Qur'an: balagha/aesthetic effectiveness 13–14; evidence of God's existence 5; feminist interpretations 132–3; i'jaz and stylistic inimitability 10–15, 116, 127, 132; as Muhammad's miracle 9–15, 97, 104

Rachamim (Compassion) 32, 36, 141
racism: Japanese racism 012, 69
radical incarnation theology 51–2, 117, 145
rational mysticism 44–5, 90, 134
Ratzsch, Del 7, 8

168 Index

reality: and truth 41
reason: absolute rationality 56, 94; dangers of 148; and embodiment 148–9; and faith 137; and passion 94, 127; women and 108–9
Recanti, Menahem 40
Rechian psychotherapy 93
Reconstructionism (Judaism) 96
Rees, Martin 136
Reich, Wilhelm 93
relationality 161
religion: problem of 'authority' 99; survival of traditional forms 99–100
religious belief: and common-sense beliefs 22; ethical dimension 22–3; informed belief 20; justification of 23; and ordinary perceptual beliefs 21–2; parity argument 16–17, 97–8, 129; philosophical scrutiny of 125–6; rationality of 15–23, 126–7, 128, 137; rationally compelling arguments for 5, 9, 125; rationally defensible arguments for 5, 23, 125; religious experience and 15–23, 126, 129; and religious practice 70, 88, 96, 113; and spirital dimension of human life 98–9, 130
religious experience: authentic versus delusory experiences 20, 23; credulity principle 17–18, 19–20; and rationality of religious belief 15–23, 126, 129
religious practice: without belief 70, 88, 96, 113, 154–9
Renaissance 118, 138
resurrection 146–7
Rippin, Andrew 9–10
Rorty, Richard 40
Rose, Deborah Bird 65
Ross, Floyd H. 159
Rowe, William 6, 20
Ruether, Rosemary Radford 49, 50–1
Russell, Letty 50

Sabbateanism 141
Said, Edward 63
salah/ritual prayer 4
Sarug, Israel 30
sawm/fasting 4
Scholem, Gershom 26, 138–9
Schüssler Fiorenza, Elisabeth 104–5
scripture: absences in 101, 104; status of 105

Second Vatican Council 131
Sefer Ez Chayyim (C. Vital) 28
Sefer ha-Bahir (anon) 28
Sefer Yetzirah 39
Sefirot (Value Archetypes): actualization 31–2, 37, 38, 45; as axiological elements 29, 136; and coordinated values 36–7; development and adaption of 28; groupings 30; as lenses 35; list 29; logic to 36; as questions 26
Sellars, Wilfred 40
Sen'yukai 162
sexual difference 56–7
sexual inequality 53–4
sexuality: control over 147
sexual theology 58–60
shahada 4
Sharia Law 132
Shekhinah (Femininity) 32, 37, 141
Shevirat ha-Kelim (Breaking of the Vessels) 30, 32, 34, 38, 119–20, 141
Shimon bar Yochai 27
Shinto: afterworld 77; as agnostic pantheism 73–6, 102, 160–1; appeal of 73; collective will 156, 158; compulsory shrine worship 156–7; correct morality 155, 156, 157, 158; ecological aspect 78; and gender stereotypes 117; and Japanese nationalism 69, 72–3, 76–8, 101, 102, 113; and militarism 69, 79; mythology 74–6, 80, 155; norito/prayers 158–9; outside of Japan 77–8, 156–8, 162–3; philosophy 68–9; political aspects 72; possibilities for 78–81, 96; practice and belief 70, 88, 96; purification 68, 76; rational inquiry into 74; religious status 68–71, 101, 163; on sexual desire 117; Shrine Shinto 69, 158, 162–3; spirit and souls 76; State Shinto 69, 70, 71, 72, 74, 78; way of kami 111, 112–13, 117; see also kami/spiritual beings
Shinto priests 71
Shiva, Vandana 65
Shrine Shinto 69, 158, 162–3
signifier/signified distinction 38–40
Sitra Achra (Other Side) 30, 34
situational ethics 159
Six Pillars of Faith 4
'Slim For Him' programme 60

somatic psychology 149
Sophia 107
Stanton, Elizabeth Cady 104
State Shinto 69, 70, 71, 72, 74, 78
Steinsaltz, Adin 31–2
Sunni Islam: core beliefs 3–5; faith 4; perfection of faith 4; practice 4; as rationally compelling 5–15, 125–6, 128; as rationally defensible 15–24, 126, 129
Supernal Torah 35
Susanoo 75, 155
sustainable development 103, 161–2
Suzuki, Daisetsu T. 68–9
Swinburne, Richard 17, 129

Taiwan: practice of Shinto 157
Takamimusuhi 75, 114
Talmud 25, 38, 99
Taryag Mitzvoth: performance of 37, 45
Taylor, Mark 41
tehom 118
tehomic ethic 65
Teresa, Mother 86
terrorism: 9/11 attacks 22
testimony, principle of 129
theism: and atheism 135; belief and practical commitment 88–91; cosmological argument 6–7, 97; design argument 7–9, 97; parity argument 16–17, 97–8, 129
things: and words 38–41
Tifereth (Beauty) 32, 36
Tikkun (Emendation) 31, 32
Tikkun ha-Olam (Repair and Restoration of the World) 31, 32, 33, 37, 45, 45–6, 138
time: arrow of time 119; directionality of 119, 140
Tishby, Isaiah 26
Torah 30, 35, 37, 39, 40, 97
Torah commandments 37, 45
truth: and reality 41
Tzaddik (Righteous, Saintly One) 36, 37

Tzimtzum (Contraction/Concealment) 29, 32, 33, 34, 36

Ueda, Kenji 74, 114, 156, 160
Umar ibn al-Khattab 3
United States: religion and imperialism 102
universe, the: ambiguity of religious accounts 99, 130–1

'video game God' 136
Vital, Chayyim 28, 35

Wadud, Amina 132–3
waka 121
'walk' 145, 146
war dead: as martyrs 116, 128; reverencing as kami 71–2, 79, 80–1, 162
war memorials 71, 80
Warner, Michael 106
Watsuji, Tetsuro 114–15, 155
'way': concept of 111–12, 114, 145, 161; rational defensibility of a 115–16
'Weigh Down' programme 60
Wittgenstein, L. 39, 40, 114
Wolfson, Elliot 26, 39, 141
women: and Islam 86; making of 53; nomadism 55–6; as outside language 54–5, 107–8, 142–3, 150; patriarchal ideology and 53–4; prophets 104; and reason 108–9; reception in theology 152; recovery of history 104–5; sexuality 57, 58, 59
Women's Bible 104
words: and things 38–41

Yasukuni faith 71–2, 79, 80–1
Yasukuni Shrine 71–2, 79, 80–1, 114, 162
Yesod (Foundation) 36, 37

zakat/alms tax 4
Zalman, Schneur (of Lyadi) 27, 39, 135
Zohar/Book of Splendour 27–8, 34, 38, 39, 44, 97